FUEL, FIRE
AND FEAR

FUEL, FIRE AND FEAR

RAF FLIGHT ENGINEERS AT WAR

COLIN PATEMAN

FONTHILL

This book is dedicated to the 4,357 flight engineers who lost their lives flying operations and to the 428 flight engineers lost in flying accidents during the Second World War. Lest we forget. For those brave men who gave their lives so we could live ours.

Fonthill Media Language Policy

Fonthill Media publishes in the international English language market. One language edition is published worldwide. As there are minor differences in spelling and presentation, especially with regard to American English and British English, a policy is necessary to define which form of English to use. The Fonthill Policy is to use the form of English native to the author. Colin Pateman was born and educated in Sussex; therefore, British English has been adopted in this publication.

Fonthill Media Limited
Fonthill Media LLC
www.fonthillmedia.com
office@fonthillmedia.com

First published in the United Kingdom and the United States of America 2018

British Library Cataloguing in Publication Data:
A catalogue record for this book is available from the British Library

Copyright © Colin Pateman 2018

ISBN 978-1-78155-675-7

The right of Colin Pateman to be identified as the author of this work has been asserted by him in accordance with the Copyright, Designs and Patents Act 1988.

Typeset in 10pt on 13pt Sabon
Printed and bound by CPI Group (UK) Ltd, Croydon, CR0 4YY

Foreword

As a flight engineer currently serving in the Royal Air Force, I consider it an honour to be asked to contribute to this excellent book on my own, little-known, flying branch. Flight engineers are a rare breed that face extinction; the first flight engineer brevet was issued in 1942 and the last was presented in 2003. Although flight engineer training continued at RAF Cranwell until 2005, trainees graduated with the new title of weapons system operator (air engineer) or WSOp(E). Those later individuals were presented with a generic single-winged RAF brevet, but if you graduated before 2003, you proudly wear the original 'E' badge seen in many wartime photographs.

The Royal Air Force currently employs a select few flight engineers, or WSOp(E), on two remaining aircraft types: the Sentry at RAF Waddington and our single Lancaster (PA474) based at RAF Coningsby. These RAF stations are now modern centres of airpower; in a way, nothing has changed because in the Second World War, they were Bomber Command stations operating the latest four engine machines. Not surprisingly, Lincolnshire remains affectionately known as the 'Bomber County'.

My personal route to becoming a flight engineer was via the Halton engineering apprenticeship scheme described in this book. Like many of my forebears, my conversion from ground crew to aircrew seemed a natural progression. Despite sound advice to avoid the 'dying trade' of engineer, I volunteered for flying duties and predominantly flew on Nimrod maritime patrol aircraft out of RAF Kinloss, Scotland. I now have the immense privilege of flying in the Lancaster bomber, which is unquestionably the pinnacle of my aircrew career. Although I have served on operations across the world, the 'action' I have seen bears no relation to the bomber war fought in the skies over Germany and Europe in the Second World War. However, the engineering side of the job remains the same: to monitor fuel, hydraulic, engine, and electrical systems; record gauge readings; diagnose faults; and strive to continue the mission without loss of the aircraft or its crew.

Colin Pateman's creation of a book dedicated to this little-known aircrew specialisation is a fitting tribute to my predecessors, who flew on various aircraft types. Although Lancaster bombers immediately spring to mind, it should be remembered that Sunderland flying boats, Halifax, Stirling, etc., also had an engineer on the crew. The brave, unassuming men who were flight engineers in the Second World War are truly unsung heroes who helped to save many lives in the air and on the ground. As they saw it, they were simply carrying out their duties like every other crew member. The heroic exploits of many flight engineers are described in this book, but the vast majority of selfless acts went unrecognised. The refusal to self-publicise is something I see in every Bomber Command veteran I have the honour to meet, but this is particularly true of the flight engineers still with us today. For example, my dear friend Warrant Officer Stanley Wilson, a Lancaster flight engineer who flew with 626 (Special Duties) Squadron out of RAF Wickenby, still has the German 50-calibre explosive round that ripped through his seat in 1943. Not surprisingly and like so many other flight engineers, he received no official recognition for his heroics on that night. Another survivor, Flight Lieutenant Edward Stocker, was lucky to be recognised and has the honour of being the most decorated flight engineer—perhaps this is not surprising, considering he flew an astounding 108 operational missions. I cannot over-emphasise the importance of this book in telling the story of other brave men like these.

The war is still very real to our veterans, and a visit to the RAF's single remaining Lancaster invariably brings them close to tears. The feel, smell, and sound of the aeroplane transports these men back to the best and worst days of their lives as part of a bomber crew. The comradeship of the bomber boys is difficult to replicate, or even appreciate, in civilian life. The bond created between men with shared traumatic experiences held the crews together. This bond often dissolved as they went their separate ways after demob. The reticence of Bomber Command aircrew was not only characteristic of their generation, but was often because no one could possibly understand what they had been through, so why bother even mentioning it? In fact, Stanley Wilson did not start talking about his wartime exploits until his daughters were teenagers. Yet once a veteran is back inside our bomber, the personal stories that have been locked up for years are unleashed. Unbelievably, the flight engineer's exemplary technical knowledge also remains, despite the intervening decades. Among all the distant memories, fuel consumption rates emerge, nitrogen purging systems are described, tank capacity figures are quoted, and engine balancing procedures are recounted in detail. These men were consummate professionals, and remain so to this very day.

Flying the Lancaster bomber today is an entirely different experience to that of a wartime bomber crew. However, in 2015, a Lancaster crew found themselves again fighting against the spectre of a burning engine. The title of this book perfectly sums up my emotions and duties as the flight engineer on that day. Fuel management is the flight engineer's bread and butter, and occupies a large amount of his time in the air. Yet when an engine fire is introduced, fuel management potentially becomes a life or death activity, for it is fuel that keeps a fire alive. It was when all the emergency drills were done, and the fire continued to burn, that the fear kicked in for me. Putting the fear element into context; mine lasted minutes, but bomber crews on a Berlin raid for example, suppressed and coped with the fear of death for up to ten hours. Statistically, a flight engineer in Bomber Command had only a one in two chance of surviving a standard thirty mission tour. What is incomprehensible to me is how these men and the rest of the crew faced that fear of almost certain death, night after night.

Lancaster PA474 forms an integral part of the RAF Battle of Britain Memorial Flight, and is an airborne tribute to the air and ground crews of all aircraft types operated by Harris's Bomber Command. Every flight is eagerly anticipated by the crew and public alike, crowds gather at display venues and flypast locations to see her and hear the unmistakable roar of four Merlin engines. As we transit at relatively low level across the British countryside, couples out walking look up and wave, football and cricket matches stop, and people literally run out of their houses as they hear us approach. The BBMF Lancaster is a flying memorial to the brave men and women of Bomber Command who gave so much for the freedom we enjoy today.

Lest we forget.

Flight Sergeant Mark Fellows
Flight Engineer, Royal Air Force Coningsby, 2018

Preface

An entire generation of men fought for freedom during the Second World War. The Royal Air Force, together with Commonwealth counterparts, comprised of volunteers and young men from all walks of life—academics, tradesmen, and those direct from schooling. Boys under military service age also served as apprentices in order to join the ranks of the Royal Air Force in an aviation-related trade. The common denominator between all of them was the determination and willingness to fight for freedom. Among these men, an army of engineers developed their skills to ensure the aircraft remained in the air. Many of these men would later become flight engineers.

Thousands of men took part in Bomber Command operations, which grew from initially being ineffective into a force of immense capability, designed for the specific purpose of winning the war. The destruction of the enemy with their highly competent military force and heavily industrialised war effort engaged endless young crews in bomber aircraft high above occupied Europe and other areas of military conflict. Aircraft with now iconic names like the Short Stirling, Avro Lancaster, and Handley Page Halifax were fundamental in the development of flight engineers. The story of these men deserves explanation because of their unique duties and courage during the war.

Approximately 125,000 aircrew served Bomber Command, of which 55,573 lost their lives. The Commonwealth War Graves Commission to this day maintains a significantly large proportion of the graves of these brave men. The Reichswald Forest Cemetery near Cleves contains 3,971 aircrew casualties, more than any other from the thirteen cemeteries within Germany. The Commonwealth War Graves Commission has registered 347,151 casualties recovered from across the services in the Second World War, all with graves commemorated and cared for in perpetuity. There remain an additional 232,931 personnel who are registered as missing. These casualties are commemorated by individually inscribed names upon many memorials across the world. The principle air force memorials recording these losses are at Alamein, Singapore, Malta, and the large Runnymede Memorial in Surrey, south-east England. The essential criteria in deciding where an airman was to be commemorated depended on where he was based, and not necessarily the area in which he was presumed lost. The Runnymede Air Forces Memorial itself commemorates over 20,000 airmen and women of the Commonwealth Air Forces who died over North Western and Central Europe, the British Isles, and the Eastern Atlantic who have no known grave.

I am full of respect and admiration for the men who served in the Royal Air Force, many of whom were inexperienced in life, yet they did more than anyone could have asked of them. The stories I have had the privilege to tell within this book are those of boys and young men who served in the particular position of flight engineer. The brevet that they proudly wore upon their uniform did not exist when war was declared. As the war progressed, however, it became recognised and respected by their peers, as the men who wore it were responsible for saving many lives within the Commands that served in the air.

A pre-war mechanic, Pennell Bates from London, typifies those who volunteered, trained, and flew with Bomber Command wearing the flight engineer brevet. Sergeant Bates would ultimately be awarded the Distinguished Flying Medal in 1945. The recommendation for that award embodies the duties and bravery of flight engineers:

This Non-Commissioned Officer has completed 19 sorties as Flight Engineer. During this time, he has displayed extraordinary skill in his trade and great personal gallantry. A typical instance of his devotion to duty was given on the night of the 20/21 February 1945 when he was the Flight Engineer of an aircraft detailed to attack Dortmund. In the target area, the aircraft was hit by flak, the shell bursting in the port inner engine, wounding the Bomb Aimer and damaging the aircraft extensively. Sergeant Bates, in addition to working on the controls and trying to repair the airspeed indicator, nursed the Bomb Aimer, bound up his wounds and stopped the bleeding. On top of all this, he promptly extinguished a fire which broke out in the electrical system. Course was set for an emergency landing in this country and attempts were made to lock the severely damaged undercarriage in position. A normal approach to land was made but, on the aircraft touching down, the undercarriage collapsed, the port outer engine caught fire and fire again broke out in the electrical system. This was promptly put out by Sergeant Bates whose conduct throughout this hazardous flight was beyond praise. On another occasion when detailed to attack Cologne in daylight on 2 March 1945, the aircraft was hit by flak while in the target area causing damage to the port outer and starboard inner engines. The port outer engine had to be feathered almost immediately and the starboard inner engine soon afterwards owing to a coolant leak. Once again, Sergeant Bates rose to the occasion and, owing to his skilful manipulation of the two remaining serviceable engines, the captain was able to bring the aircraft safely back to base. Sergeant Bates bearing in these two attacks did much to sustain the morale of his crew and his conduct throughout has made him an asset to the Squadron. For his great personal bravery, skill and magnificent operational spirit, he is recommended for the award of the Distinguished Flying Medal.

The King awarded many gallantry awards to both commissioned officers and non-commissioned men who wore the flight engineer brevet. The King also pinned the Victoria Cross beneath the flight engineer brevet worn by Sergeant Norman Jackson. No greater accolade to gallantry could be awarded and during the post-war years; Norman repeatedly characterised the duties of a flight engineer when he stated, 'It was my job as flight engineer to get the rest of the crew out of trouble'.

Colin Pateman
Sussex, 2018

Acknowledgements

The author would like to recognise Flight Sergeant Mark Fellows MSc BSc MRAeS, flight engineer attached to the Battle of Britain Memorial Flight. His foreword and unstinting assistance has been invaluable. Also, Squadron Leader Andrew Millikin (Officer Commanding Battle of Britain Memorial Flight), the original compilers of the flying log books and other associated material that has been used to assemble the foundation to this work, William Readhead, Paul Gees, Harold Stannus, and Thomas Smith. Additionally, Philip Jackson CVO, Lieutenant Colonel Jonathan RD Hipkins, Min Larkin (Archivist RAF Halton), Bob Marchant (Guinea Pig Club), Alan Cooper, Douglas Vince, Gordon Leith (RAF Museum), Pino Lombardi, Simon Muggleton, Matthew J. Poole, Simon Lannoy, Pete Tresadern, Søren Flensted, Jamie Hibberd, Duke Newstead, Susan Watkins, Gabrielle Stannus, Genevieve Stannus, Stuart Soames, and my wife, Sarah-Jane. If I have omitted to acknowledge anyone, please forgive me.

Photographs

Wherever possible, known contributors have been duly accredited, Additional photographs have been included from the author's collection. The terms of the Open Government License facilitate the use of historic material from the National Archives while other material, particularly photographic work, sits within the public domain created by the Government prior to 1957.

Contents

1

Halton Cadet School of Technical Training and the Developing Royal Air Force

In December 1919, the Royal Air Force Boy Aircraft Apprentice Scheme was created from the vision of Hugh Montague Trenchard. That same year, the War Minister Winston Churchill had appointed Trenchard to be the Chief of Staff of the Royal Air Force. In that capacity, he had the foresight to create colleges for air officer cadets and staff officers and by introducing a system of short-service commissions, he subsequently built a structured reserve for the developing Royal Air Force.

Boys were invited to sit selection examinations held around the country where they competed for a three-year aircraft apprenticeship. Admittance was strictly limited to boys between the ages of fifteen and seventeen and the Royal Air Force assumed legal guardianship of those selected to become an apprentice. Trenchard believed that the only way to fulfil the need for high-quality mechanics for the ever-more technically developing service was to train them internally. The recruitment of educated boys capable of absorbing the necessary technical training meant they would complete their apprenticeship in three years instead of the standard five years in civilian life.

In January 1920, the first intake of 235 boys began their apprenticeship at RAF Cranwell, which itself was only officially opened on 5 February that year. The program was initially restricted to British subjects many of whom were unprepared for the intense schooling and practical training that took place throughout their five-and-a-half day working week. Additionally, they were assigned fatigue duties in the cookhouses, peeling potatoes, and vegetables, coal heaving, and washing up. These boys became known as the 'Halton Cadets'.

The substantial six-floor dormitory accommodation at Halton was at that time still being completed. The boys would initially be assigned to trades of carpenter, sheet metal worker, fitter, or electrical. In March 1920, the Training Schools at Halton and Cranwell were eventually named No. 1 and No. 2 Schools of Technical Training respectively. The Air Ministry Order 500 in 1919 had instructed that boy apprentices were given a distinguishing badge. A die-cast four-bladed propeller manufactured in a circle of gilded metal brass would be sewn onto their uniform. Known as the wheel badge, it was worn on the left arm only of the jacket and greatcoat. In 1924, blue material uniforms were universally issued to all apprentices with each wing at Halton identified by a strip of coloured banding affixed to the cap of the wearer. This system allowed for instant recognition by the staff. The sixteen blocks of accommodation at Halton were completed in 1924, enabling 2,000 apprentices to be accommodated. These boys came into the service for three years as apprentices, following which they then committed to serve for ten years from the age of eighteen with a further commitment to serve in the reserve for a minimum of two years thereafter.

By late 1924, the fulfilment of Trenchard's vision to create a Reserve Air Force, which later became known as the Royal Auxiliary Air Force, enabled him to modestly expand the actual strength of the Royal Air Force. The men of the regular pre-war air force were joined by those from the Auxiliary. The RAuxAF volunteers were locally recruited in a similar fashion to the established Territorial Army Regiment structure. It proved to be a natural progression for the service and many of the Auxiliary serving officers became vital to the development of the modern Royal Air Force. Over the next two years, twenty-five auxiliary squadrons were created, and the introduction of the short-service commission scheme proved to be useful in providing some of the regular manning of these new squadrons. Trenchard also instigated the University Air Squadron Scheme. This combined foundation created an infrastructure of men who would eventually fly in the Battle of France and become fundamental to the few who participated in the Battle of Britain.

Halton cadets were provided with aspirations of great achievement by the developing Royal Air Force. In September 1931, Flight Lieutenant J. Boothman won the Schneider Trophy flying a Supermarine seaplane powered by a Rolls-Royce engine over the Lee-on-the-Solent waters. This aircraft was to be the foundation of what arguably became the most important aircraft to defend the British Isles—the Supermarine Spitfire.

In 1932, a reorganisation took place at Halton when the facility consolidated the number of apprentices, who would jointly receive training on both airframes and engines. This would change once more when separate specialisations in training evolved further. In January 1936, the thirty-third entry commenced at Halton. This was an 'expansion entry' reflecting on the acknowledgement that the Luftwaffe was seen to be a very serious threat in the light of the deteriorating relations with Nazi Germany. Some 700 boys arrived at Halton for training. Most boys were selected for the trade of fitter, engaging in the maintenance and repair of all aero engines and aircraft at that time. A lesser number started their training as fitter armourers. An early pre-war casualty from the 1936 entry was Aircraftman Robert Keogh, serving with 52 Squadron. It was commonplace for these young men to take advantage of any opportunity to fly. On 18 October 1939, he flew with Pilot Officer John Anderson in one of three Fairey Battle aircraft engaged in formation flying practice. A collision occurred, and his aircraft crashed one mile west of Dorchester, Oxfordshire, killing both occupants.

The competition to enter Halton was significant. Out of 1,000 boys who applied, only 300 would progress and the stringent medical procedure would subsequently eliminate swathes of boys who would be sent home. The successful boys would eventually be interviewed and, in order of examination attainment, be allocated the technical course appropriate to the service needs. Courses at Halton covered every aspect of aeronautical engineering. The introduction of new engines dictated the intensity and duration of courses needed to effectively train to the required levels of proficiency.

The Royal Air Force Volunteer Reserve was formed in 1936. Initially, the Reserve composed of civilians recruited from the catchment of interest that surrounded the Reserve Flying Schools, which included applicants originating from universities. The Reserve Flying Schools were operated by appointed civilian contractors who also engaged instructors from the Reserve of Air Force Officers. These were men who had previously completed a four-year short service commission as pilots in the Royal Air Force. Volunteers into the reserve were men of between eighteen and twenty-five years of age who undertook part time training as pilots, observers, and wireless operators. The strategic vision was to create a reserve or pool of trained aircrew for use in the event of war. The Air Ministry employed the Reserve as their principal means for aircrew to volunteer and enter the service.

On 3 September 1939, Halton received an Air Ministry signal announcing that war had broken out with Germany. At that time, 4,000 apprentices were accommodated with approximately 1,000 in each of its four large wings. The last pre-war intake had produced 2,135 apprentices and thereafter the training periods intensified to increase productivity of trained personnel. Boys under military age continued to be recruited with particular attention to those to be trained as fitters. The apprentice workshops held among others two Hampden light bombers and several biplanes, including Gipsys and Tiger Moths; an early production Spitfire; and the pre-curser to the Avro Lancaster, the Manchester.

Many ex-Halton brats who served in engineering as fitters and engineers on both engines and airframes would subsequently volunteer for flying duties in the Second World War. The Halton archives estimate that after it was formally established that ground crew personnel could volunteer for aircrew duties, some 2,000 ex-Halton boys immediately volunteered to undertake selection for the position of flight engineer.

Halton apprentices that went through wartime service were boys engaged from within the first to the forty-fourth entries. The roll of honour records over 1,600 young men who made the supreme sacrifice. Tragically, 475 of these brave men were ex-Halton apprentices who have no known grave and therefore, they are commemorated on various memorials across the world. The actual roll of honour to old Haltonians consists of many pages; almost every page in that historical document records the loss of an apprentice who had served as a flight engineer.

It is worthy to note that in January 1936, Halton expansion entry injected many young boys into the apprentice scheme. Sobering statistics from that particular Halton entry alone confirm that thirty of those boy entrants lost their lives flying as flight engineers between 1941 and 1944. The youngest known Halton casualty was Aircraftsman Harry William Clack, who was fifteen years old when he commenced training at Halton in 1939. The outbreak of war created accelerated courses, which in respect of Harry Clack resulted in a posting to Cambridge on aircraft salvage and repair duties. On 25 October 1940, he was fatally electrocuted when a crane jib being used to salvage an enemy Dornier Do 215 aircraft touched overhead cables. Harry Clack was buried in Cambridge City Cemetery and like so many others, his grave continues to remain cared for by the Commonwealth War Graves Commission.

In all probability, the most historically recognised apprentice, Frank Whittle, commenced his training as a metal rigger in September 1923. His first attempts to join the service had failed as a result of his small stature. On his third attempt to volunteer, he was accepted as an apprentice at sixteen years of age. Frank rose to the rank of air commodore and is recognised for his innovation and foresight in developing jet engine technology during the Second World War.

2

Interwar Duties

The formation of the Royal Air Force Technical Branch came into existence when senior non-commissioned officers and warrant officers began to receive commissions in engineering, armament, and as signals officers. These technical officers were pilots within the General Duties Branch of the Royal Air Force and they alternated between the Technical and General Duties Branches as their careers progressed, which enabled them to undertake tours in different fields. Several men later rose to senior ranks, all of which would have witnessed the evolution of flight engineers.

Squadrons equipped with large flying boat aircraft utilised ground crew engine fitters and mechanics to fly with the aircrew. Broadly speaking, both fitters and mechanics were separated between engine and airframe categories. The fitter, however, had a superior trade status to the mechanic and so they were engaged in monitoring engine performance on what were at that time comparatively long-distance flights. These men were often referred to as 'engine minders' and would carry out repairs as and when necessary. They became anomalies within the official rankings of aircrew personnel of that time.

Flying boats were among the largest aircraft to fly during the first half of the twentieth century and the Southampton flying boat was one of the most successful to be used by the Royal Air Force. In 1928, four Supermarine Southampton flying boats of the Far East flight flew to Melbourne, Australia. This achievement was considered fundamental in establishing that flying boats had evolved to become reliable means of long distance transport. With a reputation for reliability, a tribute to the aircraft designer, Reginald Joseph Mitchell, the Southampton proved to be exceptional and established not only the name of the designer but that of the Supermarine company in military circles. The Southampton eventually equipped six squadrons and established Britain at the forefront of marine aviation. Reginald Mitchell has another supreme legacy to military aviation: the Supermarine Spitfire fighter, designed by him between 1934 and 1936.

By 1931, mail from Britain was reaching Australia by air in around sixteen days, halving the time taken for the previously established sea routes. That same year, government tenders on both sides of the world invited applications to run new passenger and mail services within the then British Empire. The service established itself and rapidly outgrew its capability to carry the trade. The solution to the problem was found in 1933 by the British government who requested the aviation manufacturer Short Brothers to design a larger new long-range monoplane. The Short S23 'C' Class Empire flying boat met the British Air Ministry requirements for a long-ranged four-engine flying boat. Known to Short Brothers as the 'Imperial Flying Boat' and powered by Bristol Pegasus radial piston engines, this aircraft would eventually become famous as the Short Sunderland, which served with distinction in Coastal Command throughout the Second World War and beyond. Early engine minders and later flight engineers would become essential crew to these important aircraft.

The interwar period witnessed the Royal Air Force development of what are now collectively known as medium bombers. They were the Handley Page Hampden, Armstrong Whitworth Whitley, and the Vickers Wellington together with the later Avro Manchester. These aircraft paved the way towards the decision to commission Short Brothers to build the Short Stirling heavy bomber. The wing of this aircraft would have direct connectivity to their Empire flying boat design. Structurally, the wings would bear four Hercules engines across its significant width and be fed by fourteen fuel tanks, seven individual tanks in each wing. The Short Stirling effectively dictated the need to obtain the best possible performance from the engines by having a member of the crew dedicated to control the fuel and manage the engine instrumentation. The ensuing Halifax and Lancaster bombers simply consolidated the need.

Winston Churchill addressed the House of Commons on 24 October 1933, providing an early warning to his country by stating that Germany was well on the way to becoming the most heavily armed nation in the world. At that time, Germany was still bound by the Treaty of Versailles, banning it from rearming itself after the end of the First World War. It is noteworthy to mention that Germany did not officially declare the formation of the Luftwaffe until March 1935. In the following year, the Royal Air Force Volunteer Reserve was formed followed by the Royal Air Force Maintenance Command in April 1938.

3

Flight Engineer School: An Overview of Technical Training

Air Ministry Order 493 of 1936 announced that a new school of technical training would form at Royal Air Force Station, St Athan in Glamorgan, South Wales on 1 September 1938. It was to be known as No. 4 School of Technical Training and administered by No. 24 Training Group, Training Command.

The primary function of St Athan was for the training of drivers, flight mechanics on engines, and flight riggers responsible for airframes. The more advanced trade of airframe and engine fitters, from which many flight engineers were remustered, was swiftly added to the training output.

St Athan was a very large complex establishment cut into two sectors by grass runways. The station although far from complete, had been brought into use in September 1936. The ambitious building programme continued and by 1939, the station had been virtually completed. Workshops, stores, married quarters, an amenity block with its church, gymnasium, drill hall, swimming bath, and cinema had by that time been built. St Athan was planned and divided into two main camps—East Camp in which the School of Technical Training resided with a general hospital and the School of Physical Training, and West Camp, which was facilitating the repair and maintenance of aircraft and engines. St Athan was home to thousands of service men and women. It provided major servicing support for the heavy aircraft of the operational commands. Night and day, seven days a week, the air reverberated with the roar of engines under test. The station was a gigantic production line into which aircraft arrived, had their engines removed, tested, and replaced in many cases all in the space of a few hours.

As war progressed, other areas of instruction and education developed at St Athan. One of the greatest achievements made by the School of Technical Training was in connection with the development and training of aircrew flight engineers. Air Ministry Order 190/41 announced the need for an onboard technical expert to operate engineering systems on the latest four-engine heavy bombers—namely at that time, the Short Stirling and the Handley Page Halifax.

In June 1942, the School of Technical Training officially began the program of training aircrew flight engineers. All student flight engineers within the entire structure of the Royal Air Force would eventually be instructed at St Athan. The Commonwealth Air Training Plan would only marginally enhance the training of flight engineers during the final years of the war. No. 4 School of Technical Training consistently remained the centralised hub for flight engineer training. Post-war, a memorial board hung in one of the aircraft hangers at St Athan, which stated 'In this workshop between the years 1941 and 1951, 22,599 Flight Engineers received their ab initio training'. '*Ab initio*' is a Latin term meaning 'from the beginning'. The memorial board survives and is now on display at the Newark Air Museum. The statistics of Royal Air Force flight engineers who passed through St Athan between the years 1941 and 1945 was an incredible 17,885 qualified airmen. The Air Ministry specification for aircrew flight engineers was itself officially described as follows:

> Accepting the responsibility for the technical maintenance of his aircraft on the ground, or in flight. Before flight, testing the serviceability of the engines, instruments and ancillary equipment, the calculation of fuel requirement relative to the bomb loading and to ensure the safe return of the aircraft and crew safely to base. In flight ensure economical use of fuel, periodically record all instrument readings, operate emergency systems if required, carry out emergency repairs, and act as Second Pilot or Air Gunner when required.

Becoming a qualified flight engineer required each student to undertake a six-month technical training course undertaken in two parts, the first being seventeen weeks duration followed by a further seven weeks. St Athan was able to sustain the consistent flow of personnel for training in a regimented and highly organised program. That efficiency was reflected at its peak when it created an output of men as high as 500 a week. The year 1944 saw an absolute peak of personnel movement at St Athan and it became necessary to divert some cadets to No. 5 School of Technical Training at RAF Locking for their preliminary phase of initial ten weeks of instruction before being reintegrated into the St Athan stream of instruction.

The preliminary phase of the seventeen-week instruction course consisted of the following subjects:

Preliminary Airframes (one week)
Preliminary Engines (two weeks)
Carburettors and Magnetos (two weeks)
Electrics and Instruments (one week)
Radial Engines/In-Line Engines (two weeks)
Hydraulics (one week)
Propellers (one week)

After a five-day leave period, trainees continued with the intermediate phase of the course, which incorporated the following:

Merlin Engines (two weeks)
Typical Airframes (one week)
Typical Hydraulics (one week)
Propellers/Instruments/Electrics (one week)
Aerodrome Procedures (two weeks)

After a further week of leave, the trainees progressed to the final phase of the course. This ideally, but not always, provided specific training on the airframe and engines that would be present in the squadron that they would eventually be posted into. This was however by no means a certainty. Frequently, it fell to the Royal Air Force to dictate over choice primarily because all too often the older Stirling was under subscribed. It should be remembered that Coastal Command also required flight engineers for the heavy flying boats and, eventually, the American B-24 Liberator.

Cockpit sections were used to provide a simulated flight environment to enable trainees to practise pre-flight checks and take-off procedures. Working in flying kit, these exercises created some realism to their training. A tethered airframe enabled the trainees to run the engines up to full throttle. Undoubtedly, the noise, vibration, and feel of four engines operating at maximum efficiency would be most inspiring to these young men.

The final instructional phase at St Athan incorporated the following dedicated training:

Airframes (two weeks)
Electrics/Instruments (one week)
Fuel Logs/Fuel Systems (one week)
Engines (one week)
Engine Handling (one week)

Throughout the training, flight engineers were exposed to assessing damage inflicted by enemy action. In some instances, parts recovered from aircraft crash scenes were displayed, creating a sobering representation of enemy anti-aircraft shell fire. The course exhaustively explored remedying actions for emergency situations while flying over enemy-held territory. It was expected that each man would memorise every system on the aircraft, not just how it worked or how to fix it in an emergency, but where it was located within the aircraft. They needed to be able to find them in the dark under potentially stressful and most challenging conditions.

Manufacturer courses eventually became well established and became an integral part of the training structure for both ground and air staff. Differing designs and aspects of engineering associated to the Halifax, Stirling, and Lancaster aircraft provided broad areas of experience. The factory facilities often included large open layouts of hydraulic and electrical systems. Various mock-up installations had been constructed in class rooms and these were enhanced by display boards with large scale factory plan drawings. Fuel tank systems, lubrication systems, and hydraulic and electrical layouts were present, creating very visual representations. Piping was often coloured to identify the fluid or gas flowing through it, which helped make clearer the exact function. This also made it easier to follow the piping through mechanical intricacies and the route taken through the fuselage sections.

Throughout their technical training, trainees were required to continue with the physical fitness programme and development in the subjects of Morse code, navigation, and armaments. Practical emergency flying drills also continued throughout the training program. For example, the immediate actions in the event of an engine catching fire would have been learned by rote and become second nature. Emergency egress drills evolved throughout the war, designed to ensure a quick, safe exit from a distressed aircraft. Crash landings, ditching into the sea, and abandoning by parachute required consistent practice to become automatic responses regardless of crew position. Flight engineers would play a significant role alongside the pilot in effecting a difficult ditching manoeuvre. Symmetrical power to all engines was necessary in order to ensure minimal rudder inputs. Working as a team, the pilot and flight engineer aimed to achieve the flattest approach possible on the sea to help avoid cartwheeling. The speed of approach was lowered by the use of flaps to lessen the impact. Also, the objective of controlling the point of impact on the sea, aft of the aircrafts centre of gravity, helped prevent the nose tipping into the water. If done correctly, the aircraft would float, allowing the crew sufficient time to access the dinghy stored in the starboard wing root.

Hypoxia (the lack of oxygen when flying at great height) was a very real danger to aircrew because it is very difficult to detect in yourself. Flight engineers therefore needed to have good knowledge of the oxygen supply system. However, all crew were trained to recognise the symptoms of hypoxia in others, should an oxygen supply be lost or as sometimes happened, with masks not being worn correctly or becoming the subject of damage during flight.

The austerity and rationing measures due to paper shortage are brought into focus when noting that the Royal Air Force Standard Technical Training Notes published as document AP3042 advised students that their issued copies were for the course duration only and they were unable to remove them from St Athan. The content of that Air Publication provided extensive information on the internal combustion engine, carburettors, magnetos, air-cooled engines, liquid-cooled engines, components, variable pitch propellers, and servicing and airfield procedure. It was common practice for all of this information and the plethora of diagrams to be copied into text books, which were able to be retained as reference points for these men on their eventual postings to operational duties.

At the conclusion of the technical course, each student was required to pass two formal examinations—one written theory and an oral examination on mechanical knowledge. Students achieving pass marks of 70 per cent or over enabled them to be considered under recommendation for a commission into officer rank. This was, however, only achievable if the individual concerned had displayed a sense of discipline, leadership skills, a determined personality, and had presented intellect throughout the entire course. All successful students normally paraded to receive their flight engineer brevet and were immediately promoted to sergeant rank. Remarkably, flight engineers, on completion of training, would have had little if any practical air experience. The physical distribution of these newly qualified flight engineers onto respective squadrons appears to have had no formal process. During the research for this book, one veteran advised that they were lined up shortest to the left and tallest to the right. The tallest were allocated the Short Stirling by virtue that the aircraft supposedly had good headroom. Another instance the veteran recalled was being called aside if their service number ended with a zero. Groups selected by this process and other numerical permutations were simply allocated an aircraft type.

Statistics taken from the post-war Air Ministry Flying Training Policy document AP3233 provides an understanding of the quantity of flight engineers that were trained during 1940–1945. The staggered years are due to the calculations being collated annually, September to September:

1940–41: UK trained 154
1941–42: UK trained 563
1942–43: UK trained 6,022 and India trained 14
1943–44: UK trained 6,705, Canada trained 207, and Australia trained 175
1944–45: UK trained 4,441, Canada trained 1,706, Australia trained 194, and South Africa trained 79

Although the Royal Canadian Air Force did not open a specialised Flight Engineer School until the summer of 1944, it had been training flight engineers on an *ad hoc* basis since at least mid-1943. This was in response to needs for such duties in their maritime home defence squadrons on both the east and west coasts of Canada. In all probability, Canadian ground crew aero engineers and mechanics already overseas were able to volunteer to be trained in flight engineer duties. By example, Sergeant William Cardy deserves mention, a Canadian flight engineer who received the rarely awarded Conspicuous Gallantry Medal. William Cardy had enlisted in Canada and trained as an engine fitter, serving in that capacity for over two years before he sailed to England. He later volunteered for flight engineer duties and qualified at St Athan. Serving in the

Halifax-equipped 427 Squadron, his third operation was to attack Kassel on the night of 3 October 1943. During an enemy fighter attack on their Halifax LK637, two crew members were instantly killed at their stations while a 2,000-lb bomb came away from its bomb bay mounting and fell through the bomb doors. The flight engineer received terrible debilitating injuries to his right arm and left eye, all inflicted by enemy munitions. Significant blood loss from his injuries incapacitated him on several occasions but on regaining consciousness, he assisted his pilot as best possible. The damage to the aircraft was momentous and the flight engineer was required to supervise and instruct on an emergency lowering of the undercarriage, which necessitated introducing high pressure air into the hydraulic pipeline to drop the undercarriage.

The pilot was recommended for a Distinguished Flying Cross and the prestigious Conspicuous Gallantry Medal (Flying) went to the flight engineer. These were published in the *London Gazette* on 9 November 1943.

There were no qualified engineers, airframe, or engine personnel sent to the United Kingdom from New Zealand and very few from Australia, which explains why, when volunteers were required for flight engineer duties in the late 1942 and early 1943 period, no pool of men from those commonwealth countries were available. Frank Dunkin, an airframe fitter from New South Wales, was one of the rare exceptions for Australian flight engineers. Aged twenty-one, he was posted to 1661 Heavy Conversion Unit at Winthorpe to join his new crew. In the early hours of Saturday, 10 April 1943, his Lancaster ED823 took off from Winthorpe on a night exercise and crashed in Halam, Nottingham. All seven crew members were killed. The Australian records on the post-crash scene report impact marks, indicating that the aircraft struck the ground on an even keel and that all engines were still under power. The report further noted that three of the propellers and reduction gears were within 15 yards of the point of impact. No technical faults were found on the aircraft, leading to an inconclusive deduction as to the loss of life to the entire crew just 8 miles from their airfield. Nowadays, this incident would be referred to as 'controlled flight into terrain'.

In the vast majority of cases, the United Kingdom-based Commonwealth squadrons were always required to draw upon Royal Air Force flight engineers for their heavy bomber squadrons. Canada alone recognised the bravery and commitment of United Kingdom-trained flight engineers and, by the end of the war, had recommended 125 flight engineers for gallantry awards. In February 1944, Squadron Leader G. A. Adams from the Royal Air Force Flight Engineer School at St Athan went to Canada to serve as the liaison officer on flight engineer training in Canada. It was not until the Royal Canadian Air Force started flight engineer courses at Alymer in Ontario that the dedicated Canadian squadrons slowly began to fill the position of flight engineer with Royal Canadian Air Force personnel. In total, 1,913 flight engineers were trained in Canada. Squadron Leader Adams later assumed command of the Canadian facility.

By 1944, the swelled training structure had created many surplus multi-engine pilots. These men, many of whom were most unlikely to receive operational postings as pilots, were invited to apply for flight engineer training. A significant number of pilots qualified in this new and probably unexpected route to operational flying. One such man, Sergeant Jeffery Wheeler, had trained as a pilot in Rhodesia but remustered in 1943 to be a flight engineer. He returned to England, qualified in 1944, and eventually received a posting to the Lancaster-equipped 101 Squadron. Flying to Bremen in daylight in 1945, his Lancaster was struck by flak along the starboard side. Jeffery was himself hit by flak fragments, which tore through his clothing and penetrated deep into his thigh. He remained at the flight engineer station until safely away from the target and only then drew attention from the navigator, who dressed the wound as best as possible. Aware that two engines needed to be monitored closely as a result of being damaged by flak, Jeffrey refused to be taken to the rest area. This enticing term refers to a small padded bunk, situated between the main wing spars, where injured men were given first aid and put on oxygen. Sergeant Jeffery George Wheeler also became the recipient of the Conspicuous Gallantry Medal (Flying). The *London Gazette* published the recommendation on 1 June 1945:

> Sergeant Wheeler was Flight Engineer in an aircraft detailed to attack the heavily defended target of Bremen in March, 1945. While over the target area the aircraft was hit and damaged by enemy fire. Sergeant Wheeler was seriously wounded in the thigh. Although in great pain this resolute airman concealed the fact until well clear of the target. After receiving attention, Sergeant Wheeler insisted on being allowed to carry on with his duties. Two of the starboard engines had sustained slight damage but so well did this engineer fulfil his tasks that his captain was enabled to have full use of the four engines throughout the homeward flight. In spite of much physical distress, Sergeant Wheeler displayed outstanding devotion to duty, setting a splendid example to all. This airman has completed a large number of sorties and has invariably displayed a high degree of skill.

The extent of his injuries was disclosed by the fact that this flight engineer was detained in hospital for the duration of four months. It should be acknowledged that in total, only thirteen flight engineers received the Conspicuous Gallantry Medal (Flying) during the Second World War.

4

Flight Engineer:
Air Gunner, 1940–1942

The Short Stirling entered service with the Royal Air Force in August 1940 and it was 7 Squadron who were to be initially equipped with the new heavy bomber. Among high expectations, this mighty aircraft was assessed with some scrutiny which resulted in a deferred introduction to operational service until early 1941.

Trials and assessments established that flying with less than all four operational engines, the Stirling would suffer an overall general incapability to maintain height. Among many other engineering matters of concern, the primary electrical systems (which were heavily reliant to many controls, including the mighty undercarriage) was proving to present problems. Likewise, the electronically driven tail wheel retraction mechanism raised concerns over the entire undercarriage system. The Stirling tail configuration was rather unusual, incorporating an anti-shimmy system. This was a safety feature designed to ensure stability of the tail section. Once the tail wheel unit made contact with the runway and accepted downward pressure, hydraulic fluid was forced into the controlling arms of the complex assembly. This process restricted movement of the tail wheel, essentially keeping the twin wheels parallel and in line with the fuselage, therefore creating a very stable and controllable aircraft on landing.

Examination of the Operational Record Books for 7 Squadron in 1941 reveals that squadron personnel, normally leading aircraftsmen, were recorded on crew listings as engineer/air gunners. These men were essentially very experienced ground crew fitters from within the squadron strength who had received an introduction to basic air gunnery. In respect of the Short Stirling, the Royal Air Force had made no provision for, nor at that time had they put in place, the trade of flight engineer. A remarkable situation bearing in mind that the Handley Page Halifax was also waiting in the wings to be revealed as the second four-engine heavy bomber to join the command. The Halifax would likewise only become operational in early 1941.

The men undertaking engineering duties in the air were officially designated as 'Fitter II—Air Gunners'. This was however promptly changed to 'Flight

Engineer—Air Gunner', an indicator as to the lack of formal structure and evaluation of duties that was taking place at that time. The only possible brevet that could be worn by the men operating as engine minders was the air gunners' brevet. The Royal Air Force had seen the development of air gunners take place during the interwar period, but it was not until 1939 that air gunnery became a full-time trade and the appropriate brevet designed and awarded. Those rather changeable times saw experienced engine and airframe fitters occupying the engine instrument station within the Short Stirling; it was a position that had been constructed away from the flight deck. This was a rather unique position because thereafter all other heavy bombers had flight engineer stations situated in much closer proximity to the flight deck or cockpit areas.

The Aeroplane and Armament Experimental Establishment at Boscombe Down formally advised the Royal Air Force upon the Short Stirling handling trials conducted by them in early February 1941. The technical aspects of these trials revealed, among many matters, the necessity of duties with a flight engineer position. The duties imposed upon flight engineers were further explained in the published pilots pre-flight and take-off instructions:

> Before engines are started, each throttle lever should be moved to the priming position slightly beyond full throttle position, should be held in this position for a few seconds against the exactor spring then brought back to the closed throttle position very slowly. When the engine fires on the starter magneto each engine should be switched on. Throttle levers should not be moved during the process of starting up. Then start the engine with the propeller in fully fine position. During run out with engine speeds about 2,500 revs, replane airscrew pitch levers by moving them to the fully coarse position and holding them to the stop against the springs, then slowly return levers to fully fine position.
>
> Close gills, release brakes, open throttle as quickly as possible, leaving one outer lever in half way position. If the aircraft should tend to swing follow up slowly with the remaining throttle so as to counteract tendency to swing to the right. Alternatively, all throttles may be fully opened and the outer engine on the side opposite to the swing may be throttled back slightly.
>
> Raise the tail as early as possible and at 100 mph ease the aircraft off the ground, raise the undercarriage which takes 53 to 55 seconds, open cooling gills when undercarriage is up, raise flaps, trim the aircraft while the flaps are closing.

The fact that the huge undercarriage took so long to stow properly is quite significant. The complicated mechanism would prove to be a constant area of concern to the Stirling flight engineer. Retracted or lowered in two separate operations by electric motors, the retraction motors were eventually relocated inside the fuselage to allow for manual retraction in the event of motor failure. Also mentioned were the electronically driven engine gills, simple devices that allowed engine temperatures to be controlled by cooling or increasing temperature. The Stirling had four Bristol Hercules VI or XVI air-cooled radial engines that were fitted with a fully feathering constant speed propeller and normally started electrically. The aircraft's power supply for the electrical system was provided by two 24-volt, 1,000-watt generators, connected with four 40-amp batteries on each inboard engine. Later aircraft had two 24-volt, 1,500-watt generators connected to feed the extensive electrical systems within the aircraft.

A total of 2,692 gallons of fuel could be carried between two independent tank systems carried in the wings. The systems could be interconnected between each wing if necessary by the flight engineer operating an inter-system balance cock situated in the centre section of the fuselage. The flight engineer controls and his ancillary equipment were primarily situated about the centre section and along the starboard fuselage side, forward of the front main spar frame. There was an instrument panel mounted just aft of the armoured bulkhead on the starboard side. The list of gauges, controls, and relative equipment that fell within the responsibility of the flight engineer in a Stirling consisted of a complex arrangement of nearly fifty components or systems.

No. 35 Squadron in Bomber Command was chosen to receive the second heavy bomber supplied to the Royal Air Force: the Handley Page Halifax. Originally designed with two engines, the Halifax materialised as a four-engine aircraft, which had by then received a dedicated engineer station. This was situated much closer to the main cockpit than its counterpart Stirling. Ground crew mechanics and fitters from 35 Squadron were selected for training to man the engineer station. The 35 Squadron Operational Records for February 1941 provides detail of these events:

> It being necessary for an Engineer to be included in the Air Crew to fly the Halifax aircraft, the following airmen of Fitter trade were specially selected and trained in this Squadron by Sgt S. L. C. Watt and passed out as Flight Engineers and were promoted to the rank of Sergeant on the date with effect from 1 February 1941.
> 568825 Corporal Aedy R. G. (Fitter II)
> 569526 Corporal Ogden G. H. F. (Fitter II)
> 567891 Corporal Wheeler H. E. (Fitter II)
> 902598 Aircraftsman First Class Hill F. W. (Fitter IIE)
> 922470 Aircraftsman First Class Willingham N. (Flight Mechanic E)

These men were immediately promoted to the rank of sergeant, issued with three stripes to be worn on their uniform, and received financial remuneration as aircrew. Their counterparts in 7 Squadron, however, were not so fortunate. They carried out such duties without any promotion in rank and the first operational sorties over enemy held territory were undertaken with leading aircraftsmen and corporal engineer—air gunners. Throughout this complicated scenario, these men were essentially still regarded as tradesmen, undertaking an engineering trade within an aircraft and not regarded in many respects as true aircrew. The five fitters from 35 Squadron all flew operationally as flight engineers.

Sergeant Aedy flew his first sortie to France in Halifax L9489 on 10 March 1941. Although the sortie was successful, tragically, they were shot down in a 'friendly fire' incident while returning over Surrey. Only the flight engineer and pilot survived with their lives with Sergeant Aedy suffering injuries in these most wretched and questionable of circumstances.

Sergeant Hill in Halifax L9501 flew to Duisburg on 28 August 1941 as the crew flight engineer. He and his crew failed to return. They are all buried in the Reichswald Forest Cemetery, Germany.

Sergeant Willingham in Halifax L9560 flew to Berlin on 2 September 1941. In unknown circumstances, five members of the crew including the flight engineer were killed in action. Sergeant Willingham and his fellow crew members all rest in the Berlin War Cemetery.

Sergeant Ogden in Halifax L9512 flew to attack the Scharnhorst on 24 July 1941. After a successful attack, their Halifax was encircled by several Luftwaffe fighters and during the attacks, the flight engineer received leg wounds. Although three engines were on fire, the crew managed to escape by parachute. Remarkably, the ex-Halton apprentice Gordon Ogden and his crew all survived the war as prisoners of war.

The wearing of the air gunner brevet did nothing more than complicate matters for these early flight engineers. One contingent of advisors advocated that as they were trained in air gunnery, they should wear that recognised brevet. An alternative view was that the duties they were carrying out were ancillary to air gunnery and more akin to that of air observers who at that time were still proudly wearing the long established 'O' brevet, which had been in existence since 1916. These inconsequential matters were taking place despite the explanatory notion placed by the staff, Deputy Directorate of Technical Engineering, Wing Commander Rowland Costa. He had encouraged a brevet to be issued supporting the 'FE' flight engineer lettering in the exact style as the 'AG' gunners brevet. It would, however, be nearly a full year before the matter of revising the regulations governing the service of flight engineers be resolved and published. In the meantime, the men of 7 Squadron flying with leading aircraftsmen and corporal rank were, by June 1941, finally wearing sergeant stripes and presumably, but not confirmed, the air gunner brevet.

Flight Engineer Initial Provision— 1941 Fitters and Mechanics

Air Ministry Order A/190/1941, dated 20 March 1941, formally outlined the training requirements for ground trades qualified Fitter I, Fitter II, Fitter II (Engine), and Fitter (Aero-Engine) that were nominated to be mustered for flight engineer training. These men were volunteers, predominantly within the ranks of leading aircraftsmen and corporals who had been previously trained at various Royal Air Force Technical Training Schools across the country and were regarded as highly skilled within their respective trades. As potential flight engineers, these qualified men were initially directed to undertake a three-week course of air gunnery at No. 7 Air Gunnery School, Stormy Down, and No. 1 Air Gunnery School at Pembury. This course was predominately ground-based with technical handling and simulated aerial gunnery exercises in power operated turrets. The mainstream training of dedicated air gunners was at a premium and accessibility to the courses became problematical. Coastal Command and General Reconnaissance Squadron flight engineers had priority over Bomber Command flight engineers. Eventually, the requirement to be trained in air gunnery was eliminated for flight engineers entering Bomber Command.

Technical training in engineering was frequently undertaken at an aircraft manufacturer's works. This shop floor instruction appears to have been flexible and, in some cases, extended to several weeks while other students had fleeting experiences. These instructional periods became known as 'manufacturers courses'. The concept had been developed in 1939 for Royal Air Force airframe fitters and electricians. Initially, only three factory facilities were accessible, but they were the footprint for significant growth; eventually, these courses became of great importance to the enhanced training infrastructure that followed.

Matters were complicated when considering the deployment of the Stirling and Halifax bombers by Bomber Command during early 1941. Both aircraft were designed and constructed with engineer stations, but initially flown with a crew containing a first and second pilot with a ground trades fitter or mechanic. Ground trade flight mechanics (engines) were highly skilled and a course of just seven weeks was deemed necessary for these men to become fully trained. Ground crew personnel operating as flight engineers required a flexible approach. The early initial course infrastructures advised ground trade fitters II (airframes) were also highly skilled and just one additional week of training was necessary while the ground trade flight mechanics (airframes) were deemed to require thirteen weeks of training. Mainly due to the time required to instruct on the engine components of training, ground trade fitters II (engines) were initially allocated very limited training. Being the most highly qualified volunteers, they eventually bypassed this technical training altogether. These men undertook an attachment to a manufacturers course, engine handling, and general airframe skills before passing out of the entire examination structure in around thirty-eight days.

The Technical Training Command within the Royal Air Force managed this training infrastructure. Aircraft manufacturing courses provided more than just a technical perspective. They exposed many facets of construction and repair. Frequently, operational aircraft categorised as requiring repair but damaged beyond the capabilities of station facilities were dismantled into their originally constructed sections of manufacture. These large sections were transported to the civilian contractors, normally the company that originally produced the aircraft. Inevitably, this exposed the stark reality of operational flying to those who viewed the carnage inflicted by enemy action. The fitters and mechanics benefited from such technical exposure and gained an understanding of how the Aeronautical Inspection Department produced inspection reports. These essentially detailed the repairs and importantly instructed that modifications be undertaken to return the aircraft into operational service in the best possible configuration. In many cases, sectional unions took place between several differing aircraft used to create one air worthy example. Residue sections damaged beyond repair were consigned into the effective metal salvage and recycle procedures that existed.

The exposure to aircraft manufacturing also provided flight engineers with an understanding of many other aspects of aircraft engineering—for example, the use of industrial alcohol and its derivatives of acetone, butyl alcohol, and acetic acid. Those products were used in the manufacture of liquid coolants for aircraft engines, hydraulic fluids for aircraft landing gear, and de-icing products for propellers. Heavy bomber wings were also pasted with a protective covering to combat icing—another example derived from industrial alcohol.

Bomber Command Crews—Air Ministry Policy 1942

In February 1942, Bomber Command considered the strategic option of flight crews operating with a single pilot in Halifax, Whitley, and Wellington aircraft while flight crews in Stirling, Lancaster, Manchester, and Liberators were to be facilitated with both first and second pilot strength. There appears to have been no continuity with these considerations. The question of why the Halifax was excluded from the four-engine contingent of aircraft that appear to have been requiring a second pilot remains unexplained.

The Air Ministry conference on 12 February 1942 discussed the training of pilots and the duties undertaken within operational training units. Primarily, this looked at the level to which pilots should be trained and their subsequent conversion status from second pilots into full captains. Statistically within Bomber Command, operational injuries to first pilots necessitating the need for second pilots to take over command of the aircraft had proved exceptionally rare. The captaincy and the need for someone to relieve the first pilot in emergencies were obvious requirements, but it was thought that it need not be a highly trained pilot. As a result, the conference recommended that second pilots should be abolished and the previously conceived fatigue argument, which initially heralded the requirement of both first and second pilots, was henceforth disregarded.

On 27 February 1942, it was advocated that aircraft should have mechanical automatic pilot capabilities and that flight engineers should be carried in Stirling,

Liberators, Halifaxes, and Lancasters. Additionally, one member of the crew should be in possession of basic flying skills and be capable of bringing the aircraft back in an emergency; a provision was made for pilots to get operational experience before they took charge of aircraft on operational sorties.

The National Archives flight engineers training records, AIR10/3714 and 3715 AIR2/8348 1940–1942 provides extensive reference material indicating that the flight engineer role became policy within the Air Ministry on 27 February 1942. It could be concluded that prior to that time, terms of reference relating to engine minders or flight engineers must have been regarded as locally appointed solutions. These significant developments saw Bomber Command propose to change the established observer role to that of navigator and air bomber. New basic training courses were introduced for navigators, air bombers, wireless operators/air gunner, air gunners, and flight engineers. The new course structure for these crew positions began in April 1942.

The first flight engineer course at St Athan started on 30 May 1942. Initially, flight engineers were simply absorbed from the ranks of the serving ground crew. These engine fitters and mechanics swiftly passed through the initial courses in around three to four weeks. As the demand for heavy bomber crews escalated, the supply of suitable ground crew to take flight engineer conversion training had begun to slow. It soon became obvious that the concept of employing highly skilled fitters as a means to fulfil the duties in the new heavy bombers would never be realised. The policy in respect of formalising the status and structure of flight engineers was finally addressed in mid-1942. Air Ministry order AMO A746/1942 also settled the situation of aircrew brevets. The historical 'O' observers brevet was replaced with an 'N' navigators brevet and the bomb aimer was to wear the 'B' brevet. The long-awaited engineers brevet was designed in exactly the same way displaying a simple 'E'. The King sanctioned these matters formally and in September 1942, they were introduced and were awarded to flight engineers who successfully qualified. Men who were still wearing the 'AG' brevet would, at the earliest opportunity, exchange them. Prestigious outfitters normally supplied officer ranks with their uniforms and brevets were also supplied by these outlets. It became commonplace for these to be provided in quality silks and enhanced padding applied to accentuate the brevet. Flight engineer brevets became no exception to this rule as officer ranks progressed in that new trade during the ensuing years of conflict.

The year 1942 witnessed most of the pre-war generation of regular aircrew decimated in strength. They had taken the initial air war to the enemy in the early years and many became casualties while others remained imprisoned behind barbed wire in occupied Europe. Many by age and experience were promoted into leadership duties as the new generation swelled into the recruitment and training processes. These young men would be those who would climb into the new heavy bombers that commenced cascading out of the aircraft production lines.

5

Flight Engineer
Conversion Units

The introduction of heavy four-engine bombers into the Royal Air Force infrastructure had seen the most basic of measures put into place to accommodate the training of personnel. Those measures clearly had no long-term sustainability. Both 35 and 76 Squadrons carried out their own conversion training in co-opting qualified ground mechanics and fitters onto crews to fulfil the requirements of flight engineers. Conversion flight aircraft carried the squadron number but were appended as conversion flight.

In December 1941, the situation of attached strength conversion training was enhanced by the policy of delivering four additional heavy bombers onto nominated squadrons. This provided for dedicated conversion training to take place independently from the strength of aircraft required to maintain airworthy aircraft for operational duties. Initially, several of these aircraft were especially adapted with dual flight deck controls. This development enabled parent squadrons to facilitate training to their established crews while ensuring newly formed crews joining the squadron were facilitated with a programme of both dual and solo flying. These early training sorties tended to be of between thirty, sixty, and ninety minutes in duration. Extended flights were also undertaken to allow the newly appointed flight engineers to engage with exercises in transferring fuel loads between the various wing based fuel tanks. These exercises were also undertaken while carrying full war loads, no doubt a necessity at that time for flight engineers to experience flying fully laden with both fuel and bomb loads.

By example, Sergeant 'Tam' Readhead, who features within other chapters of this book, joined 76 Squadron Conversion Flight in July 1942. This was seven months into the planned programme of conversion flight training. He spent four weeks on supervised training and accumulated seventeen hours in the air, all of which were conducted from his home station at Middleton St George, Durham. Initially, 10, 35, 76, 78, and 102 Squadrons all created their own Halifax-equipped conversion flights and operated a program of training based upon an average of twenty hours' instruction. Other squadrons followed, and a flexible approach was required in respect of personnel. By example, in early spring of 1942, several 76 Squadron ground staff were posted to the 158 Squadron conversion flight at Linton to gain experience in the maintenance of Halifax aircraft.

Training sorties were diverse, and accidents readily took lives in numerous circumstances. On 16 July 1942, 158 Conversion Flight saw Halifax BB203 depart, carrying three pilots and two flight engineers in a morning training flight only for them all to lose their lives. The Air Ministry accident card recorded that experienced instructor Pilot Officer Craig was with two under training pilots. The flight engineer station was manned by Sergeants Place and Dunn. Alexander Dunn had volunteered to serve in 1940 after his younger brother serving as a junior engineering officer on board MV *Domala* had been killed. The incident took place off the Isle of Wight on 2 March 1940. The engine room was hit with a bomb dropped by a Luftwaffe aircraft with severe damage and an ensuing fire. Lifeboats and rafts were launched, which were then raked by machine guns from the Heinkel He 111 bomber. Along with exposure to the weather, these were the factors that accounted for the 108 deaths that took place. Alexander's brother John was irretrievably lost, presumably in the engine room explosion.

Alexander Dunn at the flight engineer station on board Halifax BB203 made preparations for a landing as they were returning to station. At the controls was Pilot Officer Withy, who overshot the turn onto the final approach and made a tight turn to enable him to line up with the runway. This caused the aircraft to stall and it crashed at 11.37 a.m. at Manor Farm, Cornborough, near Sheriff Hutton, Yorkshire. The Dunn family in Fife Scotland had already lost one son in the sea with no grave. His life is commemorated at the Tower Hill Memorial situated close to the Tower of London along with other men and women of the Merchant Navy and fishing fleets who died with no known grave in both world wars. The body of Alexander, their eldest son, was extracted from the crash scene and subsequently transported to Scotland to be buried. Wartime engineering at sea and in the air had taken a great toll upon the Dunn family.

During the closing months of the attached flight conversion period, 408 Squadron also added a conversion flight to their strength. The Royal Air Force was expanding rapidly, and a review of training resulted in the disbanding of these early conversion units. The early conversion flights had effectively paved the way forward for training and instruction in the modern four-engine heavy bombers. Those initial facilities were to amalgamate and develop their resources of men and equipment to form what were to become better defined and dedicated heavy conversion units.

6

Flight Engineer Heavy Conversion Unit Training

The term heavy conversion unit came into use on 7 October 1942 and replaced the early conversion flights, which were no more than aircraft directly attached to operational squadrons. The development of the heavy conversion unit effectively formalised and consolidated a more encompassing facility where crews both experienced and novice progressed swiftly onto the heavy bombers. These units were independently distributed within the Bomber Command structure and were until late in 1944, geographically administered by their respective bomber group.

In simplistic terms, during 1942, Bomber Command groups consisted of a number of areas. No. 3 Group were equipped with Short Stirling aircraft, 4 Group with the Handley Page Halifax, and 5 Group with the twin-engine Avro Manchester, which at that time was in the throes of being replaced by the superior Avro Lancaster. Heavy conversion units were parented alongside their respective operational group squadrons spread across central England with no attachment to any particular squadron. Each of the nineteen conversion units were uniquely identified by a four-digit number sequence, by example, 1651 Conversion Unit within three Group at Waterbeach in Cambridgeshire. These units would no longer impede upon operational squadrons and were stationed independently in a lot of instances at satellite aerodromes in relatively close proximity to the primary operational stations.

Bomber Command's heavy four-engine bomber crews were formed in two stages. The differing training programmes for the various crew members essentially dictated that process. It was commonplace for all but the flight engineer to come together at an operational training unit. This process was somewhat informal with men drifting around creating mutually agreed teams of six specialists. The pilot in effect acquired his navigator, wireless operator, bomb aimer, and air gunners by consent to create a crew which would then undertake operational training. Exceptions obviously existed within the consistently rolling program. Sickness alone would potentially disrupt this process.

The one exception of attendance at an operational training unit was the flight engineer. These men would in effect simply fill the vacancy of flight engineer when the established crews commenced training at a heavy conversion unit. Experienced twin-engine crews would also be converted to the heavier four-engine aircraft. In these instances, an additional mid-upper air gunner and flight engineer joined many previously established five-man crews. Heavy conversion units effectively consolidated the heavy bomber crews and would prepare these differing combinations of men to finally operate against the enemy. Men who arrived from the operational training unit would have already experienced both night and day training over an eight–ten-week period and recorded in their individual flying log books an estimated eighty to 100 hours of flying experience. Often, they would have taken part in operational sorties over enemy territory, dropping leaflets or supporting Bomber Command in attacking targets. These novice crews would then be posted for a further four to six-week period of instruction at a heavy conversion unit and only then did the flight engineer himself finally gain experience in the air.

It remains unclear if the flight engineers were officially issued with tool boxes at these units. Photographic evidence reveals that some men carried a canvas-elongated webbing-type holdall that was understood to contain tools. These bags are uniformly identical—16 inches long, 8 inches high, and 7 inches wide, fitted with a locking clasp and a pair of canvas loop handles. However, unlike the vast majority of issued equipment, these bags are devoid of any official Air Ministry markings. This factor suggests that these tool bags were in all probability personal items that simply enhanced the basic tools available to a flight engineer in the aircraft.

With the entire crew finally together, the last components of operational training were undertaken. This final course was divided between ground and air instruction. The crew now totalled seven men and, depending on the nature of the flying lessons throughout the course, the crew establishment would vary from four to seven actually flying. The weather was always a dominant factor but essentially wherever possible, ground training was conducted in the mornings and flying instruction took place in the afternoon. Clearly, the final training content would be relative to the particular aircraft in which the crew were to operate within. The syllabus of instruction naturally evolved and changed over the years with elements being removed that were not regarded as being of importance while the arrival of new equipment or methods influenced additional elements of training. By example, the initial concept of training flight engineers in transferring fuel between tanks in flight was later assessed as not necessitating flying time to achieve that competency.

A typical Halifax crew on heavy conversion unit duties *c.* 1944 would have included many flying exercises that engaged with flight engineers simulating mechanical malfunctions. These included simulated emergencies with feathering propellers procedure, three-engine flying procedure with three engine landings or overshoots on three engines. Inevitably the instructor also incorporated fire drill actions in event of engine fires and the ultimate ditching and emergency escape procedures.

Pilots were tested with cross wind landings, overshooting and the testing situation of flying three engine exercises that reduced to just two engine flying. Gunnery practice, aerial combat, general evasive flying, and instruction with the defensive corkscrew were all included. The corkscrew was instrumental in saving many crews from night fighter attacks. It was effective if executed sharply and violently diving and turning at the same time, it was not for the faint hearted. Many exercises were flown with the instructors before solo experience took place.

Trainees and instructors were exposed to dangerous and demanding challenges with all instructional training being paired down to the minimum time possible in an effort to be as productive as possible. The heavy conversion units were large substantial units with significant workloads and so the aircraft strength on each unit was usually greater than that on an operational squadron. Not surprisingly, the aircraft strength consisted of some elderly airframes that were always likely to become burdensome to the engineering staff.

Flight engineers required a detailed understanding of the engine driven superchargers. A supercharger impellor increases the manifold air pressure, or boost pressure, of the fuel–air mixture entering the cylinders. This ensures sea-level engine power is maintained at altitude, despite reduced atmospheric pressure. This is not to be confused with the carburettor, which controlled the fuel–air ratio. The ideal ratio is fifteen parts air to one part fuel, referred to as stoichiometric. The supercharger was ultimately added to the engine in order to provide a denser combustible mixture after it passed through the carburettor. Simplistically, the increased charge density achieved by impellors produces more power at the engine. The supercharger mechanism created the additional boost to counteract the predictable drop in power of an engine that takes place when an aircraft climbed high and entered lower atmospheric pressure. However, a high-speed supercharger can produce too much boost pressure at sea-level, possibly leading to rupture of the inlet manifold. So, what was required was matched performance at both lower and higher altitudes. The answer was the development of the two-speed supercharger. Flight engineers were required to have a thorough understanding of how this worked when in high speed gear at altitudes, where it can better a medium speed performance and when it worked at a medium speed gear for lower altitude flying. Effectively, at lower altitudes, the supercharger impellor was driven slower using less power, to prevent excessive boost pressure damaging the engine. These matters all affected fuel consumption which was the flight engineer's responsibility.

Each flight engineer carried out their own pre-flight checks, which included a test of the supercharger's gear-change system. In respect of the Lancaster with the Merlin engines, it was customary to start an inboard engine first, followed by the outer on each wing. The throttle was set with a small opening and the propeller pitch set to fine, to off load the engine during the start. The supercharger was set in

'M' gear, the engine air intake control was on cold, radiator shutters in automatic, and the fuel tank selector cocks selected onto number two tanks. The priming pump in the undercarriage bay was operated by the ground crew; in the cockpit, the ignition and booster coil were switched on before the starter button was pressed by the flight engineer. As the engine gave a few preliminary combustions, the priming pump continued to activate until the Merlin picked up on the carburettor and spontaneously fired regularly. This process would be repeated on each of the engines. After all four engines had started, the pilot would run the engines with the wheels chocked to 1,500 rpm. This enabled the eight magnetos to be checked and then to 3,000 rpm to check the boost. Further mandatory checks took place and just prior to taxying, the flight engineer checked that the bomb doors were closed, booster pumps were as required, radiator shutters open, and that the instrument panel vacuum pumps were showing the correct minus registration.

Flight engineers were aware that the two-speed supercharger was not the complete solution to managing engine capabilities; the throttle position also played a part. The balance of throttle used with the two-speed supercharger came from understanding that the speed or gear as it was known only partially determined engine boost pressure. That situation created the need for pilots and flight engineers to change from 'M' to 'S' on a climb but not at the time when the engine boost began to fall away, indicated by the boost dial indicators falling into the negative sector. A balancing act was required in many circumstances, adding to the complexity of understanding and using the two-speed superchargers. Ideally, a smooth uninterrupted climb was achieved by gradually opening the throttle to maintain boost pressure up to the full throttle height. Full throttle height is where the throttle valve is fully open and cannot maintain boost pressure with increasing altitude. Increasing the supercharger speed during the climb had the effect of increasing the full throttle height. Flight engineers and pilots were instructed to change gear smartly and firmly. It was a mechanical high speed changing process that did not appreciate operation by a faltering hand. Crucially, if the flight engineer mishandled the throttle and supercharger during the climb, fuel could be wasted and the aircraft may arrive over the target at a lower altitude; this therefore made the crew vulnerable to bombs dropped from above and anti-aircraft fire from below, not to mention the possibility of running out of fuel before reaching home.

Subsequently, Rolls-Royce developed two-stage superchargers for fighters with both impellors effectively running as one combined unit on one shaft. This created fewer complications for application in flight, undoubtedly seen by some flight engineers as beneficial.

As 1944 progressed, dedicated Lancaster finishing schools had undertaken specific training on that particular aircraft. The remaining seventeen heavy conversion units spread across the Midlands continued to process crews in predominantly Halifax and Stirling aircraft. Bomber Command losses both in the air and on the ground in accidental circumstances were, by 1945, significant.

Within those statistics was a young man from Dundee wearing a newly presented flight engineer brevet on his uniform. Alfred Keith Moncur had volunteered aged sixteen, having been a member of his local Air Training Corps Squadron. Born in November 1926, it must be assumed he provided a false date of birth on his application to serve and this had not been detected. After eighteen months of technical training, Alfred joined a newly formed crew at 1661 Heavy Conversion Unit, Winthorp near Newark, Nottinghamshire. On 20 July 1944, during a training flight, he experienced problems with all four engines on Stirling EF444. The pilot, Sergeant Bowden, ordered his entire crew to bail out over the Yorkshire countryside and everyone other than the young flight engineer managed to escape successfully. The young flight engineer perished in the aircraft as it crashed to earth. Sergeant Alfred Moncur was just seventeen-and-a-half years old when he was laid to rest in Dundee. In all probability, he was the youngest-qualified flight engineer to have lost his life in the Second World War. His short life had been subject of great adventure. In September 1939, just after war had been declared, Alfred, then aged twelve, had been playing when he fell into the docks at Dundee. On 11 September 1939, the Dundee *Courier* reported the bravery of a mill worker who had rescued him, advising that the boy's recently widowed mother was overjoyed. That same newspaper published an article reporting his death on 22 July 1944.

Engine fires on training flights frequently presented life and death scenarios for many crews under training at the heavy conversion units. A simple night navigation exercise for the crew of Halifax DG403 at Sandtoft, North Lincolnshire on the 24 May 1944 resulted in the twenty-year-old novice flight engineer, Sergeant Raymond Fowler, having to make some critical decisions. The starboard outer engine started to stream thick black smoke and immediately, a decision was taken to return to the aerodrome. The starboard inner engine then failed as they committed to land. With all power lost on the starboard wing, an emergency forced landing took place. All seven crew sustained injuries as the Halifax burst into flames and completely burnt out in the ensuing fire. The flight engineer, Sergeant Fowler, sustained torrid burn injuries to his hands, which resulted in multiple operations of specialist surgery at the East Grinstead Burns Hospital, the result of which entitled him to join the ranks of the Guinea Pig Club.

The complexities of building large heavy bomber aircraft were also challenging to those men and women who worked night and day in the factories that constructed them. These were complex aircraft and mechanical faults naturally occurred in the air. It fell upon the shoulders of the flight engineers who were expected to resolve such matters and get the aircraft and crew safely back on the ground. In May 1947, the Air Ministry published several statistics, the most pertinent of which have a direct association to flight engineers. It reported that 4,200 wounded men had returned safely from operations over enemy-held territories. Without doubt, those statistics would have been influenced by the specific duties of flight engineers assisting in bringing home any aircraft if it was at all possible to do so.

7

Heavy Bomber:
Fuel Tanks and Fire

During the inter-=war period, a typical rating for aviation fuel was 87-octane. The Royal Air Force began to investigate the use of 100-octane fuels, and would do so throughout the Second World War. Commonly seen are two octane numerical ratings for aircraft fuel—one for lean mix and one for rich mix, the rich mix always being the greater number. Therefore, by example, a common British aviation fuel of the later part of the war was 100/130 grade. In broad terms, fuels with a higher octane rating are used in higher performance. The higher the octane number, the more compression the fuel can withstand before the combustion process.

The protection of aircraft fuel tanks had seen the concept of using armour plating for the fuel tanks and feed lines. It was, however, impracticable as aircraft performance would have suffered catastrophically with such additional weight. The Luftwaffe had developed the idea of combining layers of rubber to protect fuel tanks. That concept was developed further, resulting in a vulcanised rubber manufacturing process, which was put into place within their Second World War aircraft production.

The British-made Henderson safety fuel tank was a crash-safe concept supplied to the Air Ministry in 1939. The Henderson Safety Tank Company built thousands of safety tanks supplied from their works at Elstree, Hertfordshire. The development was to create a fuel tank capable of sustaining disruption or damage during flying accidents and it was primarily fitted to training aircraft. Another company, Fireproof Tanks Ltd, was formed in 1939 in response to an Air Ministry requirement for the development and manufacture of self-sealing fuel tanks. These were fuel tanks or fuel bladders that prevented fuel from leaking after sustaining damaged by enemy ordinance. They consisted of multiple layers of rubber and reinforcing fabric, one of vulcanised rubber, and one of untreated natural rubber, which was capable of absorbing fuel. When a fuel tank punctured, the fuel would seep into the layers, causing the swelling of the untreated layer, and effectively sealing the puncture. The term flexible fuel bladder was used as a means to differentiate collapsible fuel containers from conventional solid fuel tanks.

The early solid tanks were of welded aluminium structure with the sealing material applied as a composite layer on the outside. These tanks had the potential to develop a problem with weld decay and fatigue. The welded seams were exposed to vibration while flying and research revealed that this factor was primarily responsible for such failures. Additionally, it was found that the exit of any penetrating ordinance, as opposed to the entry, was creating the greater problem. Inevitably, as with all ballistic trajectories, a large exit hole was created when sufficient velocity projected the ordinance through the tank structure.

Fireproof Tanks Ltd first installed their self-sealing tanks in the Fairey Battle light bomber, with other versions installed in Supermarine Spitfire and Hawker Hurricane fighters. The heavy bombers followed in succession. By 1942, Fireproof Tanks had developed the first flexible fuel bladders as range extender tanks for the Spitfire. These tanks were flexible fuel cells, made of a laminated self-sealing rubber material. Clearly, development of the tank engaged collaboration between experts in metal and chemical fabrication processes.

The Air Ministry approved the company Linatex rubber to manufacture fire-proofing products to protect aircraft oil tanks and fuel supply pipes. The well-known manufacturer Dunlop, who specialised in rubber products, was involved in producing various types of rubber-based protective coverings. There was no doubt that several other companies contributed to the success of self-sealing fuel tank research and development. Heavy bombers sustained terrible damage from marauding Luftwaffe night fighters, many of their pilots purposely targeted the fuel tanks in their wings. The non-discretionary fragments of anti-aircraft flak that penetrated at will in the sky over occupied enemy territory always had the potential to tear open fuel tanks regardless of the technical achievements attained to try and ensure the safe return of Allied aircrews.

The Operational Research Section within Bomber Command reviewed aircraft vulnerability and in respect of fuel tanks, they regarded the compartmentation of tanks was of the utmost importance. British-made fuel tanks were compartmented by unpainted age-hardened aluminium alloy baffles. These baffles reduced fuel movement as the aircraft manoeuvred, otherwise rapid control inputs could make the aircraft very difficult, if not impossible, to control with gallons of fuel sloshing about. Fibre baffles were thought to be less vulnerable to spark if a metal fragment was to strike it with any significant velocity. The Avro Lancaster has three self-sealing tanks fitted in each wing, each tank reducing in size from the fuselage towards the furthest tank at wing end:

No. 1 tank (Inner): Between the fuselage and the inner engines, 580 gallons in each.
No. 2 tank (Centre): Between the inner and the outer engines, 383 gallons in each.

No. 3 tank (Outer or Reserve): Outboard of the outer engines, 114 gallons in each.

1,077-gallon capacity in each wing.

2,154-gallon capacity in total.

The flight engineer controlled two tank selector cocks, which selected No. 1 or No. 2 tank situated within each wing. No. 3 tank, the outer fuel tank also known as the reserve, only replenished No. 2 and did not feed the engines directly. A cross-feed cock, referred to as the balance cock, jointly connected the port and starboard supply systems. The flight engineer accessed the balance cock on the floor just forward of the front spar, the control handle being visible through a hole in the spar cover. As the name implies, the balance cock was used to keep the aircraft laterally balanced by prioritising individual tank use, in effect moving fuel between wings. The flight engineer panel on the Lancaster had six fuel content gauges, together with six booster pump switches and a single power switch, which had to be selected to the on position to supply power to the gauges. A contents transmitter was incorporated within each fuel tank. The engineer panel also held four fuel pressure warning lights. Each was connected through resistors on the port side of the engine mounting members to pressure-operated switches in the main fuel supply system. The switch was operated by the pressure of fuel on a diaphragm, which held open a pair of contacts. If the fuel pressure fell below the setting of 6 lb per square inch, the contacts closed, initiating the warning to the flight engineer. The reason for a resistor in series with the pressure switch and warning lamp was to protect the filament of the bulb. If the warning system activated and the bulb instantaneously blew, the flight engineer would have no idea the engine was about to fail. For example, a reliable warning system allowed the flight engineer to save the engine by putting on the booster pumps.

Little doubt exists that the greatest threat posed to flight engineers in the air was that of fire, a danger that the Air Ministry was well aware of and became the subject of extensive consultation. In 1942, it was suggested that the risk from explosions and subsequent fire in fuel tanks was greater in tanks that had been drained during flight. Liquid fuel is surprisingly stable; however, fuel vapour is highly combustible. The feasibility of leaving fuel in each tank was discussed, as were the factors of temperatures and air pressures endured by fuel tanks during operational flights. It was known that flight engineers managing fuel consumption frequently ran an engine on a tank feed until the engine misfired. Even so, this practice always left a small amount of residue fuel, which resulted in a highly volatile fuel–air mixture in the tank. The Avro Lancaster fuel system used electric booster pumps in No. 1 and No. 2 tanks to maintain fuel pressure at altitudes of approximately 17,000 feet, but they were also used for raising the fuel pressure before starting and to assist in re-starting an engine during flight. Flight engineers were well versed in all aspects of fuel management. If one engine failed during take-off and the electric fuel pump was not in the on position, it was possible air could be drawn back into the main fuel system through the failed engine before its master (engine shut-off) cock could be closed. Potentially, that could cause the failure of the other engine on the same wing. It was therefore essential that all the main tank booster pumps were on, which also guarded against fuel system failures during take-off as an immediate supply was available by quickly activation of the tank selector cock. The pump in each tank should also have been switched on at any time when a drop in fuel pressure was indicated by the low pressure light on the flight engineers control panel. In order to maintain or correct lateral balance, it was possible to run all engines from one fuel tank. This was achieved by selective use of the booster pumps and by opening the cross-feed cock.

The Ministry of Aircraft Production scrutinised a series of flight engineer logs and other data relating to operational flights. This was to assist in the calculations of the fuel–air mixture strength likely to be found with fuel levels in a tank at various stages of the flight. The Royal Aircraft Establishment also carried out extensive trials and calculations on the atmosphere likely to be found in the voids above fuel level in aircraft tanks. The ideal ratio for combustion is fifteen parts air to one part fuel, which is safely utilised in an engine combustion chamber, but not in a wing fuel tank that may receive a bullet at any time.

Another fire risk in the heavy bombers was the possible presence of explosive vapour in the voids that existed within the mainplanes, a reference term for the wings. This was investigated by the deployment of vapour concentration measurements obtained during and after tank refuelling. The Wellington, Halifax, Lancaster, and Stirling bomber aircraft were subjected to these measurements. They revealed that instances existed of ground crews allowing considerable quantities of fuel to overflow from the top of the tanks during the refuelling process. With the possible exception of the Stirling, it was found that mainplane construction provided for excess fuel spill to flow away before any dangerous concentrations of fuel vapour could build up. It was assessed that this vapour risk was negligible.

It must be assumed that ground staff was under instruction to prevent fuel overspill as best as possible. The processes of ensuring tanks were up to full capacity was critical in many circumstances and it was understandable why these occurrences took place. It was common place for flight engineers to work alongside the ground crew and fuel bowser crews. An example of the accountability of refuelling duties is portrayed in the events that befell Halifax L9487. This early production aircraft, having been recently delivered from the factory, was flown on a standard fuel consumption test. The nominated crew was to carry out the test at a designated height at which they were to cruise for an hour during which the flight engineer measured the fuel consumption. About half an hour following take off, the aircraft was seen at a lower altitude and a trail of vapour spewed behind the port side of the aircraft. One of the port engines was also seen not to be working. The vapour then ignited, and a large fire was seen on the port side of the aircraft after which the aircraft entered a steep dive before crashing near Baldersby, Yorkshire. All of the crew perished. The subsequent inquiry deduced the cause of the fire to have been caused by the failure of ground crew to replace the fuel-filler cap onto one of the port fuel tanks after it had been refuelled. The flight engineer was twenty-one-year-old Sergeant Francis Leslie Plowman of Doncaster, Yorkshire. He was buried alongside some of his crew at Dishforth Cemetery, Yorkshire.

Among the many fire prevention modifications that were issued, it was emphasised that the greatest factors for overcoming engine fires was the fully feathering propeller. Feathered propeller blades produce minimum drag and cease to accelerate mass airflow rearwards over the engine. Initial instructions to flight engineers had been to turn off the fuel supply to the engine and open the throttle, actions designed to combat carburettor intake fire. As a result of consultation instigated out of the high loss of aircraft and personnel to accidental fires, the drill in respect of an engine fire was changed to a sequence that commenced by warning the entire crew. Immediate actions were closing the throttle, feathering the propeller, turning off the fuel supply, and switching off the ignition. This was followed by a final action of activating the Graviner extinguisher once the engine had come to rest. The importance of the feathered propeller is that the extinguishant gets to work on the fire instead of being blown away by the propeller slipstream.

The Graviner Manufacturing Company produced the Graviner extinguisher, which operated a fire suppression system to prevent fuel from catching fire in an aircraft crash. The flight engineer was able to activate the extinguisher manually and independently. Extinguishant was released into the carburettor intakes and around the inside of the engine cowling. This effective fire extinguisher system was installed in the engine nacelles, each extinguisher being electrically operated by push buttons within the respective aircraft cockpit. In the event of the pilot being unable to activate these push buttons, an automatic operation was provided to assist with forced landing or crash scenarios whereby an inertia switch in the nose of the aircraft was capable of activating the extinguishers.

The Operational Research Section, in addition to their own inspectors responsible at group level who collated enemy aircraft damage, sought to obtain intelligence from returning bomber crews who had witnessed aircraft fires caused by enemy action. Essentially, that information was needed to access and establish what proportion of missing aircraft fell in flames due to flak or fighters. They estimated that between mid-August to end of October 1942, it seemed likely that about 40 per cent of aircraft missing had been shot down in flames.

The period of May to August 1942 examined incidents of aircraft successfully returning after having had fires in the air. That information disclosed eighty-one varied incidents of fires; however, remarkably, forty of these appeared to have had no correlation to enemy action whatsoever. Enemy flak was without doubt the primary reason for those fires.

Each heavy bomber engine had its own oil tank with a capacity of just over 37 gallons of oil. Some 150 gallons of lubricating oil were carried to cater for oil consumption, which was normally 1–2 gallons per hour, per engine, depending on its condition. An engine exceeding a usage of more than 2 gallons per hour would be identified by the flight engineer and preferably be exchanged. The aircraft oil tanks were also self-sealing and constructed in a similar fashion to the larger fuel tanks. The Operational Research Section advised the Air Ministry by letter in July 1943 detailing all known strikes on self-sealing oil tanks, together with remarks on the efficiency of the self-sealing covers. The research advised that operational experience provided little evidence to contradict the experimental results obtained at the Royal Aircraft Establishment showing that the self-sealing on an oil tank could rarely be of value. Consultation with the Ministry of Aircraft Production subsequently agreed that the saving in crude rubber, of which the supply was critical, would be substantial. It was agreed to substitute the oil tanks self-sealing covers with crash-proof felt coverings.

In November 1943, concern was expressed that self-sealing fuel pipes were sealing themselves internally and cutting off the flow of fuel to the engines. It must be assumed this information was ascertained from unexplained low fuel pressure warning lights preceding an engine failure, crash investigations, or maintenance engineering. The Operational Research Section found that during a four-month period of assessment, there were twenty-five cases of damage to fuel pipes and of those cases, the self-sealing was certainly unlikely to be effective in half the instances. It was suggested to the Ministry of Aircraft Production that the self-sealing on the main fuel feed lines to the engines might safely be removed. It was later agreed that self-sealing pipes ceased to be fitted in the production of heavy bombers. This removed any risk of fuel lines involuntary closing.

The Department of Scientific and Industrial Research was a department of the British Government responsible for the organisation, development, and encouragement of scientific and industrial research. This department became engaged in undertaking experiments instigated by the Air Ministry to discover the effects of firing fragments of metal through inflammable mixtures. This was to determine if ordinary flak fragments had sufficient velocity, as was suspected, to cause ignition of fuel or vapour. Various technical applications were applied to this research and two cases out of eight replica firings of flak fragments caused fires.

In respect of incendiary ordinance, experiments took place with small capacity self-sealing fuel tanks filled to a quarter capacity and cooled to replicate altitude flying. When a single incendiary bullet was fired above the fuel line into the void area, the fuel tanks exploded and burst into flames. This apparently convincing evidence was brought to the attention of the Air Ministry and to the Ministry of Aircraft Production.

In January 1943, the Royal Aircraft Establishment had carried out further incendiary bullet firing trials using various fuel tanks. Those experiments consolidated the previous findings with identical explosions and fires taking place. Mr Mowatt, attached to the Bomber Command Operational Research Section, arranged for the Bomber Development Unit to carry out monitoring to determine the temperatures endured inside fuel tanks during operational flights. It has been unconfirmed but presumably, this data was supplied by a temperature bulb similar to those in the engine coolant and oil temperature gauge systems. The flight engineer would monitor and record these additional readings in his log, which was assessed immediately upon the return from operations.

The Bomber Development Unit had good communications within the other sectors engaged in research and development. It was, however, the primary resource used to test new equipment often associated with electronic devices. In respect of the task to assess temperatures in the Avro Lancaster, the temperature readings obtained from the No. 3 fuel tank once empty resembled closely the outside air temperatures. The remaining fuel tanks retained a slightly higher temperature caused by the heat from the engines. The fuel tank temperatures flying in sunlight were found to be remarkably higher. This higher tank temperature will encourage fuel to evaporate and produce a combustible fuel–air mixture more readily than a cold tank. It was deduced that any part-empty fuel tank struck by an incendiary bullet above the fluid line would inevitably cause a disastrous explosion or fire, with certain destruction of the aircraft leaving any crew with no possible chance of escape.

Previous experimentation involving inert gas nitrogen being introduced into fuel tanks eventually eliminated the risk of fire and explosion completely. Nitrogen pressure not only supresses fuel vapour production but also overwhelms any emergent fire. In or around May 1943, with the approval of the Commander in Chief Bomber Command, the Air Ministry was advised and agreed to introduce the nitrogen scheme as a matter of priority. In July 1943, the Air Ministry reported that the Ministry of Aircraft Production was making satisfactory progress with introducing nitrogen installations. Matters of additional weight to be carried by the heavy bombers necessitated further consultation as the combined installation of new methyl bromide firefighting equipment with the nitrogen installations became a serious concern.

The process of bartering between the various departments saw questions asked about the need for the methyl bromide fire extinguisher system, which was designed to quell entire fuel tank bays. The significant evidence of methyl bromide tests undertaken on the half-scale Avro Lancaster wing was reiterated, however a predicted weight gain on a heavy bomber with both nitrogen and methyl bromide fire safety systems in place was approximately 500 lb. The significance of this meant that less fuel or bomb weight would have to be carried, both of which were most undesirable.

The first Bomber Command heavy bomber to be equipped with the nitrogen system commenced operations in April 1944. Very few aircraft carried this facility and it encountered technical issues with rubber used in valves wrinkling on exposure to the fuel allowing nitrogen to escape. No doubt this was frustrating bearing in mind the extensive efforts to reach eventual production in the aircraft construction factories. The Bomber Command Research Unit dispatched this unfortunate news to the Headquarters Bomber Command on the 6 June 1944. The most significant military invasion in history had just commenced and it must be assumed instructing the Royal Air Force groups equipped with nitrogen systems, to discontinue the use until further notice, was a most unwelcome annoyance. This situation eventually eased in early July when flight engineers received instructions to ensure the nitrogen system was turned on as soon as the aircraft was airborne. This necessitated taking a record of the pressures in the system every thirty minutes until the pressure fell to a pre-prescribed limit. Records disclosed that by September, flight engineers reported high instances of nitrogen not being exhausted on operational flights and in the following month, the Research Unit undertook analysis of the effectiveness of the nitrogen system. Due to poor record-keeping, this analysis was basically inconclusive in its findings. Worryingly, in November 1944, the Air Ministry received notification that an estimated 80 per cent of missing aircraft were thought to have been lost in flames. This represented significant losses in aircraft and men, but it was based on probable flawed intelligence. The scrutiny of that intelligence gathering process revealed nothing specific. The Bomber Command Research Section had clearly recognised and evidenced that fire risk was the major hazard associated with the operations of bomber aircraft. They had engaged in experimental development in order to establish remedial measures, working tirelessly to protect the men from the tragedies of fire and explosion while flying over occupied Europe. The fight to conquer fire on-board heavy bombers was actually never won and the awesome responsibilities of fuel management remained a primary duty for flight engineers until victory was achieved for the Allied forces in the Second World War.

8

1943 Direct Entry Flight Engineer Students

The Military Training Act of 1939 required all men born between 4 June 1918 and 3 June 1919 to register at the local Ministry of Labour office. These young men were to be called up for six months of military training, and upon completion transferred to what was known as the reserve. To ensure that the call up did not take men away from vital industries and other important services, the Government introduced a schedule of reserved occupations. These were men meeting the age criteria laid out in the schedule, but were reserved in their present occupation. After the declared war on Germany, Parliament immediately passed wider reaching measures. The Armed Forces Act imposed conscription on all males aged between eighteen and forty-one who had to register for service. Those medically unfit were exempt, as were those men employed in mining, food, farming production, and engineering.

In February 1943, the concession in respect of reserved occupation status was relaxed. This assisted in releasing many young men with various elements of engineering skills. Some of these potential candidates would eventually fulfil duties as flight engineers because in June 1943, the Royal Air Force announced in its order, A538/1943, that they would accept direct entry training of civilians for the position of aircrew flight engineers. Volunteers who responded to this entry process undertook an assessment at an aviation candidates' selection board. If successful, they were required to swear allegiance to the King and Country and be formally enlisted into the Royal Air Force for the duration of the present emergency. Effectively, they were placed on reserve status. This was standard procedure at the time as the military infrastructure engaged in processing men within the broad spectrum of trades and duties required immense logistical management.

The Air Ministry subsequently published pamphlet No.167 titled 'Your place in the Air Crew Team'. This purposely explained individual aircrew duties and was issued to volunteers during their initial training. The pamphlet explained all duties and for flight engineer positions, it stated as follows:

The Flight Engineer is the member of the crew most concerned with the care and maintenance of the aircraft as a whole. When he is not flying, the Flight Engineer in a Squadron is the link between the captain of the aircraft and the ground servicing party. He takes a close interest in their work, each day he carries out for himself an inspection of a different part of the aircraft, and when the aircraft is being prepared to fly, supervises such work as refuelling, filling oil and coolant tanks and applying de-icing paste to the wings.

Just before the flight, the Flight Engineer does an engineering check of the aircraft, both outside and in, and then he helps the Pilot to start up and records the gauge readings during the ground test. During take-off, he operates some of the engine controls, watches to see that engine running limitations are not exceeded and in some cases, raises the undercarriage and retracts the flaps on instructions from the Pilot.

During flight, he is responsible to the captain for the engines. He operates such controls as the air intake shutters, cooling gills and fuel cocks and advises the Pilot how to handle the engines to fly the greatest distance for the amount of fuel carried. In his log he records engine conditions and fuel tank contents, keeping a tally of air miles per gallon. The Flight Engineer also carries a tool kit and a collection of spares so that, if small engineering repairs to the airframe or to engine controls become necessary during flight, he may do them. After landing he hands his log to the Flight Engineer Leader so that any snags may be reported to the maintenance staff and put right.

The training of a Flight Engineer covers all technical subjects. If you already have any trade qualifications, so much the better, but do not be discouraged from volunteering because you have no actual experience. If you feel sufficiently interested to want to volunteer you already have the most important qualification.

After selection within the direct entry process, formal instructions would eventually be received to report at an aircrew reception receiving centre. Basic uniform was issued, and the volunteers were formed into flights, normally consisting of sixty men. They were subjected to dental checks and inoculations against diphtheria, typhoid, and smallpox. Every student commenced wearing the fibreboard identity tags around their neck. These tags identified every man, his religion, and his personal service number. Each student was instructed to mark each item of issued kit with his unique service number. All uniform and equipment was to be kept spotlessly clean and were subject to daily and the weekly inspection. Daily routines included instruction on service law, signal skill, use of weapons, mathematics, swimming, training drills, and lectures, all of which were subject to aptitude tests. Swimming lessons were put in place for any volunteer who was unable to swim, and games were designed to create bonded participation exercises.

More formal training then took place at an initial training wing. This six-week training programme was designed to instil discipline, improve physical fitness, and provide a sound basic knowledge of the Royal Air force structure. The initial training wing syllabus included understanding the principles of flight, augmented by additional mathematics, aircraft recognition, and meteorology. Individual aptitude tests and combined tests between students often required apparatus manipulation. These were designed to test the speed of learning. The understanding of mechanical problems and the ability to apply eye, hand, and foot co-ordination was significantly important. Aptitude tests were strictly pass or fail with no second test facilitation permitted.

During the initial training wing course, the tangible connection with flying became a reality with the issue of flying clothing. These items were personal issue and in keeping with common practice, the service numbers or other means of identity were applied to each item, which included a flying helmet with oxygen and communication mask, flying goggles, flying suit (either one piece or separate Irvin jacket and trousers), a pair of leather gauntlets, a pair of inner silk gloves, flying socks and boots, life jacket, and a parachute harness.

Flight engineers would all fly wearing what was known as the observer's parachute harness. This was a somewhat cumbersome item when first seen but it actually fitted well and would ultimately be responsible for saving many hundreds of lives. The harness was manufactured in webbing material with bright plated alloy buckles and clips. The four main straps located into a quick release buckle, which would be positioned on the lower chest position. To prevent the harness straps from twisting, they passed through a rear back pad, making it as comfortable as possible. The parachute pack itself was a rectangular shape with a brown coloured canvas exterior fitted with four carrying handles, one to each side. The metal 'D' ring or ripcord directly connected to the parachute canopy. Fitted to the reverse was a pair of metal buckles with spring clips for attaching onto the hooks that fitted to the observer's parachute assembly harness. Once attached, the parachute sat upon the wearer's chest but when deployed, the harness strapping became detached by the stitching to be torn from the wearer's shoulders as the 24-foot diameter parachute rapidly inflated. This assembly was well liked by the vast majority of personnel and in any emergency, the parachute could be attached with no regard to its position. Either way up, the ring or rip cord could be pulled by the left or right hand. The personal harness was worn at all times while in the air, normally without a parachute attached. The parachute pack would be stowed and accessible at all times. It was simple to clip the parachute pack onto the harness hooks.

Maneuverability within an aircraft was of utmost importance to flight engineers. The Irvin flying jacket was an ideal garment for their use. Designed by the parachute pioneer Leslie Irvin, the first examples went into production in 1931. These were manufactured with undivided one-piece body panels requiring only the minimum of necessary seams. Although this facilitated easier assembly, it consumed large quantities of sheep fleece material. As the demand for jackets increased, a more economic method of manufacture was devised. Smaller panels of sheepskin were used, which naturally increased the number of seams. As time progressed and demand continued to increase, even greater measures were taken to reduce any waste of the valuable sheepskins. Jackets were produced with additional panels, creating almost patchwork results. Flight engineers therefore inevitably wore the multi-paneled Irvin jackets. The 'Irvin' has become an item strongly associated with airmen of the Second World War.

The lesser-known Irvin trousers were produced at the same time and were designed as a one-piece slip over thermal-insulated trousers. When worn with the jacket, the dual sheepskin outer garments provided some protection from the freezing temperatures at high altitudes. The trousers were completed with fitted braces, which enabled easy dressing. The legs were fitted with separating zips running the full length of each leg, a design crucial to allow easy removal to treat any wounds. These trousers were capable of being fitted with electrical elements that ran down both legs, enabling the wearer to gain constant warmth at high altitudes.

The successful completion of the initial training course was dictated by constant assessment and examinations, all of which had to be passed in order to progress. Those successfully qualifying from the initial training wing were awarded seven days' leave and provided with a free travel warrant to their chosen leave address.

9

Flight Engineer Watson DFM: Short Stirling

William Alexander Watson entered No. 1 School of Technical Training as a Halton apprentice in September 1934. He had an impending sixteenth birthday as he was issued with his Royal Air Force number, 567222. This young boy from Bankfoot in Perthshire Scotland was far from home as he embarked on his training to become a fitter and commence his twelve-year commitment of service. He was educated at Perth Academy and his subsequent apprenticeship examination performance in science, English, maths, and mechanical drawing all received good marks.

In 1935, as a junior aircraft apprentice, William was awarded a coveted Barrington-Kennett medal. The Barrington-Kennett Trophy had been established in 1920, in memory of Major B. H. Barrington-Kennett, who was killed in France in 1915. The trophy became a highly-prized sporting award for both summer and winter events, and was awarded twice annually to the wing of aircraft apprentices gaining the highest number of accumulated points. From 1928, medals were awarded to mark individual achievement and one of these was awarded to apprentice William Watson for his cross-country running ability.

William Watson eventually became one of only 249 apprentices who were awarded a Distinguished Flying Medal. William was preferred to be known to all as Sandy and this remained so throughout his life. In 1938, he was promoted to aircraftsman first class and served as a fitter at several maintenance units. After the outbreak of war, the official service records indicate that Sandy received instruction in air gunnery in 1941. This was prior to a posting to 15 Squadron in June 1941. This would suggest that Sandy Watson had volunteered as a result of Air Ministry Order A/190/1941, which published a request for suitably qualified volunteers to apply for aircrew selection. Sandy later served in the conversion flight attached to 15 Squadron, this effectively acted as a training flight. It would appear that he was wearing the air gunner's brevet on his tunic at that time. The following month Sandy was detached to the Short Brothers' factory. This clearly indicates his formal training for flight engineer duties, returning to 15 Squadron on 10 August 1941 when he was promoted to the rank of sergeant.

Operational flying as a flight engineer commenced on 7 September 1941. He had qualified in a rather indirect manner but the duties of being a flight engineer were thrust upon him when the troublesome undercarriage of the Stirling brought Sandy difficulties when only one wheel assembly retracted after taking off to attack Berlin. Despite all efforts, the fault was not resolved. The bomb load was dropped at a safe location as they flew with one extended undercarriage locked into place. Fortune favoured the crew when the faulty undercarriage operated correctly during a final attempt before the anticipation of a most dangerous landing. Sandy ensured both main undercarriage structures were eventually locked down and the crew finally landed. The early Stirling had three pairs of green and red lamps on the instrument panel, one set each for the main wheels and the additional tail wheel unit. When all three wheels were locked up, three red lights were illuminated. When all three were locked down, the three lights changed to green. If any malfunction took place, the electrical system needed to be switched off and rested for thirty seconds before being retested. If both red and green lights were illuminated, the system needed to be physically inspected and may well have required winding down by hand crank. To do so would have been a strenuous task requiring great tenacity and strength to complete in an emergency situation.

Sandy was not particularly tall, and the fuselage-positioned engineer station in the Stirling was suitably proportioned around him. His circumstances had seen him operating as a spare bod until Flying Officer Peter Boggis secured him as his regular flight engineer. In 2010, the late Peter Boggis recalled:

> Sandy Watson was assigned to my crew in MacRoberts Reply as a well-qualified chap, he proved to be a most efficient Flight Engineer. This crew were close and frequently got together at the Bridge Hotel in Huntingdon where we were able to socialise together. The Squadron mess did not allow that to happen because the non-commissioned officers were always in their own mess. Sandy was a jolly efficient engineer that was why he was in my crew.

Sandy had been fortunate to fly in the most prestigious and now historically important Short Stirling heavy bomber, MacRoberts Reply. The origins of this aircraft are surrounded by the great misfortune that befell the three sons of widowed Lady Rachael MacRobert. The title from their deceased father had been passed to her eldest son, Alasdair, who was killed in a civil flying accident in 1938. On his death, the baronetcy passed to his brother, Roderic, a pilot in the Royal Air Force. Roderic was lost in action just three years later on 22 May 1941 while leading a flight of Hurricanes in a strafing attack on a German-held airfield in Iraq. The baronetcy therefore passed to the youngest son, Iain, who by them was himself a pilot officer in the Royal Air Force having joined straight from

Cambridge University. Fewer than six weeks after the death of his brother, Iain was reported missing when his Coastal Command aircraft failed to return from a search and rescue mission flown from Sullom Voe airfield in the Shetlands. Adding to this final tragedy, his body was never found.

Lady MacRobert wrote to the Air Ministry. Her letter demonstrated the remarkable fortitude and resilience of a proud mother:

> It is my wish, as a mother, to reply in a way my sons would applaud—attack with great fire power, head on and hard. The amount of £25,000 is to buy a bomber aircraft to continue my son's work in the most effective way. This expresses my feelings on receiving notice about my sons ... They would be happy that their mother would avenge them and help to attack the enemy. I, therefore, feel that an appropriate name for the bomber would be the MacRoberts Reply. The aircraft should also bear the MacRoberts coat of arms the family crest, a crossed fern leaf and an Indian rose. Let the bomber serve where there is the most need of her and may luck be with those who fly her. If I had 10 sons, I know they all would have done service for their country.

The Air Ministry commissioned Short Stirling N6086 from the ministry of aircraft production with instructions for the artwork as directed by Lady MacRobert to be applied accordingly. The MacRoberts Reply arrived at Wyton on 10 October 1941 and with some ceremony, it was handed over to her first pilot, Peter Boggis, with these words:

> The best of good luck boys always, and whenever and wherever you go, I know you will strike hard, sharp, and straight to the mark. That is the only language the enemy understands. My thoughts and thousands of other mothers are with you, and we are truly grateful to all concerned. Also thanks to those of you who have the care of my 'Reply' and prepare her for her flights. May the blows you strike bring us nearer victory—God bless you all.

Lady MacRobert had a preference for a Scotsman to pilot the bomber, yet Flying Officer Peter Boggis, from Barnstaple, Devon, became her captain. Lady MacRobert will no doubt have been made aware that her aircraft flight engineer, Sandy Watson, was from Scotland. The crew were lined-up in front of the Stirling while Wing Commander Ogilvie, the officer commanding 15 Squadron, officially handed over the aircraft to them. Following the formal part of the ceremony, a number of photographs were taken for publicity purposes. Sandy Watson was fortunate to be associated to this Scottish bequest. The crew were photographed as they climbed aboard the bomber and then took to the sky to perform an impromptu flying display.

The MacRoberts Reply immediately participated in several operations against enemy targets. On 28 October 1941, over Nieuport, the aircraft sustained the first damage inflicted by the enemy anti-aircraft gunners. They returned with damage to the tail, which the airframe engineers quickly repaired. On 18 December 1941, the MacRoberts Reply accompanied four other Stirlings to attack the French harbour at Brest, where the German warships the *Gneisenau* and the *Scharnhorst* were berthed. Sandy had visited the same target four days previously but on this occasion, he saw their bomb load land just short of the dry dock and saw the *Gneisenau* issuing black smoke. Their Stirling was subjected to attacks by three Luftwaffe fighters, one of which was claimed as damaged by the crew's gunners, who had put up a stiff retort of gunfire from their turrets.

Lady MacRobert was justifiably proud of her 'Reply' and its crew. Having completed his second tour of operations, Peter Boggis was posted to 15 Squadron Conversion Flight as an instructor on 26 January 1942. Sandy Watson was likewise posted, and sent to No. 1651 Conversion Unit as an instructor a few days later.

Promoted to temporary flight sergeant in August 1942, Sandy returned to 15 Squadron for two months where he accrued a further eleven operations before being posted to 90 Squadron, where he amassed a further fourteen operations. In total, he had completed forty-four operational raids between August 1941 and March 1943. The time spent flying operationally had accrued to 240 hours and this was recognised on 28 April 1943 when the Distinguished Flying Medal was recommended and subsequently awarded to Sandy. The recommendation for that medal mentioned: 'The safe return of his aircraft on many occasions must be credited to his skill and knowledge.'

Sandy Watson had completed two tours of duty—no mean achievement. He wore a gallantry ribbon on his tunic as he commenced duties as a flight engineer 'instructor' at No. 1657 Heavy Conversion Unit. Arriving at the conversion unit based at Stradishall, Sandy was within service language, 'an old sweat' flight sergeant who would be promoted later in the year to the rank of warrant officer.

Sandy teamed up with a fellow tour expired pilot from 15 Squadron, a New Zealander called Hugh 'Wendle' Wilkie, who wore the Distinguished Flying Cross medal ribbon on his tunic for his service with 15 Squadron. During an attack on Le Creusot, France, Flight Lieutenant Wilkie had succeeded in evading persistent attacks by a German night fighter on 21 June 1943. Only a few days previously, when attacking Düsseldorf on 11 June 1943, he had seen the propeller of one engine shot away when another Stirling mistakenly opened fire upon them. The port outside propeller tore itself away from the engine while over the target area but his crew managed to return safely.

While they served as instructors, both men had extraordinary experiences to exchange with the students undertaking conversion flights in the heavy Stirling. After nearly a year together, these two men were to lose their lives undertaking what was a most basic flying exercise.

Stirling EJ108 was delivered to Stradishall in early 1944. The aircraft had previously completed a total of twenty-six operations with 75 Squadron, being badly damaged during a mine laying operation on 4 November 1943. Bad weather had prevented the mine from being dropped and as the crew departed the Denmark coastline at 9,000 feet, a German night fighter made a passing attack, which resulted in serious damage. The pilot managed to avoid further attacks by diving towards the sea. At an estimated 1,000 feet height, he pulled up despite the starboard flap having been shot away and the port elevator being badly damaged. The rear turret area had also been badly damaged, resulting in the death of the air gunner within. EJ108 was later posted onto 1657 Conversion Unit where, among other aircraft, Warrant Officer Sandy Watson would instruct his flight engineer students.

On the night of 18 April 1944, a training crew of nine, including the experienced Sandy Watson and Wendle Wilkie, took off from Stradishall to perform night landings and circuits at Polebrook, an American Air Force airfield in Bedfordshire. American bases were often used for these exercises as they were inevitably clear from operational flights at night. EJ108 was on its fourth take-off exercise when three cyclists unexpectedly appeared riding along the east to west runway, presumably having returned from an evening pass off the aerodrome. The student pilot at the controls of the Stirling was committed to the take-off and unable to avoid them, the American airmen being struck by the undercarriage structure of Stirling EJ108.

As a result of the collision, an engine from the Stirling was damaged and the emergency dinghy was automatically released from its wing void housing. This may have resulted from the initial impact but regardless, the released dinghy had in all probability damaged the elevators in the process of its release and as the aircraft gained height. The accident was subject of communication with the airfield control and in view of the circumstances, the crew were instructed to divert to the nearby emergency landing ground at Woodbridge, an airfield especially designed for aircraft in distress. As they neared Woodbridge, the aircraft became more difficult to control. This resulted in both Sandy and Wendle deciding they alone would attempt to land the aircraft. Instructions were given for the training crew to bail out—this was ironic when you think these two men had been posted to the training unit for a 'rest' from the hazards of operations.

Almost immediately after the crew had taken to their parachutes, there was a significant disruption to the airframe almost equivalent to an explosion and the aircraft immediately plunged out of control into fields close to a pond and an isolated thatched cottage. Flight Sergeant Frederick Atkins was the twenty-year-old flight engineer under instruction. He had departed the aircraft safely but appears to have failed to secure his parachute harness properly and so with the parachute attached to the harness as the canopy opened, the velocity created forced his body through the harness and he plunged to his death in horrifying circumstances. It is possible he had fallen from the aircraft with raised knees—such events inevitably induce tumbling and continued to do so until the rip cord was pulled. In those circumstances, he may have been hanging in a downwards position before departing from his harness.

Police Constable Vince from nearby Glemham Police Station reported the crash to have taken place at Moat Farm and that the aircraft had been flying in a north-westerly direction when it exploded in mid-air. The constable reported six crew safe and one deceased having fallen to his death in the fields at Pettistree, approximately 7 miles south of the crash scene. The fire units from the nearby American airfield at Parham were quickly upon the scene and, using their foam tender, extinguished the fire and recovered the bodies of Sandy and Wendle. The fire engines from Framlingham, Woodbridge, and Southwold had also attended the scene. The cottage at the far side of the pond had been slightly damaged, with doors blown open, ceilings damaged, and a window broken. The occupants, William Carter and his sister, were shaken but unharmed. The remains of the pilot and flight engineer were taken to the American air station at Parham while the American Military Police guarded the crash scene. The carnage back at Polebrook had resulted in the pedal cyclists—Sergeant D. K. Ollre, Corporal J. A. Moore, and Corporal T. B. Potocki—losing their lives in shocking circumstances.

Warrant Officer William Alexander 'Sandy' Watson was twenty-five years old when he lost his life on 18 April 1944. His parents William and Christina Watson asked that their son be brought to his home in Bankfoot where he was buried in the Auchtergaven Parish Churchyard. Proudly, his headstone advises that he was a flight engineer who had been awarded the Distinguished Flying Medal; his relatives' requested inscription at the base reads: 'We shall always remember you smiling.'

The official Royal Air Force accident card Form 1180 reveals that the release of the emergency dinghy had strewn survival aids and emergency rations along with dinghy covers on the runway after the collision with the pedal cyclists. The Stirling dinghy was actually stowed in the port wing in close proximity to the aircraft fuselage. It was tethered to the aircraft by both a steel cable and long length of cord, which would have to be purposely cut by the crew after climbing into the dinghy from the sea. Clearly, the impact caused the unintended release and spewed all of the survival equipment and rations at the same time. The standing height of the Stirling was significant, which suggests that the pedal cyclists may well have been struck by the port undercarriage and the ensuing damage was caused by bicycle components entering the wing assembly.

The report also advises that the wing and tail unit had been damaged by the dinghy fouling. The report fittingly mentions that the pilot and flight engineer were highly commended for remaining with the aircraft. The accident cards appear to have formed part of the Air Ministry S.4 Statistical Branch documentation, from which they compiled the monthly and other periodical statistical flying accident reports during the war.

Three months after the accident, five of the survivors who had bailed out from the stricken Stirling—Sergeants Faulkner, Perry, and Nairne from New Zealand and Sergeants Woodford and Stannard—all lost their lives on 30 July 1944. They had been together, flying on operations over France in Lancaster HK558.

10

Casualties and Respectful Adversaries

Flying accidents occurred across the width and breadth of the country and in particular around the aerodromes of Great Britain. Many lives were lost through the eventualities of flying in wartime conditions. Frequently, young pilots were unprepared for many unintended occurrences that took place, or they were simply incapable of controlling them. If at all possible, casualties were always recovered in a respectful manner. It should be remembered that the scene of any fatal crash, particularly with a heavy bomber, inevitably involved significant trauma and in many cases, the destructiveness of fire had taken place. The grim recovery of casualties was traumatic and disturbing for those who undertook such duties. In many instances, the next of kin immediately requested their sons or young husbands be returned to their custody for a private burial. Others sanctioned them to be buried in graveyards close to their aerodromes and alongside fellow casualties.

The Royal Air Force provided a service of remembrance normally attended by senior officers and colleagues. Regardless of the location, the Commonwealth War Graves Commission, which was at that time recognised as the Imperial War Graves Commission, would immediately instigate temporary grave markings. Further correspondence would follow from the Commission as more permanent arrangements were put into place for the care of the fallen. An opportunity would eventually be provided for personal inscriptions on the post-war permanent headstones. It was possible to have a short, chiselled inscription at the base of each erected headstone at a personal cost of two shillings per letter.

In operational scenarios over enemy-held territory, any recovery of casualties could be delayed for a great many reasons. It was, however, commonplace for immediate graves to be dug and the military transmission of details eventually passed to the Red Cross. The Air Ministry was efficient at informing the next of kin that their relative had been killed, wounded, or were missing. Those messages were delivered personally by the Post Office telegram service, normally a young boy in Post Office uniform riding a pedal cycle. The dreaded sight of such a person holding the small buff-coloured envelope brought anxiety and complete distress to endless families. Despite this efficiency by the Air Ministry, it was unprepared for the scale of losses that developed as war progressed.

Early on in the war, the Casualty Branch commenced as a small department. Sir Arthur Street, the then permanent Under Secretary of State for Air, engaged in developing the efficiencies of the branch. Ironically, his son, Flying Officer Denys Oliver Street, became the subject of being reported as missing and Sir Arthur Street himself received one of the Air Ministry telegrams. Good fortune saw his son's status changed to that of being reported as a prisoner of war. The information exchange regarding prisoners of war was itself reformed with the International Red Cross Committee to create an exchange of prisoner of war agreement via Geneva. Flying Officer Street later took part in the 'Great Escape' from Stalag Luft III on 24 March 1944. Among those men recaptured after the escape, fifty men had been shot on the direct orders of Adolf Hitler. 'Shot while escaping' was the language used to describe these atrocities and tragically, the son of Sir Arthur Street was among those men who were effectively executed.

The initial casualty telegrams issued by the Casualty Branch were followed by a confirming letter from the Air Ministry, normally received within the following week. The Air Ministry regulations stated that a relative should also receive a personal letter from the casualty's commanding officer. It was also common for the station chaplain to send a short letter and over the following weeks and months, additional letters and official documents would arrive. Personal items of the missing person were sent from the aerodrome to be held at the central depository at Colnbrook, near Slough. All service material, including their flying log books, would be retained while other personal items were eventually sent to the next of kin.

In respect of bomber crews, it became common practice for next of kin to be provided with details of fellow crew members also lost. Communication was frequently taken up between bereaved families spread across the country, each family desperate to acquire more information, none more so than the mothers and wives of the young men who were simply known to be missing. For these men, the Air Ministry established the Missing Research Section in late 1941.

A great many men were simply regarded as missing. Bomber Command engaged in flying over significant stretches of water and events took place which were not witnessed by anybody and normally during the hours of darkness. Often, there was no crash scene to be investigated and unless the aircrew had been fortunate to escape into a dinghy, there was very little likelihood of anything being visible to identify a location. The sea had the capability to devour and consume a heavy bomber and its crew within a few minutes. This danger was present on every operational raid undertaken during the war and the English Channel alone took many aircraft and men to their unmarked graves.

The expanse of the North Sea also consumed a great many crews. Heavy bombers attacking targets such as Rostock, Lübeck, Kiel, and Flensburg in northern Germany also flew over the Baltic Sea. By example, Halifax DT620 crashed in to the Baltic Sea on 14 March 1943. Halifax DT620 was from the Special Duties 138 Squadron, flying from the secret Tempsford aerodrome in Bedfordshire. The Halifax had taken off at 5.50 p.m. that evening, tasked with dropping supplies into occupied Poland. The destination was coded as a delivery to the special operations executive at drop zone, Wrona 614. The British flight engineer in Halifax DT629 was twenty-one-year-old Arthur Cyril Sixsmith from Liverpool. He and his crew had, on the previous day, flown to France and dropped supplies to the SOE. They were experienced in these individual special operations. Flying to Poland, their Halifax was at a low altitude progressing east over the Baltic Sea. Onboard were two Canadians, one New Zealander, and three British men who completed the mixed commonwealth crew.

Oberstleutnant Martin Drewes, a Bf 110 night fighter pilot of significant skill and experience, was directed by his radar controller towards the plotted route of Halifax DT620. Drewes hunted down the British bomber, sighting the Halifax at an estimated 600 feet above the sea. At a distance of 240 feet, the Luftwaffe pilot opened fire with a short burst from his machine guns. The Halifax immediately started burning and exploded in the air. At 9.42 p.m., Halifax DT620 crashed into the Baltic Sea off Harvig, Denmark. The aircraft had been rapidly approaching the coastline and the crew were no doubt anticipating a gain in height when they were shot down. Unsurprisingly, the entire crew perished in the tragic event, which took only a few seconds to unfold around them. Flight Sergeant Leslie Smith was the pilot; Sergeant Horace Harrap was alongside him as second pilot; Sergeant Thomas Mairs was wireless operator; Sergeant Colin Chambers was navigator; Flight Sergeant Eugene Masson was air gunner; Sergeant Donald Ross was air gunner; and Sergeant Arthur Sixsmith was flight engineer.

Three hours after the crash, at 12.30 a.m., a body presumed to have come from the crash was found washed onto the beach. At 6.30 a.m., a second body was found nearby, along with several pieces of aircraft wreckage. Both bodies were taken to the fishing town of Rødvig and handed over to the Wehrmacht, who transported them to Fliegerhorst Kastrup (Copenhagen Airport Denmark). The two casualties were immediately identified as the two Canadians, Masson, and Ross.

The following translated orders were written at Kastrup by the Luftwaffe Air Force Commandant. A funeral was ordered by the *Oberstleutnant* (German Air Force rank equal to lieutenant colonel) and the *Fliegerhorst* commandant. These orders illustrate the dignity and respect paid to the two Allied casualties that they were responsible for at that time:

16 March 1943
  Air Force Command L Kastrup
  Special Order No. 7

Subject: Funeral of two dead Canadian airmen.

On Friday 19 March 1943 at 11.00 a.m. the internment of both the bodies of the Canadian airmen will take place at the Bispebjerg Cemetery. In accordance with L.V. B1, 1941, 36th Edition, page 651, line 1075, the burial must take place with military honours. Care is therefore to be taken to see that personnel from the Swiss Consulate in Copenhagen take part in the funeral. An Evangelical clergyman will also be present. Oberleutnant Gombert, Ln. Unit, is appointed leader of the funeral procession.

In addition, Ln. Unit will provide: 1 Ensign 8 Men.

Headquarters Company: 1 N.C.O. and 4 Men.

The Seeland Anti-Aircraft Unit, as promised by telephone by the Commander: 1 N.C.O. and 8 Men.

Dress: Service uniform without overcoats, with helmet and carbine, no gas mask.

N.C.O. Ernst of the Photographic Unit will take part in the funeral and will make 3 different pictures which will be placed with the deceased documents.

Group Command of the Air Force Command L, Kastrup will procure the two wreathes prescribed in accordance with the above mentioned order. Oberleutnant Gombert will maintain contact with Group Command for the purpose of receiving the wreaths in good time. The coffins will be borne into the Chapel of the Bispebjerg Cemetery and from there through the Seeland Unit detachment to the open grave and lowered into it. The salute of honour will be ordered by Oberleutnant Gombert after the consecration of the bodies in the open grave.

Departure of the Air Force Command L. Kastrup detachment (revolving door) on 19 March, 10.00 a.m. The bus will travel to the Cemetery and back.

Assembly point for the Seeland Anti Aircraft Unit detachment about 10.45am in the Cemetery Chapel at Bispebjerg.

Costs arising from the internment are to be booked to Kap. VIII E 230 in accordance with the above mentioned order.

Signed Volbehr

Oberstleutnant and Air Force Commandant.

Distribution: Local Authorities Copenhagen; Army Command Copenhagen; Gen. d. lw. In Dk. Abt. Kdo. Fl.Ber. 2/XI Seeland; Anti-Aircraft Unit, Seeland; Headquarters Company; Ln. Unit; Group Command; Photographic Unit; Hfz. Command; z.d.a. Command; Captain and Staff Officer of the Air Force Command

Two days after the funeral, another body was washed ashore near Rødvig. The body was recovered by the Danish police and taken to the hospital at Store Heddinge. The body had suffered terrible injuries and was dressed in a blue grey uniform with three chevrons and a gold crown on the right upper arm. This factor identified the deceased with the rank of flight sergeant. The Wehrmacht took possession of the body on 22 March 1943. The deceased was identified as the pilot Flight Sergeant Smith, who was also laid to rest in Bispebjerg Cemetery on 26 March 1943.

Ten days after the initial funeral on 29 March, a local fisherman brought the body of another casualty to Rødvig harbour. The Wehrmacht had engaged a number of fishermen to look for the plane wreckage in the sea, and in doing so, they were able to recover a body. It was the body of the New Zealander Sergeant Harrap, who was subsequently buried in Bispebjerg Cemetery on 7 April 1943. Fisherman Jens Hansen recovered a further body on 14 April 1943. Exactly one month after the crash into the sea, the remains were taken to Store Heddinge hospital. That same day, the remains were removed under instructions of the air commander from Kastrup. It appears that the remains were thought to be that of Sergeant Mairs but as a confirmed identification was not achieved, the remains were initially buried as an unknown in Bispebjerg. It has become apparent that this was later confirmed as having been the remains of Flight Engineer Sergeant Sixsmith. He is now commemorated appropriately in Bispebjerg Cemetery.

At 8.30 p.m. on 4 May 1943, Sergeant Chambers' body was found washed ashore next to Villa Hage in Bjerred between Malmö and Halskrona. He was found wearing a parachute harness but no parachute. The body was left where found for the night, guarded by military personnel from the local barracks. In the morning, the body was examined by the local police, laid in a coffin, and taken to the local chapel in Fjelie. Sergeant Chambers was laid to rest in Fjelie cemetery on 26 May 1943 with full military honours. Military clergyman E. Eberhard performed the graveside ceremony. The remaining crew member, Sergeant Mairs, has no known grave. His body was never found, and he is duly commemorated by the Commonwealth War Graves Commission upon the Runnymede Memorial.

Flensburg was the most northerly port in Germany, near the Danish border. This location facilitated the construction of submarine and shipbuilding for the German Navy (*Kriegsmarine*). The route by Allied bombers to and from the target was predominantly across water and on 1 October 1942, Bomber Command ordered Flensburg to be attacked by a force of twenty-seven Halifax aircraft from 4 Group. No. 10 Squadron would suffer the loss of nearly thirty men from twelve Halifax that never returned from that particular operation.

Sergeant George William Spowart was a flight engineer who served with 10 Squadron from Doncaster in Yorkshire. At twenty-two years old, he was another young man in charge of the engineering complexities of a Halifax heavy bomber. His story also serves to endorse the tragedies of those men who fell into the Baltic Sea off Denmark and were later recovered by the occupying military when given up by the sea. When compared to the oceans, the Baltic Sea is a small and shallow body of water. The average depth of the Baltic Sea is around 160 feet, with some significantly deep basin areas comparable to the oceans. The Baltic Sea is linked to the North Sea via the narrow Danish straits.

Flight Engineer George Spowart enjoyed the company of a crew complimented entirely of sergeants, two of which were Canadians. The morning of 1 October 1942 followed the normal routine for an early evening departure. The selected aircraft were made ready and serviceable whereupon the flight commander and eventually the squadron commander passed orders advising their compliment of crews were able to fulfil the numbers of aircraft required of his squadron.

Once confirmation was received that the operation was on, aircrews set about their normal business. Pilots and navigators attended a short pre-briefing and later, all the crews involved received the formal briefing with meteorological predictions for the weather across the sea route. George and his crew had been allocated Halifax DT520, which was ready for a take-off against Flensburg at 6 p.m. The seven sergeants were delivered in the open-backed truck, which parked near the hardstanding apron. George made his final exterior inspection of the Halifax before his pilot signed and accepted his aircraft. Sergeant David Campbell and George climbed aboard followed by the bomb aimer, Sergeant Leslie Smythson; wireless operator Sergeant Robert Gourlay; two air gunners, Sergeant Donald Ivers and Sergeant Herbert Moore; and the navigator, Sergeant Henry Sullivan, who made his final preparations.

The outbound flight went well but at 10.08 p.m., Halifax DT520 was hit by anti-aircraft flak shells fired from a unit based on southern Langeland, Denmark. Langeland Island is located between the Great Belt and Bay of Kiel, effectively due east and parallel to the target of Flensburg. The damage was instantly disabling to the aircraft and insufficient time existed for any escape. Burning intensely, it crashed into the Baltic Sea off the Nordenbro Vesteregn peninsular. This location indicates that the aircraft had been hit while over the target or possibly immediately after their bombing run.

The following day, the body of the Canadian Sergeant Robert Gourlay was found as it drifted ashore. His body was taken to the Magleby chapel in the outskirts of Copenhagen where it was collected the next day by *Unteroffizier* (Corporal) Martinsen of the German Wehrmacht. He removed the body, taking it to the Luftwaffe base on Zealand Island, Copenhagen. Arrangements were put in place and Robert was laid to rest on 7 October 1942 in the cemetery at Svino, a small village in Southern Zealand, overlooking Dybsø Fjord, south-west of Copenhagen.

The German Kriegsmarine were constantly sweeping the Baltic Sea for aerial mines dropped by Allied aircraft. On 6 October 1942, the area close to the crash scene was being swept for mines when they came across the body of Flight Engineer George Spowart. He was taken by the minesweeper to Bagenkop Harbour. The body was formally identified and taken to the Magleby chapel. On 7 October, his body was collected and taken to the Luftwaffe base at Avnø. Arrangements were put into place and George was also laid to rest in Svino cemetery on 9 October 1942.

On the morning of 11 October, the body of Sergeant Herbert Moore drifted ashore at Langeland near Ristinge. The body was formally identified and placed in a coffin in the church at nearby Humble. On 13 October, the body was collected by

Martinsen of the Wehrmacht and brought to Odense on the island of Fyn. Herbert Moore was laid to rest in Odense (Assistens) Cemetery on 14 October 1942. The German field priest Johannes Vorrath officiated at the graveside ceremony.

On 14 October, the body of the remaining Canadian casualty, Sergeant Donald Ivers, was found having drifted ashore at Nordenbro Vestereng. It was now nearly two weeks since the crash; however, the temperature of the water was cold in October, which had slowed the process of decomposition. It presented little problem in identifying the body. Donald Ivers was in keeping with all of his crew placed in a coffin in Magleby church.

On the morning of 15 October, the body of the pilot Sergeant David Campbell was found in the sea off Ristinge. His body was taken to a farm in Hesselbjerg where he was formally identified by Doctor Demmagaard and Mr Oppermann from the Danish police. The body of David Campbell was then placed in a coffin and taken to the church at Humble.

On 16 October, the body of Sergeant Henry Sullivan was found, having drifted ashore on Langeland Island. The body was taken to Magleby chapel and placed in a coffin before being positively identified. On the same day, it was once again *Unteroffizier* Martinsen of the Wehrmacht, who arrived to transport the casualties from the chapel. He took the coffins of Sullivan Campbell and Ivers to Odense where the three of them were laid to rest in Odense Assistens Cemetery on 17 October 1942. A German field priest officiated at the graveside ceremony.

On the morning of 18 October, the body of Sergeant Leslie Smythson was retrieved from the crash scene. This is not detailed in any respect but may indicate further *Kriegsmarine* sweeping activity as the body was taken by boat to Bagenkop harbour. The body had been in the water for seventeen days and was taken to the chapel at Magleby. The identification was achieved and once again *Unteroffizier* Martinsen of the German Wehrmacht collected the body on 19 October. Martinsen transported the remains of Sergeant Smythson to Odense. He was laid to rest in the Odense Assistens Cemetery on 23 October 1942. A German field priest officiated at the graveside ceremony.

The Assistens Cemetery contains a plot of twenty-three Commonwealth burials, most of them airmen. The local people have subsequently erected a monument in the form of a square column, surmounted by two bronze eagles. This memorial is dedicated by them with the inscription: 'In memory of British and Canadian airmen who gave their lives in the battle for freedom during the war 1939–1945'. The parents of Flight Engineer Spowart, George Bertram and Jeannie Spowart, requested that Sergeant 547329 G. W. Spowart's headstone receive a personal inscription when it was installed at Svino during the post-war years. Chiselled at the base of the headstone are the words 'Treasured memories of our dear son and Brother George Till we meet again'. Svino Churchyard contains a Commonwealth plot of sixty-two burials, all of which are airmen, eight of them unidentified. Two of those unknown men rest in a plot with the

Canadian wireless operator Sergeant Robert Gourlay. Immediately next to him rests his friend and fellow sergeant, Flight Engineer George Spowart.

The families of the deceased received two photographic images of the grave and would have also received a wealth of official correspondence from the Royal Air Force on the subject of their tragic loss. Eventually, the Post Office delivered a small brown card box addressed to G. B. Spowart Esq, 16 Danum Road, Doncaster, Yorks. The family then held in their hands the contents of the box, four medals: the 1939–1945 Campaign Star, Air Crew Europe Star, Defence Medal, and the War Medal.

Contained in the box was a small certificate with the following words:

> The Under Secretary of State for Air presents his compliments and by Command of the Air Council has the honour to transmit the enclosed Awards granted for service in the war of 1939–45. The council share your sorrow that Sergeant G.W. Spowart in respect of whose service these Awards are granted did not live to receive them.

Thousands of these small cardboard boxes were delivered, and endless families relived the grief that they had suffered from the enormous casualties suffered between 1939 and 1945. These short accounts illustrate the respect that took place around the waters of the Baltic Sea, echoing other events that took place elsewhere. However, it must be said that during the latter years of the war, such protocol as evidenced within these instances was not adopted. The horrors of war brought circumstances that simply failed to allow, permit, or normalise the respect that should have been present when a body was recovered. Many airmen were not identified at the time and were simply buried close to their crumpled and tangled mass of metal, which was once a heavy bomber. Others were impossible to identify by virtue of the trauma suffered and sadly, many young men had been simply obliterated in vast explosions and fire.

The shallow waters of the Baltic were sympathetic to the casualties that fell within them. The masses of water in the other seas were not so accommodating. Many cases exist where those seas gave up the remains of men that had been immersed for many extended weeks. They were simply impossible to identify despite the best intentions to do so. The Royal Air Force Missing Research and Enquiry Service (MRES) was tasked in 1944 to commence with the duty of investigating the circumstances and deaths of all allied missing casualties. At that time, 42,000 personnel were listed as 'missing or believed killed' in a vast number of incidents and either the Germans or other local authorities had interred casualties in graveyards close to the scene of their death or, in the case of prisoner of war camps, in close proximity. The MRES arranged for proper exhumation and formal identification wherever possible and in many cases, identity discs or dog tags and scraps of uniforms with the various brevets assisted greatly in establishing some formal identification.

Geographically, this work was undertaken in many remote areas. By example, flight engineer Sergeant Vincent Nelson Taylor and his crew failed to return from operations over Germany on 11 December 1944. Lancaster PD263 of 57 Squadron simply disappeared and all next of kin received official notification that they were missing. Sergeant Taylor was a married man and his wife later received notification from the Air Ministry in August 1945 that wreckage and remains had been located in the deep and extensive woodland at Gemund Forest, western Germany. The recovery process identified one body by unique artificial dental work, which strongly suggested the wreckage was that of Lancaster PD263. The MRES later confirmed the facts that those remains recovered were the missing crew from Lancaster PD263. The recovered remains were interned in the British Military Cemetery, Rheinberg, Germany. The one crew member identified by the teeth was buried in an individual grave while the remaining crew members were buried collectively in one plot.

The MRES became very effective and were able to account for over two-thirds of missing personnel. Those found were identified if at all possible and reinterred in Commonwealth War Graves Commission plots. The work of this unit continued unabated until it was disbanded in 1952.

11

Flight Engineer Readhead DFC: Handley Page Halifax

William Folger Readhead was a boy apprentice who joined the sixth Royal Air Force Halton intake in August 1922. William was allocated service number 363236, which was not only his identity as a Halton cadet in the Royal Air Force but also through his service until commissioned as an officer during the Second World War. He was born 17 April 1906 and became readily known and addressed throughout his life as Tam; the reason for this has not been fully established.

The aircraft apprentice service equipped Tam with engineering skills, which were put to good effect when he was posted to serve in India during the latter interwar years. Many apprentices were posted to the North-West Frontier, usually for a five-year tour of duty. Tam served as an engine fitter, but opportunities to fly as air gunners were frequently taken up by these young men serving on the North-West Frontier. This sporadic flying, when undertaken, was effectively non-official and no official records were maintained. These duties were simply short interludes between their ground duties.

The Indian North-West Frontier (now Pakistan) was divided into three geographical areas, which were policed in the air by the Royal Air Force. The northern area comprised the region to the north of the Khyber Pass up to the foothills of the Himalayas, an area often referred to as 'the roof of the world'. The second or central area lay south west of the Khyber Pass, roughly between the rivers Kabul and Kurram. This was mountainous terrain, criss-crossed by deep valleys. The third region was the southern area, which lay to the south-west of Kohat, from the Kurram river down towards Fort Sandeman and Baluchistan. This was dominated by Waziristan, the centre of the frontier and the stronghold area of fierce tribal resistance.

The 1908 India General Service Medal was awarded for service in military operations in and around India between 1908 and 1935. Tam became a recipient of the medal along with the North-West Frontier 1930–31 clasp. This was a clasp awarded to 1,350 members of the Royal Air Force for service during the Red Shirt and Afridi Rebellions on the North-West Frontier between 23 April 1930 and 22 March 1931. The Afridi uprising was a traditional frontier tribal revolt, but the Red Shirt Rebellion was essentially political, motivated by the Indian Independence movement that was gradually unfolding within British India. Leading Aircraftsman Tam Readhead became recognisable thereafter as a veteran of the North-West Frontier operations by the green and blue medal ribbon displayed on his uniform. By the end of the war, Tam would be the proud wearer of several other medal ribbons on his uniform, including that of recognising gallantry in the face of the enemy and significantly the brevet identifying him as a flight engineer.

During his service in India, Tam married his first wife, Esther, on 23 September 1933, in Karachi. The following year, they returned to England, where he resumed his engineering duties and witnessed the progression to war with Germany during his ensuing five years of service. Responding to the request for qualified ground trades personnel to volunteer for flying duties, Tam subsequently applied and as a skilled fitter II engine mechanic, he progressed through the selection procedure with ease. He attended St Athan and was selected for the shortened seven-week course of instruction to qualify as a flight engineer. With effect from 27 June 1942, he was awarded the 'E' brevet along with the sergeant stripes and took leave before progressing onto his next posting.

Tam joined 76 Squadron Bomber Command, which was also operating with a Handley Page Halifax Conversion Flight on the aerodrome at Middleton St George in County Durham, 5 miles east of Darlington. In command of the conversion flight was Squadron Leader Charles Cranston Calder, who was addressed by his peers as 'Jock', a nickname clearly associated to his place of birth in Morayshire. Jock had been awarded the Distinguished Flying Cross in February 1942 and in the summer of that year became responsible for organising the 76 Squadron Conversion Flight. No. 76 Squadron had recently suffered a depleted strength, which occurred through crews being detached to the Middle East theatre. A possible explanation for Tam being posted to Middleton St George may have been the need for experienced men to join the conversion flight. Without doubt, his engineering experience of some twenty years was exceptional and stood him apart from the vast majority of young flight engineers appearing through the training programme. Jock Calder was some fifteen years junior in age to Tam. Having such an experienced man around him will have made Jock's duties in organising the conversion flight an easier task. Destined for additional rank and awards, Jock later became the personal pilot to Air Marshal Sir Arthur Harris towards the end of the war.

In July 1942, Tam was issued with his personal flying log book. His first duty was certifying his qualification as a flight engineer on the Avro Lancaster at St Athan and adding his flight engineer qualification on Halifax Mk I and II aircraft at 76 Conversion Flight. Jock Calder added his signature to that entry on 17 July. On 29 July 1942, Jock and Tam flew together on what was simply recorded as a sea search for just over three hours in daylight. No. 76 Squadron, although depleted in strength, was still required to support Bomber Command wherever possible. On 26 July, 76 Squadron dispatched three crews to reinforce an attack on Hamburg. Tragically, one of the Halifax flown by Sergeant Butt failed to return.

Tam Readhead joined the depleted strength of 76 Squadron after a short introduction to the Halifax. His flying experience at that time was just twenty hours and ten minutes, with only one hour having been flow in night conditions. Also, joining the squadron at that time was a new commanding officer, the now famous Squadron Leader Leonard Cheshire, a subsequent recipient of the Victoria Cross. Squadron Leader Cheshire was charged with rebuilding 76 Squadron into an effective body of men and machines. Probably by coincidence and nothing more, Squadron Leader Cheshire joined the squadron following in the footsteps of his younger brother Christopher, who had been serving in the squadron when he was shot down on operations over Berlin in August 1941. Christopher Cheshire survived the war as a prisoner of war.

Squadron Leader Cheshire was renowned for setting and maintaining extremely high standards of technical competence for aircrews and ground crews alike. Tam was exceptionally skilled in engineering, but this was balanced by having had little operational experience. He would have witnessed several no-nonsense briefings from Squadron Leader Cheshire, who frequently advocated that general flak, if not targeted towards them should be ignored because it was just as easy to fly into a shell as away from it.

Sergeant Alastair Moir was to become Tam's regular pilot and no doubt, the young twenty-two-year-old sergeant was delighted at having an experienced thirty-six-year-old flight engineer in his crew. Alastair was known within the crew as Al and they first flew together on 20 August 1942 in an aircraft with the serial R9365 and the identity letter 'C' displayed on her fuselage. They flew an air test that proved problematical. Tam recorded the starboard outer engine boost falling on any climb in altitude. He advised his pilot that he suspected an air leak on the suction side of the engine super charger. The Halifax returned and landed safely. Tam documented the fault for engineering works. This confident diagnosis in the air would have provided confirmation to his crew that they were in safe hands. The same Halifax was flow on 22 and 23 August, when other mechanical problems were identified, including the malfunction of the braking system to the starboard undercarriage. On the morning of 28 August 1942, Halifax R9365 was once again air tested and this time, it was given a clean bill of health. That same night, the crew would fly on their first operational sortie to attack Saarbrucken in Germany.

Bomber Command was to send 113 thirteen aircraft to bomb Saarbrucken, while another heavier force was also attacking Nuremberg. Halifax R9365 reached the target area without incident and they successfully dropped their bomb load. The port inner engine developed a heavy glycol leak and immediately overheated. The engine was feathered, leaving the propeller turning in the slipstream without any power. These were serious matters for Tam to contend with on his first venture over enemy-held territory. Flying on three engines at night brought forth narrow differences between normal flight and stalling when flying at the maximum speed possible on three engines. The imminent redesigning of the Halifax tail construction would later assist in reducing tail stalls for crews flying on three engines. On this flight, after six hours and forty minutes, they experienced foggy conditions over some areas of the Midlands and so were diverted to the Pocklington Bomber Command aerodrome in Yorkshire. The damage to the Halifax and the added adverse weather conditions proved significant, resulting in the crew remaining at Pocklington until 31 August.

On 31 August, the crew were allocated a replacement Halifax at Pocklington, serial BB196, which was to be flown on the short journey back to Middleton St George as soon as the weather cleared. In the early afternoon of 31 August, Al Moir took off from Pocklington at 2.20 p.m. Tam could not have predicted that this short flight would become so challenging. Soon after taking off, the port outer engine completely failed, resulting in the aircraft being unable to climb higher than an estimated 300 feet above ground level. With smoke pouring from the engine manifolds, Al crash-landed the aircraft at nearby Catfoss aerodrome. The emergency landing was made downwind and the undercarriage subsequently collapsed as the aircraft slewed across the ground and struck a parked Blenheim, serial number Z7302. Although the crew survived the crash uninjured, Tam deduced that a con rod had punctured through the crank case in the engine block, causing the terminal failure of the engine at a critical height. The crew had been lucky to survive, the aircraft not so fortunate. Halifax BB196 was written off and scrapped.

The first two operational flights had proved challenging for Tam, each involving engineering failures. These immediate situations must have seemed daunting and they would continue into the first week of September 1942. The crew were allocated Halifax W7812 'B' Beer, which had been air tested on two short thirty-minute flights in preparation for the next operation. Bremen was to be the target, taking off at 10.30 p.m. on the evening of 4 September with a very specific briefing instruction to bomb on illuminated markers. Just an hour into the flight, once again, technical faults took place with their aircraft. Tam investigated a failure in both the oxygen supply system and the intercom system. Additionally, he was required to deal with the port inner engine boost mechanism that was inducing poor engine performance. This combination of faults forced a decision to return to base. Tam recorded a comment in his log book that the port inner 'S' gear was the source of the problem. It must be assumed his comment was referring to the gearbox operating the supercharger.

Squadron Leader Cheshire was striving to achieve improving performance statistics for 76 Squadron. The performance thus far for Al Moir and his crew was likely to draw attention as they were failing to complete operations. Although bad luck in respect of aircraft performance was evident, the question of LMF (lacking in moral fibre) was an issue that Bomber Command could well have associated to any underperforming crew, a subject restricted from the public domain by the Air Ministry. In an era when individuals were expected to maintain a stiff upper lip in times of personal adversity, great stigma and humiliation existed to those men who were simply unable to cope. It was not unknown for individuals to simply disappear off station and be removed to dedicated locations. Although these men had rank, their brevets would be removed from their uniforms, and disgrace and humiliation pervaded in abundance.

On 6 September, just two days after having returned from the ill-fated raid to Bremen, Tam along with his crew were scheduled to fly to Duisburg in yet another replacement Halifax, which displayed the identity letter 'H' on her fuselage. Crew orders noted that they were to be joined by the soon to be appointed station commander, Group Captain William Neil McKechnie, who wore the medal ribbon of the George Cross on his uniform, a medal as revered as the Victoria Cross. The award of the George Cross to McKechnie related to an incident that occurred in June 1929 when an aeroplane crashed on landing at Cranwell aerodrome and burst into flames. The pilot, a cadet, although stunned, managed to release his safety belt and fall out of the machine in a dazed condition. McKechnie himself a cadet at that time, landed in close proximity and ran at full speed towards the scene of the accident. The petrol had spread and was in full blaze, with the cadet lying in it semi-conscious. McKechnie ran into the flames and rescued the cadet, who had been badly burned. He was himself scorched and superficially burned but had undoubtedly save the life of the cadet pilot.

It is unknown if McKechnie was to accompany Al Moir and his crew as a result of their less than notable success thus far against the enemy. Regardless to that fact, such a distinguished pilot on the flight deck would have added to the pressure upon the young pilot and his crew. At 12.43 a.m., Halifax 'H' departed from the aerodrome, one of three aircraft from 76 Squadron engaged in the operation that night. The major port of Duisburg was going to be attacked by over 200 aircraft, but foremost no doubt in Tam's mind were thoughts of the starboard outer engine low fuel pressure readings, which came to light in their morning air test. He had supervised the replacement of the accelerator pump to that engine and maintained a close eye upon its performance before it was rendered serviceable.

Al Moir, with the group captain sitting alongside, saw a thick blanket of haze covering the target area. Such conditions were likely to obstruct accurate bombing and in some instances, prevented the dropping of bomb loads, despite the great endeavour taken to reach these targets. Regardless, Al opened the bomb doors on the bombing run and the bomb aimer dropped the bomb load with the greatest possible accuracy given the conditions. Having completed the bombing run over Duisburg, the standard procedure of closing the large bomb doors became problematical. Tam had previously noted poor oil pressure and the bomb doors repeatedly failed to close properly. The hydraulic accumulator for the bomb door system was situated mid-section of the fuselage and despite this being accessible to the flight engineer, the fault was impossible to rectify. An isolating cock was fitted between the bomb door accumulator and the hydraulic jacks and an additional selective closing valve accessible to the flight engineer was fitted into the complicated system. The malfunction caused the port wing to be forced downwards and the pilot needed to apply correctional force to maintain stable positioning. The open bomb doors increased significant drag to the aircraft, which induced increasing fuel consumption and a reduced air speed. The return flight was going to be fraught with dangers. Group Captain McKechnie assisted the pilot in holding the aircraft steady. Moreover, he had personally witnessed the bad luck with mechanical failures and the great endeavour of the crew in undertaking a successfully attack on the target in adverse circumstances. Eventually returning to their aerodrome safely, they landed five hours and thirty-five minutes after departure. Once again, mechanical faults had dogged their operational record. The squadron operational record written immediately after the above-mentioned Duisburg raid recorded that seven crews had been available to 76 Squadron. However, it further noted that only four aircraft were serviceable.

The growth of the squadron was slow and severely troubled by serviceability. On 8 September, six aircraft became serviceable and the crews were briefed to attack Frankfurt, departing at 8 p.m. Flight Sergeant John Eric Nicholson was flying Halifax W1228. Twenty minutes after take-off, the aircraft caught fire while flying over the area of York. The aircraft subsequently exploded at a low altitude, suggesting the pilot was attempting an emergency landing at Pocklington. The mid-air explosion resulted in wreckage being scattered over a wide area and all on board the aircraft were killed. The subsequent investigation found that it was likely that the photoflash bomb had detonated in the bomb bay and ignited the fuel lines that ran across the fuselage floor. A photoflash bomb was a pyrotechnic device dropped by aircraft, which would ignite and allow a photograph of their bombing to be taken. These were commonly carried within the bomb load and deployed on the vast majority of sorties undertaken within Bomber Command. The court of enquiry into this incident led to a change in the carriage of photo-flash devices, a directive that was instrumental in creating better safety in the carriage and deployment of photoflash bombs.

Al Moir, once again flying Halifax 'C' R9365 with second pilot Sergeant Tom Gallantry alongside him, had taken off five minutes before the ill-fated

Halifax had burst into flames. They had been spared the sight of that tragedy and successfully reached the intended target. The return journey saw frantic calculations and the management of fuel by Tam as he calculated a shortage of fuel was rapidly becoming critical. The navigator instigated a direct flight to the first aerodrome possible, which was the fighter station at Tangmere on the Sussex Coast. Tam recorded in his log book that the flight concluded with a forced landing after seven hours and twenty-five minutes. On 9 September, Halifax 'C' left Tangmere at 2.40 p.m. The transit flight was two hours in length, during which the port inner engine started smoking heavily at the exhaust manifolds. The ground staff engine fitters would once again be called to investigate the engine.

The following day, 10 September 1942, became eventful but in far better circumstances. The American publication *Life* had obtained authorisation to produce an article with pictures at Middleton St George aerodrome. Clearly being censored and supervised, Tam and his crew had been selected to feature. The crew were allocated Halifax W7812 'B' Beer, the aircraft that had previously suffered the engine boost issue on the port inner earlier that month. Reports record them taking the Halifax on an air test at 2 p.m. in preparation for their operation that night to revisit Düsseldorf. Photographs were taken, including the crew walking away from the aircraft; souvenir postcard-size examples were later provided to the crew, the image aptly titled, 'Halifax bomber crew of 'B' for Beer go out for a practice run before Düsseldorf raid'. The article was later published with several photographs, and read:

No air force much likes to be photographed setting out on a bombing mission and coming home, sometimes with gaps in the Squadron, but the Royal Air Force gave *Life* permission to cover one of Bomber Commands night raids on Germany. As luck had it, *Life* photographer Hans Wild walked in on one of the biggest attacks of the year, the raid to Düsseldorf. On these pages are seen one cheerful Squadron loading up, getting instructions, taking off into the dusk and, at length, arriving back home with one loss, and wolfing bacon beans and beans on toast.

Over six hundred big bombers attacked Düsseldorf in one busy hour on the night of 10 September. Losses were thirty-one planes. This crew had done seven jobs before. There was no moon, suddenly in the dark they could see ahead the glow of Düsseldorf. Like the lights of a country club dance in peacetime. Pathfinders had already dropped flares and the first fires were springing up. The Halifax was caught in the searchlights, but side slipped out, made its run, dropped its bombs and a few empty bottles and sailed home.

The operation to Düsseldorf was a complete success and the aircraft developed no faults. The crew no doubt hoped they had broken the spell of bad luck and four days later, they attacked Wilhelmshaven. Despite heavy defences, they returned safely with no damage. The short spell of stability at Middleton St George was interrupted when orders were received that 76 Squadron was to take up residence at Linton-on-Ouse, at an aerodrome situated 10 miles north-west of York on 17 September 1942.

The arrival at Linton-on-Ouse saw Handley Page Halifax serial number DT556 become a regular aircraft for Tam and his crew and on 23 September, they boarded the aircraft to attack Flensburg. The target was the German submarine pens that were known to be heavily defended. Thick cloud over the Kiel Bay shielded the target and the aircraft was forced to penetrate below only to be attacked by effectively co-ordinated light flak defences. Sergeant Tam Readhead recorded in his log book: 'Bombed target from 3,000 feet engaged heavily by light guns all high explosive load on U Boat yards, landed Leconfield aerodrome'. This was presumably the result of bad weather conditions; however, they were able to take advantage of recent extensive concrete runway developments at that aerodrome and only stayed a short time before taking off to return back to Linton-on-Ouse after lunch on 24 September.

On 26 September 1942, Halifax DT556 was once again bound for Flensburg. Regarded as a vital target, the submarine pens were again targeted by Bomber Command. The Halifax wireless operators within the twenty-eight aircraft engaged on that operation all received a recall message approximately two hours into the flight. Al Moir responded by aborting the attack and upon reaching England, was yet again diverted to another aerodrome. They landed at Driffield, another location that was being developed with extended concrete runways. During late 1942, the Midlands were being subjected to intensive aerodrome developments across its geographical width and depth. The crew departed in the early afternoon on 27 September and following the short twenty-minute hop back to Linton-on-Ouse, Al was met with congratulations having been promoted to the rank of flight sergeant.

Submarines would once again figure in a briefing for their next operation, but on this occasion the target was the workshops that facilitated those deadly boats in and around Kiel harbour. The shortening days allowed a take-off at 6.40 p.m. on 13 October 1942. Almost 300 aircraft were engaged in the attack during which the enemy deployed decoy fires to confuse targets. Al and his crew had difficulty in establishing the target and decided to bomb the German stronghold of Heligoland as an alternative. Tam needed to apply his flight engineering skills to a fractured pressure pipe on the hydraulic system to ensure a safe arrival back at Linton-on-Ouse.

Cologne, a city synonymously connected to Bomber Command, was written into Tam's flying log book on 15 October 1942. Close to 300 aircraft were sent to attack the city, but the weather conditions were erroneously predicted. The winds were strong, and the Pathfinders had great difficulty in combating a significant German decoy fire, which successfully pulled a lot of aircraft away from the actual target. Eighteen allied bombers failed to return to England and Halifax BB237 'C' being flown by Flight Sergeant Al Moir came close to being the nineteenth. They had successfully dropped their bomb load, but the hydraulic system soon became problematical. The undercarriage activated on its own accord and would not respond to being retracted. The undercarriage system was fitted with mechanical up-lock controls accessible above the rest seat area, but the fault did not appear to relate to that mechanism. The up-lock system had red light indicators in the cockpit, which remained on if they were not engaged. Emergency circuits operated by the flight engineer were provided to lower a defective system, while a hydraulic hand pump was provided to override the system should the engine driven pump itself malfunction. It would appear no measures taken by Tam rectified the fault. Fortune was however on their side as they eventually made it on to home soil and they landed at Eastmoor, a sub-station to Linton-on-Ouse. It must be presumed both undercarriage assemblies operated properly to facilitate what was reportedly a safe landing.

Halifax BB237 'C' was repaired but it had unknowingly been on its penultimate sortie and never survived from the next operation to Genoa on 23 October. The operation involved six crews led by Wing Commander Cheshire. Tam and his crew were flying in Halifax DT556. They took off at 5.45 p.m. and as they did so, the port inboard cover for the bomb loading point detached itself from the upper wing and flew off. This was a winching point cover that the armourers removed to set into place a small hand winch, which loaded bombs into the small inner wing bays. No damage had been caused to the fuselage or tail section as it was ripped off in the slipstream and the general performance to the aircraft was unaffected. The flight to Genoa, Italy, was to be the furthest distance travelled thus far by Tam. As they approached the target, they saw no blackout precautions and no opposition took place. However, the cloud base caused problems in preventing the identification of the docks, the primary target. Wing Commander Cheshire was approached by an Italian biplane, but it proved to be easily distracted by his rear gunner's actions and disappeared after two unaggressive attacks. On safely returning to Linton-on-Ouse, Tam recorded that the sortie had taken nine hours and twenty minutes. He handed in the flight sheet detailing fuel consumption to the leading flight engineer and reported the missing bomb loading point cover, which would be investigated. Tam's flying log book was also submitted to the 'B' Flight Squadron Leader in order to be certified. At the close of October 1942, Tam had recorded sixty-six hours and thirty minutes operational flying at night, with just under 117 hours in total. Eleven operations had been completed against enemy-held territory.

Italian targets were to continue appearing on the briefing boards in November 1942. In general, these operations were regarded as easier to undertake than into Germany, despite the long runs over the Alps. Among the crew, they became known as 'Ice Cream Runs', Italy being synonymous with ice cream. These operations were undertaken in support of the recent Eighth Army El Alamein offensive. On 7 November, returning to Genoa Halifax DT556, a worrying oil leak developed from the port outer engine cooler on the Merlin engine. Rolls-Royce had developed the Merlin into an exceptionally reliable engine. The practice of selecting random engines from the assembly line and testing them continuously on running rigs until they eventually failed was instrumental in continuing development. Each engine was then completely dismantled to establish which part had failed. This programme assisted in the Merlin developing into one of the most reliable aero engines in the Second World War.

There were no mechanical issues to trouble Tam on the ensuing operations to the Italian target of Turin, which was attacked on 18, 20, and 29 November. That trio of operations added another twenty-seven hours and forty-five minutes operational flying to his flying log book.

Halifax DT556 returned to German objectives in December 1942 with Turin only appearing on one further occasion. Frankfurt on 2 December witnessed nine crews from 76 Squadron travelled to the target only to be met with thick cloud. The Pathfinders were unable to mark the target and so Al and his crew returned back to base, no doubt disappointed. The weather also forced a landing at Syerston aerodrome, where they rested before a short thirty-five-minute flight back to Linton-on-Ouse. The next target, Mannheim on 6 December 1942, witnessed almost identical events—thick cloud prevented any accuracy over the target area. Al reported that they were not certain where their bombs fell, other than probably 15 to 20 miles south-west of the intended target. On this occasion, they were forced to land at Breighton aerodrome, where after breakfast, the exceptionally short hop of just fifteen minutes saw them return to Linton-on-Ouse.

Exceptionally, it appears that Tam Readhead did not undertake an air test within Halifax DT556 in anticipation of another planned excursion to Turin on 11 December. It is possible this was done by another flight engineer but not recorded. The normally reliable and regular Halifax used by Al and his crew was about to buck the trend. Taking off at 4.50 p.m., the flight initially progressed well but cloud formations grew in their intensity. On reaching the Alps, significant icing had accumulated on the aircraft and both starboard engines lost power presumably due to icy conditions. Carburettor icing alone had the ability to lead to emergencies. Ice would form at the point that fuel was introduced into the carburettor. The moisture content of the air would then freeze as a result of the cooling induced by fuel vaporisation. Ice would also be formed when freezing moisture such as rain, snow, sleet, or cloud was present on the engine air scoops.

All flight engineers were trained to acknowledge the numerous symptoms induced by ice and the best options available to reduce those dangers. Ice was also capable of accumulating on the spinning propellers and large lumps of ice were capable of spewing off and hitting the fuselage. The engine coolant system was filled with glycol, which was used because of its very low freezing temperature. Additionally, the mixture had the ability to dissipate heat, which was also exceptionally important. It was usually used as a mixture of pure Glycol and water and, as such, possessed some lubricating qualities to benefit the engine function.

As Halifax DT556 progressed to Turin, the weather conditions failed to dissipate to any great extent. The combination of dangerous icing and accruing electrical storms forced a decision to drop the bomb load and return. Tam was also monitoring the starboard oil coolers, which were indicating some concerns on his engineering flight panel. After a rather precarious flight, the crew landed back at base seven hours and fifteen minutes after having departed. As they did so, Tam witnessed the sudden loss of oil pressure when the starboard oil cooler burst. The oil pumps had worked hard, forcing endless gallons of oil through the hot engine, oil tanks, and oil cooler, extracting heat from the oil and lubricating the Merlin engine for hours on end.

Tam supervised the engine fitters who replaced the burst oil cooler and examined both troublesome starboard engines. The relationship between flight engineers and ground-based engineers was important and essential in many respects. A short air test of just twenty minutes on 13 December saw DT556 ready for operational service once again. It was detailed to fly a mining operation to the Frisian Isles the following day; that operation was recorded as having been satisfactory. The crew would not fly operationally again until after the Christmas celebrations.

As the crew embarked into January 1943, the oil cooler problems would yet again feature in the delicate balance of surviving operations. Halifax DT556 remained the aircraft of choice to Al and his crew. The crew rankings at this time consisted of a single officer, three flight sergeants, and three sergeants. The officer, Pilot Officer Monkton, was a Canadian who had joined 76 Squadron direct from No. 22 Operational Training Unit. As a crew in the air, they were closely united, but on the ground, as an officer, Monkton was separated by virtue of his rank. Their first operation of the New Year was to the German submarine yards in Lorient, France, on 14 January 1943. The route to this target took them relatively close to the occupied Channel Islands. They were subjected to search lights and heavily engaged by anti-aircraft gunfire from the Islands. Escaping apparently unscathed, they later identified the target and accurately dropped their bomb load from 10,000 feet.

Photographs were taken, and three enemy night fighter aircraft were observed stalking in the darkness. The crew identified two aircraft as ME109 types but neither of them commenced an attack and later disappeared into the dark sky. Once again, during the return flight, the oil pressure became problematical to the flight engineer. The port inner engine needed constant monitoring and instructions were given to divert to Tangmere as soon as landfall was reached.

They landed at 3.05 a.m., having been in the air for four hours and fifty minutes. As they did so, the port inner oil cooler burst, spewing hot oil onto the runway.

Tam recorded in his log book that the burst oil cooler was changed on station and Halifax DT556 was made ready to leave just fourteen hours after their impromptu arrival. The crew departed from the South Coast and flew north to Linton-on-Ouse, where they arrived ready for supper on 15 January. It becomes an obvious fact that the oil cooler issues will have resulted in some attention to detail by Tam and consultation between him and the squadron flight engineer leader would have taken place. Having rested for a day, the crew attended an early afternoon briefing at Linton-on-Ouse on 17 January 1943. Tam had been aware that Halifax DT556 had received a significant fuel load, indicating a deep penetration operation and so, no doubt anticipated another 'Ice Cream Run' to Italy. The briefing board, however, revealed Berlin as the target. Air Chief Marshal Harris had decided that this was to be their first attack upon the German capital city and the first attack by Bomber Command upon Berlin for over twelve months. A combined force of around 200 aircraft—Halifax and Lancasters—were to attack the Pathfinder marked target.

Taking off at 4.30 p.m., it was estimated that they would reach the target of Berlin at approximately 8 p.m. The aircraft engaged flak as soon as they approached central Germany. The bomber force was spread out into separate groups, which was not ideal circumstances as the German flak was able to concentrate on the groups independently. Al Moir was at 15,500 feet when he commenced the bombing run onto target. Just before releasing the bombs, the Halifax was surrounded by flak explosions and struck by flak splinters. White-hot metal shards tore into the aircraft and it was just a matter of luck as to whether they missed either crew or vital aircraft components. Incredibly, their bad luck with oil coolers continued. The flak ruptured and burst the port outer oil cooler. Tam immediately feathered the port outer engine as they flew over the target.

The opposition at Berlin had been colossal and with a very long flight back to Yorkshire, the ever-present threat of enemy night fighters became even more of a concern as they were now a lame target. Fortune favoured the crew with no further incidents occurring. After nearly nine hours of flight, the three hard-working Rolls-Royce Merlin engines were finally rested on the aerodrome at Linton-on-Ouse. Halifax DT556 was battered and badly holed, and once again, a fated port engine had suffered the loss of yet another oil cooler. Unbeknown to Tam, he would never occupy the flight engineer station in that particular aircraft again.

Halifax DT767 was taken on an ice cream run to Turin by Al's crew on 4 February following which they targeted the submarine yards at Lorient in Halifax DT545. Both sorties were uneventful in all respects. The squadron had by this time a substantial number of Norwegian pilots and aircrew attached to them, the majority being experienced men drawn from those who had successfully escaped from occupied Norway. The men had come to England to fight and carried a reputation of willingness to do so within the Royal Air Force. The Norwegian, Lt Sandberg, became the first name from that contingent to be recorded in Tam's log book. On 11 February, Tam flew with him on a mid-morning air test.

Al and his crew, including Tam, flew to Wilhelmshaven on 19 February. This was to be his last operation as he became tour expired and rostered for a rest from operational flying. Commissioned as a pilot officer that month, Al departed to undertake instructional duties at the Heavy Conversion Unit from Marston Moor aerodrome situated just west of York. On 25 May 1943, Al undertook instructional duties in Halifax L9571 with an Australian trainee pilot, Daniel Veness, on a dual control training flight. The flight engineer on board was thirty-four-year-old Frederick Barns from London who had joined up in 1939. Flying in the circuit over Rufforth airfield, the aircraft's port inner engine suddenly burst into flames. Al took control and attempted a shortened circuit of the airfield to affect an emergency landing. The fire took hold as the aircraft stalled and lost height. It clipped the roof of Tockwith Vicarage and crashed, tragically killing all on board. The faulty engine was later stripped to investigate the reason of its failure and cause of the fire. It was found that the engine fire had burnt through the elevator and the rudder just prior to the crash, which, in the opinion of the investigator, was the cause of a total loss of control. The accident investigation also stated that the instructor Al Moir had experienced a similar incident while instructing at Marston Moor but had been able to land safely on that occasion. Flying Officer Alastair Moir, Flight Sergeant Daniel Veness, and Sergeant Frederick Barns all lie together in Stonefall Cemetery, Harrogate, Yorkshire.

Eleven days prior to the accident, Al had been awarded the Distinguished Flying Cross for service with 76 Squadron. It was included in the *London Gazette* on 14 May 1943:

> As a captain of aircraft this officer has flown on a large number of operational sorties. He took part in a low-level attack on Flensburg through the heaviest and most intense enemy opposition. He has also participated in attacks on Berlin, Duisberg, Bremen and Düsseldorf.

Back at 76 Squadron, Tam Readhead realised his tour of duty was reaching its conclusion. Unbeknown to him and quite unexpected, he would see his name appear alongside a further eight major operations before he was actually rested.

No. 76 Squadron received a number of new aircraft in March and April 1943. One aircraft, Halifax HR748, was flown by Squadron Leader Clive Smith, who took Tam along with him on an acceptance flight on 17 March 1943. Five days later, Wing Commander Cheshire took the same aircraft up on a handling test with Tam manning the flight engineer's station. This particular aircraft was a factory fresh Mk V model and carried several modifications instigated by Wing

Commander Cheshire. News filtered out that Wing Commander Leonard Cheshire was about to leave on promotion to group captain. Before that took place, he congratulated Tam on his commission to pilot officer. Wing Commander Leonard Cheshire had previously published a book titled *Bomber Pilot* and prior to his departure to command the Heavy Conversion Station at Marston Moor, he handed a copy of his book to Tam with a written dedication: 'I'd be proud if I knew so much about so many knobs as you do. Leonard Cheshire April 1943'.

His replacement was Wing Commander Smith, who took Tam on an operation to Stettin on 20 April 1943. Wing Commander Smith was heading a force of fourteen Halifax bombers from the squadron. The post raid debriefing for the Stettin raid disclosed that it was successful in all respects but the log book entry by Tam is conflicting because he regarded the trip as a special reconnaissance flight. On route, they flew at just 500 feet over Denmark in bright moonlight.

After the departure of Wing Commander Cheshire, Tam became a spare flight engineer, no longer part of a regular crew. Squadron Leader Vivian Gordon Bamber had Tam allocated as his flight engineer in Halifax DK202 on the operation to Düsseldorf on 11 June 1943. Visiting the intelligence room prior to the briefing, Tam looked at the latest photographic images taken over Düsseldorf, a target that he had previously visited and knew it would be well defended. What he did not know was that this operation was going to be a close encounter with potential death. Eighteen aircraft from 76 Squadron were to partake in the operation. The briefing room was a hive of activity and among the men in that room were two crews who would not return to Linton-on-Ouse. Sergeant Wilson was to command his crew on his very first operation in Halifax DK170. His navigator, Sergeant Lobban, became the only man who managed to parachute to safety, eventually becoming a prisoner of war. The second crew in Halifax DK200 fared slightly better. Four men escaped death to become prisoners of war. These losses were no more than a mean monthly average; by example, eight crews in April 1943 failed to return as did eight crews in June while in May 1943, four crews added to the devastating statistics.

Tam experienced the loss of many fellow flight engineers. Düsseldorf nearly claimed him as well. Leaving the aerodrome on 11 June 1943 at 11.02 p.m., everything went well and they reached the target area at 1.54 a.m. Approaching the target, their Halifax became coned by searchlights. Once seized upon by a leading searchlight, others coned or covered the same aircraft, bringing a crescendo of anti-aircraft flak in a quest to destroy one particular aircraft held in the beams of light. Squadron Leader Bamber was forced to drop the bomb load some 3 miles south-east of the primary target. Halifax DK202 was badly damaged, flak splinters and fragments had torn into her with terrifying velocity, and the noise even above the screaming engines was immense. Tam noticed fuel leaking from what he found to have been the port fuel control valves, which had been shot away. Remarkably, no fire had ensued. He had to facilitate a cross feed of fuel from the starboard tanks to feed the failing port engines. No doubt these actions were being undertaken while the squadron leader was taking evading action from both searchlights and flak.

They had been at 18,000 feet on approach to Düsseldorf but now at a much lower altitude, thoughts of fuel management and being picked off by marauding night fighters became important considerations. There were some thirty-three flak holes of various sizes puncturing the aircraft and the loss of the port wing fuel tanks was a significant matter to compensate for. With immense relief, Halifax DK202 successfully returned to Linton-on-Ouse, looking decidedly battle worn in appearance. The operation had taken six hours. They landed at 4.58 a.m. and as daylight broke, the mechanics and airframe fitters surveyed the extensive damage. It was common for aircraft to return with various levels of damage and great expertise existed within the ground staff who repaired them. Merlin engines were themselves often completely replaced and a team of four mechanics were capable of undertaking such a complex job in around four hours. An additional complication at this time was the imminent squadron move to Holme on Spalding Moor aerodrome, a move in consequence to a reorganisation of group boundaries within Bomber Command.

The Squadron move, completed on 16 June 1943 saw Tam promoted to acting flight lieutenant. Both his age and experience now placed him highly within the flight engineer structure of 76 Squadron and he had undertaken the role of flight engineer leader. Unbeknown to him, Wing Commander Smith typed out a recommendation that he be considered for the award of the Distinguished Flying Cross. The recommendation was dated 24 June 1943. It stated:

> This Officer has completed 25 sorties and flown a total of 170 operational hours as Flight Engineer. He has made several sorties against the heaviest defended of Axis targets, including Berlin, four to the Ruhr and six to Italy. He has at all times shown a very high degree of courage and initiative, while his tenacity, endurance and fine offensive spirit in action have inspired all those with whom he has come into contact. He is recommended for the award of the Distinguished Flying Cross.

The station commander recommended the application:

> The above officers operational tour has been distinguished by a combination of technical skill and a determination to make every possible contribution towards the success of every sortie upon which his crew has been engaged, and it is recommended that his personal record be recognised by the award of the Distinguished Flying Cross.

Air Marshal Sir Charles Roderick Carr, commanding 4 Group, endorsed the recommendation on 30 June 1943.

Tam filled the position of flight engineer in Pilot Officer Hickman's crew to Hamburg on 29 July and with Sergeant Row and crew to Remscheid on 30 July. The Hamburg sortie took the life of the Norwegian pilot Bjercke. His crew had not been on station for more than a few weeks. News arrived sometime later that the majority of crew had survived and were being held as prisoners of war.

During August 1943, once again, Pilot Officer Hickman was in need of a flight engineer to attack Hamburg. This was to be the last of the 'firestorm raids' to that particular target for 76 Squadron. As the squadron flight engineer leader, Tam was responsible for all of the flight engineers on station. Those duties involved assessing all operational reports submitted by his flight engineers and supervising all aspects of his trade within the squadron. When due to sickness or other reasons, a replacement flight engineer was needed, the leader would often step into that vacancy.

Taking off from Spalding Moor in Halifax DK195, Pilot Officer Hickman made an error of judgement and with the aircraft heavy with both fuel and bomb load, it clipped a tree with the port wing. A quick assessment indicated they were safe to continue; however, some damage had been caused to the port inner engine. It started to overheat, and heavy vibrations escalated into a serious problem as they crossed the open sea. Tam assessed a broken propeller tip to be the cause of the vibration and with escalating engine temperature, he feathered the engine. Flight engineers would always balance out the pitch controls on all four independent propellers in order to get them running evenly. Unbalanced propellers would be a source of vibration in any aircraft but with a damaged blade it would have been impossible to control. The Halifax engines drove 13 feet in diameter constant speed Rotol propellers. Imbalance caused by a failed or broken blade on a propeller under power was capable of subsequently tearing itself or the unbalanced engine itself from its wing mounting. The weather was worsening and with just three engines, a decision was made to jettison the bombs into the sea and return. To have continued into the brewing stormy weather on three engines intent to reach Hamburg would have been monumentally dangerous. Two hours and thirty minutes after having taken off, Halifax DK195 landed safely.

On 9 August, an operation to Mannheim once again saw Tam fly with Pilot Officer Hickman followed by three days later when Wing Commander Smith took Tam on a nine-hour operation to bomb Milan. This proved to be a most successful operation, but as with so many raids, success was tainted by the loss of two entire crews. This had been Tam's thirtieth operation. One more target, Peenemunde, would be entered in his log book before he was officially rested. At that time, the name Peenemunde meant very little; in fact, when it appeared at the briefing, several crews would have been relieved, thinking it was likely to be far more palatable than Berlin, Hamburg, or Duisburg. These men were to be mistaken. Within unusually secure briefings, Peenemunde was disclosed to aircrews as a secret establishment that was developing a new radar capability on the island of Usedom in the Baltic. They were not told it was in fact a secret rocket establishment. The reason to adopt such subterfuge was to enhance the awareness the crews already had for their vulnerability with the enemy's effective radar and radar-influenced night fighter capabilities.

Tam flew alongside Pilot Officer Hickman in Halifax DK266 to attack the German rocket establishment, which had developed 'V' weapons. The 'V' reference was short for *Vergeltungswaffen*, which roughly translates to 'vengeance weapons'. Halifax DK266 was one aircraft in a force of nearly 600 briefed to destroy Peenemunde. Each crew knew that if Peenemunde was not destroyed on 17 August 1943, they would return to the target the following night and thereafter until the job was done. Duncan Sandys, the Prime Minister's son-in-law and Joint Parliamentary Secretary to the Ministry of Supply, was charged with coordinating information about the development of secret weapons. Duncan Sandy promoted the decision that Peenemunde needed to be bombed, his decision greatly influenced by aerial interpretation photographs. Air Chief Marshal Arthur Harris subsequently gave the authority to launch the operation against Peenemunde.

Some 596 heavy bombers, 324 Lancasters, 218 Halifax and fifty-four Stirlings flew on the operation to attack Peenemunde. They did so from thirty-eight aerodromes on a bright moonlight period to increase the chances of success. The crews had been briefed in detail, this being the first occasion that a master bomber would control a full-scale Bomber Command operation. Group Captain J. H. Searby of 83 Squadron carried out this role. Duncan Sandy was present with him when he provided his extensive pre-raid briefing. Three primary aiming points within the experimental station were to be controlled with special Pathfinder crews acting as shifters, marking one part of the target to another as the raid progressed. The vast majority of aircraft were carrying high explosive bombs to blast apart the target and destroy as much machinery as possible. No. 76 Squadron provided twenty Halifax crews to support the Peenemunde operation. Only one Halifax, DK266 flown by Pilot Officer Hickman, carried an additional eighth man in her crew, Sergeant G. Whitehead as second pilot. The target was to be located on the seaward end of a long peninsula of the southern Baltic shore and all of 76 Squadron were to bomb after a timed run from the offshore island of Ruden. The Pathfinder force was going to be significant, deploying primary green and yellow target indicators over the three aiming points. The crews were concerned as the moon would be high in the sky and the combination of moon and ground illumination would make them very susceptible to being picked off by night fighters.

At 8.55 p.m., Tam checked the flight engineer's control panel as the pilot moved away from the hardstanding. The Halifax engines commenced the task of pulling the mighty aircraft laden with her bomb load towards the runway.

The sudden lurch that the crew had grown to expect indicated that the pilot had tested the brakes. Sitting on the runway, the Merlin engines responded to the additional power settings and the airframe strained in anticipation of the inevitable release of brakes. As the aircraft gathered speed, Halifax DK266 lifted off the ground and having gained some height, Tam, in common with all flight engineers, responded to the situation and activated the undercarriage to accept and stow the gear. Once Tam had balanced all four propellers to run evenly, it set the scene for the estimated four-hour journey to the target.

Within fifteen minutes of the raid commencing, the Luftwaffe night fighters announced their engagement with the remaining bomber force. The moon and the raging inferno on the ground created easy targets for them to attack. Several bombers became casualties despite the valiant efforts by their air gunners to defend themselves. All twenty aircraft from 76 Squadron returned with no losses. They had been the lucky ones. Bomber Command suffered a loss of forty aircraft, almost 300 men would never walk back into their mess rooms for the bacon and egg meal that greeted aircrews. Tam and his crew were diverted from returning to Holm and landed at Wymeswold where they were required to remain until the weather cleared.

Tam Readhead wrote in his log:

Ops PEENEMUNDE. Successful. DCO [Did Complete Operation]. Good Visibility. Smoke screens in operation over target area. Weather useless at base BFX [Diverted] Wymeswold. All HE [High Explosives] load on Radiolocation Experimental Station.

The log book entry recorded by Tam clearly illustrates Bomber Command's established machination over the true identity of Peenemunde. It is unclear when the crews became aware that the raid was in fact against German 'V' weapons.

Having been with 76 Squadron for a year, the Peenemunde raid marked the end of Tam's operational tour of duty. With a well-deserved Distinguished Flying Cross and having achieved the status of flight engineer leader, Flight Lieutenant Tam Readhead was posted to the School of Technical Training at St Athan. He had been selected to act as an instructor on flight engineer leader courses, a posting that endorsed his competency at the highest level possible.

In May 1944, after nine months' service at St Athan, Tam requested to leave his posting. Assessed as category 'A' and having passed final examinations, he could gain no further flight engineer qualifications and he wished to return to operational flying. Prior to commencing a second tour of operational duty, he followed in the footsteps of Al Moir and Leonard Cheshire, moving to the Heavy Conversion Unit at Marston Moor for a short period of time.

Posted to 462 Squadron at Driffield, Yorkshire, as engineering leader, Tam became personally responsible for the entire squadron contingent of flight engineers, approximately twenty-eight men of differing ranks and experience. A primary duty was applying scrutiny over every flight engineer report submitted after post raid debriefings, examining the fuel analysis statistics of each aircraft and signing off each report with general remarks. This continuity of scrutiny was capable of evidencing faults or potential failings in any particular aircrafts performance.

No. 462 Squadron had its roots buried within 76 Squadron as it had been originally formed from a direct detachment from that parent squadron and still flew the Handley Page Halifax. The squadron had become a nominated Australian squadron, manned by a high contingent of Australian men and as such was 462 Squadron, Royal Australian Air Force.

Despite the extensive experience of Tam, his operational flying against the enemy had thus far always taken place during the hours of darkness. This was about to change, attacking three targets in France and Germany in September 1944. Green ink was used to record daylight operations against Calais (25 September), the heavy guns at Cap Gris Nez (26 September), and the synthetic oil plant at Bottrop (30 September).

Adding to those experiences was the fact that they were undertaken in the new Mk III Halifax aircraft. As an operational flight engineer, Tam had only flown in the Handley Page Halifax aircraft. He had witnessed the development of various modifications made to the troublesome rudder design, a problem not completely eliminated until the introduction of the Mk III, which had a rectangular rather than a triangular-shaped rudder. In addition to the revised rudder, the Mk III took on a new appearance. The front nose section had neither the conventional air gunner's turret nor bomb aimer blister. Both were replaced with a slim streamlined Perspex nose fairing, which allowed the bomb aimer adequate downward visibility and also included a single 0.303 machine gun on a pivot mount. However, the replacement of the Merlin 'X' engines with Bristol Hercules VI radial engines created the most changes for flight engineers. The term 'radial air-cooled' meant that the engine cylinders were radially arranged in a circle. The complete circular array was called a bank. In the case of the Hercules, there were two banks, each of seven cylinders, lying behind each other. Each cylinder had metal fins around it. Air from the action of the propeller on the ground and in the air the forward motion of the aircraft forced air through the fins dispersing the heat. The Hercules engine was in essence less likely to cause a flight engineer issues with any overheating problems. Other changes included the use of de Havilland Hydromatic propellers, which operated a mechanical system in which forces applied controlled the propeller blades.

As an engineering leader, Tam Readhead will have known every flight engineer on his station. One young flight engineer, Sergeant Stuart Soames, was a member of the Australian Air Force pilot and part of Flight Lieutenant McGindles' crew. This gallant flight engineer experienced a remarkable survival, returning from an operation having attacked one of Germany's synthetic oil depots. His account is to be found within these pages. The engineer leader was the direct link to the squadron engineering officer on all stations.

No. 462 Squadron returned to night operations and on 30 October 1944, crews were briefed for an attack against the city of Cologne. A replacement flight engineer was needed for the Australian pilot Flying Officer Hourigan and so, Tam accompanied that crew to Cologne. He did so again for the same crew, attacking Düsseldorf on 2 November 1944. Both operations were flown in Halifax MZ467.

On 27 December 1944, 462 Squadron was relocated to Foulsham aerodrome, Norfolk. They became part of 100 Group, which specialised in electronic warfare. No. 100 Group was highly secret, special duties being undertaken in various guises. Wing Commander David Shannon commanded 462 Squadron and Tam Readhead accompanied him on several short test flights in the newly converted Halifax aircraft. The squadron operational record book entries, originally composed to record the crew and aircraft engagements, reveal at this time an unusually high work load for the squadron flight engineers, some of which were additionally tasked as special operators working alongside the crew rostered flight engineer. Tam flew in Halifax NA147 on 2 January 1945. The secret work they were undertaking was reflected in his log book entry: 'Operations as ordered'. This was actually an operational flight to the Nuremburg area of Germany where four Halifax aircraft created a spoof or fake impression of a full bombing raid. Each of the participating Halifax carried two flight engineers. Flight Sergeant Murray, Pilot Officer Manning, Sergeant Daughters, and Flight Lieutenant Readhead were the flight engineer special operators. Sergeants Hewlett, Hollins, Coleman, and Brown served as the crew's flight engineers. These aircraft carried and distributed the device known as 'window' dropped to a regular pattern to create spoof Allied bomber streams upon German radar. On occasions, the aircraft carried an additional small bomb load to be dropped in order to enhance the feint attacks.

No. 462 Squadron also flew as a radio counter-measures unit. Aircraft were fitted with the latest technical equipment, the most important items of which were the ABC (airborne cigar) and the electronic jammer known as 'Carpet'. The squadron's first serviceable ABC and Carpet jammer aircraft made their first operational sorties on 13 March 1945. There would eventually be eleven aircraft equipped with such secret countermeasure equipment in the squadron.

In the closing months of the war in Europe, Flight Lieutenant Tam Readhead supported his flight engineers by flying on six additional operations. The final operation took place on 13 April 1945 when he accompanied the Australian pilot Leo Britt on a five hour and eighteen-minute operation in a diversionary raid on Boizenberg, Germany. As he made the final entry in his log book, he calculated that he had flown nearly 300 operational hours against the German and Axis forces over occupied Europe.

The commanding officer 462 Squadron recommended Flight Lieutenant Readhead for an Air Officer Commanding Commendation on completion of two operational tours of duty:

> For Meritorious service and good airmanship, in that two full operational tours have been completed without having been involved in any accident or ever having an unnecessary cancelation or abandonment of an operational sortie.

The recommendation was supported by the Group Captain Commanding Foulsham and subsequently approved by the Air Vice Marshal Commanding 100 Group. Recognised within the Royal Air Force as a Green Endorsement, the small certificate was pasted into the certificate and qualifications section of his log book. The last written entry in the log book compiled by Tam Readhead was made by him on 4 July 1945. A passenger transit flight into Schleswig, Germany, was undertaken in Halifax PN423 with the previously mentioned pilot, Flight Lieutenant 'Ted' McGindle, in the cockpit. The flight engineer was the newly commissioned Pilot Officer Stuart Soames, his exploits to be explored later on in this book.

12

Flight Engineer Mallott: Short Stirling, Killed in Action

Sergeant Henry George Mallott was born in 1917 in Southwark, London. He volunteered to serve in the Royal Air Force immediately after war was declared with Germany in 1939. The military discipline and way of life suited Henry who progressed through the early training infrastructure with ease. As a qualified ground tradesman, Henry later volunteered to serve in the air and passed through the School of Technical Training at St Athan, qualifying as a flight engineer on the Short Stirling. Henry would eventually serve with 7 Squadron, Bomber Command. He joined the crew of John Patrick Trench, who, at twenty-two years old, was well respected, having progressed from leading aircraftsman into the commissioned ranks.

On the night of 10 September 1942, Stirling aircraft W7564 flew to attack Düsseldorf. This particular operation features in the account of flight engineer Sergeant Tam Readhead when the American publication *Life* obtained authorisation to create an article of that particular Düsseldorf raid.

Henry and his crew departed from their aerodrome at Oakington at 8.30 p.m., twenty minutes after Sergeant Tam Readhead, in his Halifax of 76 Squadron, had departed from the aerodrome at Middleton St George, both on route to Düsseldorf. Alongside Flight Engineer Sergeant Henry Mallott in Stirling W7564 was the pilot, Flying Officer J. Trench; the navigator, Pilot Officer C. Selman; the wireless operator, Sergeant I. Edwards; the front gunner, Sergeant F. Thorpe; the rear gunner, Sergeant W. Glendenning; and the mid-upper gunner, Flight Sergeant R. F. Jenner.

On the approach to Düsseldorf, Henry was at his engineer station. As with any heavily defended German target in the Ruhr, the flak and searchlight activity was intense. Immediately after bombing the target, Henry's Stirling was surrounded by flak, having been individually targeted by several guns. This may well have occurred during their constant speed bombing run undertaken to secure images of the attack by the photoflash bomb. It would have become obvious to the crew that flak splinters and larger fragments of anti-aircraft shell casings were inflicting catastrophic damage to their aircraft. The starboard fuel tank was holed, and the port wing oil pipes were damaged, which immediately reduced the supply of oil to the engines. After a short time, the port inner propeller and its reduction gear sheared apart, the propeller becoming separated, resulting in it flying off only to hit the aircraft in the mid-upper turret area. Although the port inner propeller had torn into the fuselage and turret at great velocity, incredulously, the air gunner escaped serious injury. Sergeant Henry Mallott will have been all too aware that a reduced supply of oil to the port wing engines would lead to terminal failures within a short period of time.

Within minutes, the complete port outer engine fell away from the wing, leaving only the two starboard engines in action, one of them not functioning to full capacity. These events serve to evidence the strength of construction of the massive wings that supported these engines. The wireless operator came to the assistance of the pilot and added immediate pressure to the rudder bar and control column, which enabled the pilot to keep the aircraft on a relatively even level as best possible in those circumstances. Owing to the wireless operator's preoccupation, no distress signal could be sent out. The flight engineer managed to isolate the cocks to the severed and damaged pipelines and had by balancing the fuel, ensured the two remaining engines were working with as much capacity as possible being fed from dual fuel tanks. Under normal circumstances, the fuel was drained systematically and sequentially from the fuel tanks by cross-feed valves and pumps. In these circumstances, the draining of the tanks needed to be managed in a manner that did not create an additional unbalancing affect because the pilot was having significant trouble keeping the aircraft in level flight. It was imperative that flight engineers ensured that fuel tank loads were always distributed evenly and used systematically, as in these traumatic circumstances, it was crucial to be able to forecast the rate of fuel usage and the time at which a tank would become empty. Remarkably, this unimaginably hazardous situation on Stirling W7564 was endured consistently over the long and fraught return journey from Düsseldorf to the English coast.

The damage inflicted upon the aircraft dictated that airspeed and height was gradually being lost. Their height had reduced down below 200 feet as they crossed the Dutch coast. This was exceptionally low and precarious. In order to maintain the little height they had, the remainder of the crew collected all removable equipment, guns, ammunition, and anything of weight, which was then jettisoned through the escape hatches. This was in itself not an easy task owing to the altitude of the aircraft and the need for care in keeping the remaining weight evenly distributed within the fuselage. This was required to ensure the best stability possible for the pilot in those perilous circumstances. Flight Engineer Henry Mallott would have been all too aware that for any Stirling with two engines out of action, it would be impossible to gain any height and maintaining the existing height was unlikely to be sustained.

As the aircraft crossed the English coast, the starboard inner engine started to splutter; after a short period, it finally cut out. Remaining in the air was now impossible. With just one operational engine, the pilot force landed in a field near Weeley, south-east of Colchester. Having been exceptionally low in the air, the aircraft crashed onto the field with an advantageous trajectory; both the pilot and wireless operator who had continued to assist on the flight deck were knocked unconscious in the initial impact. The navigator, with great courage, managed to extricate them from the wreckage and succeeded in getting them both clear of the aircraft. The remaining members of the crew had managed to extract themselves from the aircraft, with the exception of the rear gunner. The aircraft then burst into flames. Seeing that the rear gunner was trapped, Henry, assisted by another crew member, returned to the blazing wreckage in a heroic attempt to save him. Tragically, as they entered the fuselage, the fuel tanks exploded and they were both killed in the blast. They had shown immense bravery. Incredulously, the rear gunner survived, having been rescued by the mid-upper gunner, who had accessed the aircraft through a break in the fuselage, possibly created by the explosion. The extracted rear gunner, suffering severe burns, was later taken to Colchester military hospital by the attending rescue party.

The commanding officer of the squadron subsequently submitted a report requesting that four members of this brave crew should be recommended for their gallantry. That recommendation progressed to the awards of the Distinguished Service Order to the pilot, the Distinguished Flying Medal to the wireless operator, the Distinguished Flying Cross to the navigator, and the George Medal to the mid-upper gunner.

The George Medal recipient was Raoul de Fontenay Jenner, a Canadian enlisted in Ottawa who in February 1941, graduated from No. 2 Bombing and Gunnery School at Mossbank, Saskatchewan. Posted to 7 Squadron Bomber Command, he commenced a tour of operations on the Short Stirling. Pilot Officer Jenner was awarded the prestigious George Medal for outstanding bravery in saving the life of his fellow rear gunner, Sergeant Glendenning. The official recommendation for his George Medal was published in the *London Gazette* in December 1942:

One night in September 1942 Flight Sergeant Jenner was a member of the crew of an aircraft detailed to attack the target at Düsseldorf. The target was bombed successfully but, while still over the objective, the aircraft was repeatedly hit by anti-aircraft fire. The port inner propeller came off and, shortly afterwards, the port outer engine fell out; the petrol tanks were holed in many places. During the return journey, the crew displayed coolness and skill, doing all they could to keep the crippled bomber in the air. Shortly after crossing the English coast the aircraft crashed in a field and immediately caught fire. All the crew, with the exception of the rear gunner, managed to extricate themselves. The whole aircraft was soon blazing fiercely. Knowing that the fuel tanks might explode at any moment two sergeants re-entered the aircraft in an attempt to rescue the rear gunner. They went right forward to reach the place where they thought he would have been thrown, but a petrol tank exploded and both were killed. Flight Sergeant Jenner, who had seen his two comrades killed and knew that a further petrol tank might explode, then re-entered the burning fuselage. He found the rear gunner who was severely burned, and succeeded in removing him to safety. Throughout, this airman displayed extreme courage, fortitude and devotion to duty in keeping with the highest traditions of the Royal Air Force.

After this harrowing experience, Jenner spent six weeks in hospital recovering from shock. Little doubt exists that Flight Engineer Henry Mallott contributed greatly in saving the aircraft. Henry and his fellow crew member also demonstrated exceptional courage on the ground in attempting to rescue a crew member from a terrible death, a selfless action that took both of their lives. It seems remarkable that the fearless action undertaken by Henry was never to be recognised in any official manner whatsoever. He was twenty-five years old when he lost his life.

The next of kin to those courageous rescuers would have gained solace in knowing that their sons had died while trying to rescue a fellow crew member. The formal recommendation of bravery to the crew survivors is testimony to those events. Posthumous recognition of bravery is severely limited in several respects, but opportunities of recognition existed; the Mentioned in Despatches Bronze Oak Leaf may well have been particularly relevant. Abbreviated to MiD, this award, accompanied with a small dedication certificate signed by the Secretary of State for the Air, was given for gallantry and could be awarded posthumously. A total of 37,508 of these were awarded to members of the Royal Air Force during the Second World War. The Committee on the Grant of Honours, Decorations and Medals counselled upon the conditions for the award of all war medals and campaign stars, known as Command Paper 6833.

It must be noted that a quota system existed for the award in question, with a restriction to one award for every 250 persons in any unit, during any six-month period. It remains unknown if this became an influencing factor in relation to the failure to recognise Flight Engineer Henry Mallott and his fellow crew member who gave their lives in the explosion while valiantly attempting to rescue the rear gunner who was in such peril.

Flying Officer Trench, Pilot Officer Selman, and Sergeant Edwards all remained with 7 Squadron. Their battledress tunics would have displayed their gallantry medal ribbons as they continued with the war. Flying Officer Trench and Pilot Officer Selman flew together among a new crew. They lost their lives attacking Nuremburg on 8 March 1943 in Stirling R9270. Sergeant Edwards went on to receive a commission and remained with 7 Squadron. He narrowly escaped death over Köln on 2 February 1943 when a night fighter raked his Stirling R9273 with cannon fire. One cannon shell tore two fingers away from his right hand as he worked his radio set, a disabling injury that would prevent him from undertaking any further wireless operator duties.

Flight Engineer Henry Mallott was buried in Manor Park Cemetery, Essex. He lies in grave 436 and his Commonwealth Commission headstone proudly illustrates his life given that day in September 1942. His family requested that the base of his headstone should hold these words, 'At the going down of the sun and in the morning, we will remember them'.

13

Flight Engineer Moores: Handley Page Halifax, Guinea Pig Club

Francis Moores was twenty-four years old when war was declared against Germany. He subsequently qualified as a flight engineer and served with 51 Squadron, flying Halifax bombers from Snaith aerodrome in Yorkshire.

Any complex operational base within Bomber Command required hundreds if not thousands of service men and women to operate the mechanism of war. At this time, it was the flying crews who took the war to occupied Europe and beyond, but those operations were only possible through the impressive infrastructure that they left behind as they flew out on every operational sortie.

Francis Moores was a little more mature in age to many of his fellow flight engineers, but he was surrounded by many ground personnel who were older than himself. He and his crew would see for themselves the traumatic deaths of many of those men in the summer of 1943. The misfortunes of war came in a multitude of circumstances and it is fitting to explore events that took place at Snaith aerodrome in 1943.

At 1.20 p.m. on 19 June 1943, bomb loads were being prepared for the planned operations to the French Schneider armament factory at Le Creusot that night. The logistics of supplying numerous aerodrome bomb stores with a constant supply of ordinance configurations was a huge undertaking. Bomb stores were inevitable and situated a short distance away from the aerodromes for safety reasons. To protect against damage and to assist with camouflaging, wooded areas were always favoured for airfield bomb stores. High explosive bombs of medium capacity and high capacity ordinance, minus their tail fins, were stored in the open, frequently on a series of raised concrete plinths surrounded by earth revetments designed to contain the blast from accidental bomb detonation and provide a degree of protection from air attack. Concrete roads fed into and through the dump areas where individual loads would be prepared, fuses inserted, and tail fins fitted. The bomb loads would be transported from the store and onto the aircraft dispersals. The distance between the store and dispersals was not significant within the boundary of the aerodrome. Blast walls provided some protection and the armourers were well versed in safety within the busy environment that always contained immense destructive capabilities.

Incendiary bombs were also stored on site and these were carried in the aircraft bomb bay in open aluminium boxes called small bomb containers. The boxes could carry 236 individual 4-lb incendiaries, which were stacked in rows of five, six rows deep, and typically three stacks per container. The containers were fitted in the bomb bay inverted so that when released the incendiaries simply dropped as a mass. The fuse would ignite the thermite combustible pellet content, which in turn ignited the magnesium casing burning intensely for about fifteen minutes. Trying to douse the fire with water only intensified the reaction. It could not be extinguished and burned at such a high temperature that the destructive capability was exceptional. The empty containers remained in the aircraft bomb bay and on return were unloaded, checked, and refilled by the armourers. Magnesium Elektron in Swindon were the experts in developing and the supplying of magnesium alloys since 1936. The vast proliferation of incendiary bomb production saw the need for magnesium to be produced in significant quantities.

In the Snaith bomb dump, a large bomb accidently detonated after it had been armed for the Le Creusot operation. It became apparent that the blast from the explosion caused the incendiary stores nearby to ignite and a large number of high explosive bombs that had been prepared for operational use were caught in the initial blast. A number of bombs exploded with the igniting incendiaries creating a confined heat, which in itself was able to cause further explosions. The main railway line, which had a relatively close proximity to the site, was closed and despite the knowledge that many men would have been killed, it was not until 9 a.m. the following day before a bomb disposal expert was able to assess the site and advised that the area remained unsafe. It was not until 26 June 1943 that personnel were able to venture into the decimated bomb dump. Initially, ten bodies were removed to the mortuary. Nine men were identified while one casualty was initially presumed impossible to identify. The bodies of a further eight men were never found, confirming a chilling understanding of the utter devastation that had taken place.

On 30 June 1943, the ten recovered victims were all buried in the Selby Cemetery, the unidentified body was buried as an unknown. The nine identified victims were the following:

Flight Sergeant Victor Harold Benfield, aged twenty-four.
Sergeant Ernest David Francis, aged thirty-one.
Aircraftman First Class Sidney Miller Stubbs, aged thirty-five.
Aircraftman Second Class Anthony Charles O'Donnell, aged twenty-one.
Aircraftman Second Class Joseph Edward Powell, aged thirty-two.

Aircraftman Second Class Joseph Ridley Cousin, age unknown.
Leading Aircraftman Herbert Rudge, aged twenty-three.
Leading Aircraftman Hugh Smith, age unknown.
Leading Aircraftman Robert Menzies Taylor, aged thirty-five.

The eight armourers who were never found are commemorated on the Runnymede Memorial where those with no known grave can be remembered:

Leading Aircraftman Hugh Bannatyne, aged thirty-five.
Leading Aircraftman Stephan Blackwell, age unknown.
Aircraftman Second Class John Brown, age unknown.
Aircraftman First Class Oliver Richard Edward Dormon, aged twenty-two.
Leading Aircraftman Hugh Finlayson, aged thirty-five.
Leading Aircraftman Kenneth William Harris, aged twenty-two.
Leading Aircraftman Alfred Irvine, aged thirty-five.
Leading Aircraftman John Jamieson, aged thirty-six.
Leading Aircraftman James Roberton, aged thirty-seven.

Francis Moores would have inevitably known several of the victims who tragically lost their lives that day and felt the impact of their loss on base. Flight engineers were present with ground crew on pre-flight inspections; moreover, he would have seen the devastated site from the air as Operations continued regardless. On 9 July 1943, Francis was in Halifax HR859, which took off from Snaith airfield at 11.03 p.m., having been briefed to drop their bomb load upon Gelsenkirchen refinery. Bomber Command had turned its attention onto the Ruhr synthetic oil plants; these were always heavily defended. Over 400 heavy bomber crews received the briefing against this target and took off, not all of them returning. The crew in HR859 very nearly added to those who did not return. Over the target, they sustained damage by flak to their starboard inner engine. Operational records advise that they released their bombs from 19,500 feet at 1.22 a.m. and were able to bring the aircraft back to Yorkshire. The loss of an engine over Germany was always a serious situation to be in and one that required skill and determination by the crew to bring the aircraft back to base. For Francis, he was to face a far more serious incident in Halifax HR981 just four weeks later.

On 10 August 1943, Bomber Command sent 653 heavy bombers to Nuremberg. Halifax HR981 was among that number of aircraft with Francis Moores at the flight engineer station anticipating a long and arduous flight into Germany. The process of gaining height and looking for other bombers forming up for the bomber stream heading into German itself could be fraught with everyone needing to be alert. For Francis, he was, however, engaged in frantic work trying to resolve a developing hydraulic system failure that occurred after take-off.

The hydraulic systems on the Halifax were complex despite working on a most basic principle of applying a force to be transmitted to another point using an incompressible fluid. The hydraulic system followed a myriad of routes emanating from the fluid stored in the holding tank in the starboard engine recess. Flight engineers were expected to be familiar with all such matters. The hydraulic system provided important capacities to flight, not merely associated with just the undercarriage manipulation. The flight engineer was obviously expected to resolve all engineering failures and while over homeland environments, as in this case, aircraft would normally lose height for safety measures. Any loss of an engine regardless of its position required the pilot to throttle back on the opposite engine. In all probability, Halifax HR981 was flying relatively low over Lincolnshire; as the situation worsened, this forced them to jettison their bomb load in open countryside. Operating the fuselage bomb doors required hydraulics, the power from the starboard inner engine being the direct link for that power. It was possible for emergency mechanical systems to be used; that may well have taken place in order to drop the bomb load. A hydraulic hand pump was provided at the port side of the fuselage near the front wing spar. That pump drew fluid from the hydraulic tank return pipe and was capable of operating the entire system. The system also had isolating valves in place, so when in the manual closed position, the valves prevented the complete lowering of the hydraulic operated flaps and bomb doors.

It remains unknown exactly what took place that night other than shortly after 10 p.m., Halifax HR981 crashed into a house identified as Snitterby House Farm, near Kirton-in-Lindsey, Lincolnshire. The aircraft was heavily laden with fuel and the crash scene developed into an inferno of flames. The wireless operator, Pilot Officer Cyril Silvester, was killed in the crash and within the house, Mrs Olive Dickinson and her baby son John Dickinson aged just fifteen weeks, also lost their lives. Only one crew member survived unscathed—the Canadian rear gunner who was able to extract himself from his turret and assist in rescuing those he could from the terrible scene.

Flight Engineer Francis Moores suffered badly from burns to his face and hands, clearly lucky to have survived the crash. The ramifications of the crash and loss of life that took place at the remote location at Snitterby, Lincolnshire, would likely have remained with the survivors for a very long time, if not indefinitely.

The tragedy that had taken place involving a mother and young son became even more poignant when it was disclosed that Olive Marguerite Dickinson and her son John Rowland Dickinson were both buried together at Glentworth Cemetery four days after the incident, the infant and mother joining their grandmother and mother respectively who had died in 1941 and lay in the same cemetery. The names of Olive and John Dickinson joined the names of those civilians of the Commonwealth whose deaths were due to enemy action in the Second World War. The names of some 67,092 are commemorated in the Civilian War Dead Roll of Honour, located in St Georges Chapel in Westminster Abbey, London.

Francis himself faced serious deep burn injuries. Initially taken to York Military Hospital, he was transferred to the Royal Air Force, Rauceby Hospital on 14 August and finally taken to the prominent burns unit at East Grinstead Hospital on 18 April 1944. At East Grinstead, he was operated upon by Archibald McIndoe, therefore becoming a member of the Guinea Pig Club. McIndoe became the consultant surgeon to the Royal Air Force, specialising in plastic surgery. Although plastic surgery was established during the First World War, McIndoe was one of only three experienced plastic surgeons in Britain when war was declared against Germany in 1939.

Archibald McIndoe went on to achieve critical acclaim during the second world war for his pioneering work at the East Grinstead Hospital. He carried out ground breaking reconstructive surgery techniques on men who had suffered serious burns or significant disfigurement from across the Commonwealth Air Forces. It was, however, membership to the exclusive Guinea Pig Club that provided the most significant medication, the psychological reconstruction of its members. This proved fundamental to the process of keeping up morale. Established in 1941 first as a drinking club, the Guinea Pig Club ensured that the men did not feel isolated while undergoing extensive treatment at the hospital.

The term 'Guinea Pig' indicated the experimental nature of the reconstructive work carried out on the club's members, and the new equipment and procedures designed specifically to treat these terrible injuries. Full membership was open to all Allied Air Forces servicemen who had suffered injuries primarily as a result of fire, but other facial injuries were included.

Inevitably, aircrews suffered considerably from explosions and fire eruptions when involved in crashes, and ground crew personnel often risked their lives in rescue attempts, resulting in similar injuries. Reconstructive surgery operations at East Grinstead conducted by McIndoe automatically entitled the patient to Guinea Pig Club membership. The types of injuries requiring his attention frequently entailed significant numbers of operations, the piece by piece rebuilding of damaged skin tissue over weeks, months, and years.

During his hospitalisation, Francis was made aware that he and his crew had received recognition with awards being published in the *London Gazette* in October 1943. The Canadian newspaper, the *Hamilton Spectator*, provides a clue to these collective recommendations, reporting upon the crew's rear gunner's exploits:

> Back from overseas, wearing the ribbon of the Distinguished Flying Cross and with a tour of operations behind him is Flying Officer W. R. Clow, whose wife is residing at 263 John Street South. The medal was well earned. In addition, to complete

his tour of operations the veteran air gunner shot down one enemy plane, and, as the only member of the crew not seriously injured, helped rescue his fellow crew members when their aircraft crashed.

The *London Gazette* advised that the King had been graciously pleased to approve the following awards:

Distinguished Flying Cross.
   Pilot Officer William John MACPHERSON 146862, Royal Air Force Volunteer Reserve, 51 Squadron.
   Pilot Officer Francis Stephen MOORES 52574, Royal Air Force, 51 Squadron.
   Pilot Officer Anthony Trevor ELLIS 146795, Royal Air Force Volunteer Reserve, 51 Squadron.
   Pilot Officer Joseph GRUDZIEN J.22090, Royal Canadian Air Force, 51 Squadron.
   Flying Officer William Ralph CLOW J.14011, Royal Canadian Air Force, 51 Squadron.
   Distinguished Flying Medal.
   Sergeant Reginald Vaughan PAYNE 776171, Royal Air Force, 51 Squadron.

The Distinguished Flying Medal recommendation to the bomb aimer provides a little further detail as to what took place within the ill-fated Halifax:

Sergeant Payne who joined the Squadron on 19 April 1943 has completed 22 operational sorties. He has always pressed home his attack with the utmost determination in the face of the heaviest opposition. He has always shown himself to be thoroughly imbued with offensive spirit and played his part well in a highly successful crew. On his last sortie, his aircraft crashed and burned out due to hydraulic and engine failure soon after take-off. Before crashing he gave his Captain valuable assistance in his attempt to force land with one engine on fire. He is strongly recommended for the award of the Distinguished Flying Medal.

Francis Moores carried the injuries of war sustained while serving as a flight engineer for the rest of his life. He was one of only 649 men ever entitled to wear the Guinea Pig Club badge. He died in 2010.

14

Flight Engineer Horner: Handley Page Halifax, Killed in Action

Douglas Carter Horner was born in Britain yet he served in the Royal Canadian Air Force—an unusual situation but the result of him having sailed to Canada for employment in 1937. Douglas originated from Lancashire and had gained experience working in motor mechanics since the age of fifteen. Prior to departing for Canada, he had attained an engineering diploma and a similar qualification with mechanical rewiring.

Douglas started his new life in Canada when he was twenty-six-years old. Within two years, he knew that his family in Britain were going to face war against Germany. His country of birth made the declaration of war on 9 September 1939. Although this did not automatically commit Canada into the conflict, little doubt existed that the government and people of Canada would be united in support of Britain and France. Parliament debate settled the matter and Canada declared war on Germany the following day. Prime Minister William Lyon Mackenzie King promised the Canadian people that only volunteers would serve overseas.

Douglas Horner with his exemplary engineering credentials, volunteered to serve as an engine fitter in the Royal Canadian Air Force. The process of going to war took time to organise and it was in August 1940 when Douglas was swept into the initial training and mechanism of preparing to wage war in Europe. His qualifications served to have him posted as an engine fitter, servicing aero engines at the Flight Training School at Camp Borden. Canada was committed to the Empire Air Training Scheme and Douglas witnessed first-hand the enormous task of building an infrastructure of training establishments for pilots and aircrew. Canada was building upwards of eighty aerodromes during the time when Britain was engaged in what is now known as the Battle of Britain. Desperate news of unfolding events was being fed back to Canada including for Douglas, news that his family home had been subject to Luftwaffe bombing and his father had been seriously injured.

In May 1941, Douglas personally applied to his commanding officer for consideration for an overseas draft to serve in Britain, outlining the needs of his family. At that time, no policy existed for sending ground staff fitters overseas as they were desperately needed within the rapidly developing Canadian Air Force. There was no doubt, however, that compassionate grounds existed for Douglas, coupled with a statement of intent from him to volunteer for aircrew duties and so, with the evolving need for flight engineers being sought from established ground staff, Douglas was able to return home to Britain.

Very rarely was it possible to see a Royal Canadian Air Force uniform among those of the plethora of Royal Air Force uniforms arriving at St Athan for flight engineer training. Douglas had presented impressive aero engineering experience in his application. The course at St Athan held between 28 August 1942 and 23 September 1942 was condensed for him due to his experience. During that period, he attended a factory course at Rotol aircrews in Gloucester and a week at a Warrington factory concentrating on superchargers. He swiftly passed through training, was awarded the flight engineer brevet (which was sewn onto his Canadian uniform), and then posted onto a Canadian squadron serving within Bomber Command. Douglas arrived at Leeming in Yorkshire, joining the Halifax equipped 408 'Goose' Squadron on 26 September 1942.

Douglas joined a crew consisting of predominantly officer ranked Australian, British, and Canadian men. The only fellow flight sergeant was the Canadian bomb aimer Max Samuels. He had likewise been a garage mechanic, which no doubt forged their friendship even further.

As a crew, they participated in attacks upon many targets, including Italy and deep into Germany. On 14 February 1943, the crew was returning from a successful operation against Köln, a reference frequently applied to the city of Cologne. Effectively, it had been an uneventful operation, if such a thing could exist in Bomber Command. Douglas had almost completed his fuel calculations and checked the engine temperatures as his British pilot, Flight Lieutenant Robert Boosey, approached Leeming. Committed to landing, Douglas stood close to the pilot. The port outer engine suddenly erupted in flames and, simultaneously, the port inner lost power. Frantic actions between the pilot and flight engineer needed to be instantaneous to avert disaster. Additional power was applied to the engines to gain as much height as possible. The undercarriage was raised and actions to extinguishing the fires were undertaken immediately. The official Air Ministry Bulletin 9917 of 18 April 1943 has the following citation to recognise the action of the pilot:

> While serving as an operational Pilot, Flight Lieutenant Boosey has displayed courage and coolness of a very high order. He has participated in sorties against such targets as Bremen, Düsseldorf, Kassel, Lorient, and in numerous mine laying operations. He has invariably pressed home his attack with great determination,

and on several occasions, has brought back excellent photographs of the aiming point. In February 1943, when about to land, after an attack on Cologne, his port outer engine caught fire, and the port inner engine stopped when the aircraft was at a height of about 300 feet. Flight Lieutenant Boosey, with great skill and coolness, kept the aircraft under control and climbed to 900 feet where the crew bailed out safely. With complete disregard of his personal safety, the pilot then made a successful crash landing.

Douglas Horner has no mention in these events, yet he would have undertaken significant action in averting fatal consequences for the entire crew. The official operational records for that operation states, five crew escaped by parachute, one of which was the rear gunner who did so without sufficient height for his parachute to function properly, he was killed when he struck the ground. The remaining four crew members including Max Samuels survived the emergency escape sustaining minor injuries. Therefore, despite no mention of the fact, it becomes obvious that two men remained within the Halifax. Douglas Horner as flight engineer would have supported his pilot in the cockpit trying to control the aircraft with the two remaining starboard engines.

It was just before midnight when the forced landing was undertaken. The burning port engine became the only light available as the Halifax tore into the fields near Kirby Wiske, Yorkshire. Two days later, a report was undertaken, normal practice for a forced landing not attributable to enemy action. The 400 Squadron engineer officers deduced the following from his examination:

Simultaneous cutting of Port Inner and fire in Port Outer would indicate likelihood of fire starting from engines backfiring on throttle being opened too quickly. This is borne out by soot deposit on air intake of Port Outer engine. However, degree of burning around exhausts on engine while aircraft remained in flight indicates possibility of fire from overheating engine by loss of coolant. Engineers log shows normal temperatures five minutes before fire broke out.

The Halifax airframe was unrepairable and subsequently scrapped as was the Merlin engine, which had been torn away from the wing mounting as it forced landed. The three remaining Merlin engines were recovered and sent for repair and salvage. The report advises that the flight engineer at the time of the incident had accrued seventy-five hours and forty-five minutes experience.

Further evidence of Douglas's unrecognised bravery exists in the 408 Squadron operational record book entry dated 31 May 1943: 'Caterpillar Pins and membership cards were presented to Pilot Officer Mitchell, Pilot Officer Quance, Pilot Officer Giblin and Flight Lieutenant Samuels.' It becomes obvious that the exclusion of Douglas Carter Horner from that presentation means he was not among the crew who had parachuted to safety. Documentary evidence of Caterpillar Club Pins being presented to members of a crew in this fashion is exceptionally rare and it is certainly unique to the author.

Douglas and his close friend Max Samuels had by this time both received commissions. They continued flying operations with their 408 Squadron crew. The majority of operations were bombing as accurately as possible on the relevant Pathfinder target markers laid upon the industrial Ruhr. They flew with a new British pilot, Richard Symes, who had joined them from 405 Squadron. He wore an unfamiliar medal ribbon on his tunic. It was for the British Empire Medal and the circumstances of his award for that medal made clear how much this new pilot would have valued serving alongside an experienced flight engineer:

Air Ministry Bulletin 9418:

One night in November 1942, Sergeant Nichols and Sergeant Symes were Flight Engineer and Pilot, respectively, of an aircraft engaged on anti-submarine patrol duties. On the return journey engine trouble developed and Sergeant Symes was compelled to make an emergency landing. In so doing the aircraft struck a hut and burst into flames. All the crew with the exception of the Wireless Operator, who was trapped by the legs, managed to extricate themselves. Knowing that the petrol tanks might explode any moment, Sergeants Symes and Nichols re-entered the blazing aircraft and succeeded in extricating the Wireless Operator. A few seconds later the petrol tanks exploded. The courage and devotion to duty displayed by these Sergeants undoubtedly saved their comrades life.

All of the individual crew flying with Douglas were focused on completing their respective tours of duty. On station and off duty, Douglas and Max continued to appreciate their friendship. Only a few weeks after the presentation of the Caterpillar pins, the target of Le Creusot appeared at briefing. Some 181 Halifax, 107 Stirling, and two Lancasters were to fly deep into France to bomb the Schneider armaments factory and the Breuil steelworks at Le Creusot. The date was 19 June 1943.

Following the detailed and lengthy duties required for such operations, the crew climbed into the easily accessible main door in the Halifax fuselage. Douglas knew exactly what fuel load was being carried in their allocated aircraft JD 107. He expected the normal flitting between his little cubby hole engineer station and the cockpit as preparations were made for take-off. He had done it many times, and expectantly, once in the air, he put the undercarriage up, reduced the flap angle, and set the throttles for climbing. Having synchronised the propellers, he would have checked the engine temperatures and pressures and changed the gills to get the engine temperatures right. Douglas would fill in the log book as the Halifax climbed higher. With every change of engine revolutions, the log had to be filled in, essential for his fuel calculations. During the climb, a Halifax flight engineer always undertake the very important job of charging and locking of the hydraulic accumulator. This was an emergency charge of hydraulic fluid, which would hopefully be enough to lower the undercarriage and potentially the flaps in an emergency. Effectively, it was a large cylinder connected to the hydraulic system. Fluid was let into this cylinder and charged to a pre-requisite pressure. The fluid was held under pressure by the air in the cylinder and retained for any emergency.

Once the altitude they were to fly at was attained, the engine revolutions and boost were reset. High speed would be selected on the supercharger for each engine as the crew commenced the long run into occupied Europe. Douglas would also have been monitoring the engines, having attained the best possible fuel efficiency. The navigator and wireless operator were in their respective stations while Max was in the front, potentially stretched out full length looking out and telling the pilot what he could see to help avoid others in the bomber stream. These and similar circumstances would have been repeated by every crew as they headed towards the important steelworks at Le Creusot.

What followed next can be best described by two written accounts. The pilot and his Rear Gunner provided these reports two full years after the flight to attack Le Creusot. The pilot recorded:

> There was a full moon and very clear. Everything went according to plan. I flew out at 10,000 feet and bombed at 4,000 feet. I saw 2 Ju-88 night fighters, but they apparently did not see me. Owing to the fact that I had no mid upper turret and that the operation was originally intended to be a low level one, I decided to fly back from the target low. The visibility was very good. I reached a turning point on course, here I saw 2 other Halifax, one on either side about the same height as myself. Everything was quiet and I avoided all villages, towns, etcetera until I approached the French coast where I turned to starboard to avoid coastal flak and flew over Caen. 4 guns, 20 mm turret opened up all around, especially on the beams. The aircraft was hit and the port outer caught fire, but since it was still working I did not feather it. A searchlight picked me up dead ahead. The aircraft started to spin and having only one wing the aircraft crashed nose first and broke up on its back. I remember nothing about the crash. The Rear Gunner says the wing came off. I regained consciousness sometime later. The Rear Gunner and some German personal extracted me from under an engine ...

Rear Gunner Flying Officer Ball stated:

> We took off from Leeming on the evening of 19 June 1943. Headed south to the target of Le Creusot, France, bombed at approximately midnight, light flak in target area, clear sky, full moon. On turning from target to return to base, Pilot considered it best to avoid night fighter attack by descending to low level, 2 Ju-88's having

been spotted flying parallel course just after leaving the target. Passed over Caen at its western extremity, about 3 miles north we passed over a thin strip of trees and dead over a flak battery of which we were unaware of until it opened fire. The guns were in pits with soil and grain growing around and over them...An opening barrage of flak, the rear turret opened up to retaliate, aircraft penetrated through the fuselage by flak, rear turrets guns damaged and reflector sight damaged by a passing shell from starboard to port. Intercom still working, last message from pilot 'we will be out of this in a minute' port outer engine then burst into flames followed immediately by an explosion. The port outer engine and wing tip dropping away from the aircraft, with the aircraft dipping sharply to port, diving to the deck, hitting skidding on its nose and then giving a quick flip over. The rear turret becoming disengaged during the flip and I landing some 50 feet away from the tail of the aircraft on leaving the turret I crawled to the cockpit, found the Pilot held in an inverted position by his harness. I tripped the harness and made him as comfortable as possible on the ground, bound a deep gash on his temple with a handkerchief and then endeavoured to locate the rest of the crew. The mangled remains of the wireless operator was the only other member seen before my removal by German soldiers to the German billet, approximately 10 to15 minutes after the crash.

The vast majority of repatriated prisoners of war underwent a questionnaire interview. The pilot and Rear Gunner had both been detained in Stalag Luft III and therefore it appears that it was only in early 1945 when the circumstances surrounding the fate of Halifax JD 107 became known.

France granted Canada perpetual concession to the land occupied by the cemeteries that held their dead. Bretteville-sur-Laize Canadian War Cemetery is one such location with a concentration of Canadian burials. This cemetery was created as a permanent resting place for Canadian soldiers who had been temporarily buried in smaller plots close to where they had fallen. There are now 2,793 Canadian soldiers buried in the cemetery. Unfortunately, ninety-one of them still remain unidentified. A small number of Royal Canadian Air Force casualties lay among the many graves, seventy-nine airmen who had been exhumed from small isolated grave sites. Flight Engineer Douglas Carter Horner and his close friend Max Samuels were recovered from their temporary graves and reburied at Bretteville-sur-Laize cemetery on 29 May 1945. They now respectfully rest adjacent to each other for perpetuity.

15

Flight Engineer Van de Velde: Avro Lancaster, Evader

Cyril Van de Velde was born in 1924, and lived in Loughborough in the East Midlands. He later became employed at the local John Corah and Son print workshop and participated as an active member of the Air Training Corps. The Air Council had actively promoted cadets to join the Air Training Corps, which was tasked with providing the earliest possible training in order to pave the way forward into the Royal Air Force. It had been formed primarily with an objective to provide for aircrew, but also to give training for all branches of staff. They actively sought young people with high levels of intelligence, skill, and character for maintenance work.

Cyril Van de Velde married relatively young and, like his brother Maurice, volunteered to serve in the Royal Air Force in 1942. It would appear that Cyril had little if any engineering background. In all probability, he was one of the many young men who responded in the early weeks of 1943 for direct recruitment to become a potential flight engineer within Bomber Command.

Cyril passed out from St Athan, having attained his flight engineer brevet and promotion. He temporarily returned to his wife in Loughborough for his allocated leave prior to complying with orders to attend at 1656 Heavy Conversion Unit, based in Lindholme, Yorkshire. This posting was ideal for Cyril as he was roughly two hours' travelling distance from his family. The flight engineer leader at 1656 Conversion Unit was Flight Lieutenant Humphrey Phillips, a vastly experienced man who had a preoccupation in developing visual and practical flight engineer training aids. One of these was his Lancaster fuel system display with illuminated links to the fuel cocks. Another was his Lancaster undercarriage rig, which provided the full hydraulic operation and demonstrated the function of the complicated locking mechanism. Micro-switches operated an electrical indicator.

The time eventually arrived when Cyril became part of a heavy bomber crew and engaged in flying. He joined forces with a pilot, Roy Whalley, who had likewise been a member of his local Air Training Corps in Blackpool prior to his acceptance for pilot training in Canada. Roy and Cyril would spend a great deal of time together in the cockpit of the Lancaster and later experienced many operations into the heart of Germany.

Cyril's constituted crew departed the Conversion Unit in October 1943 when they were posted into 101 Squadron stationed at Ludford Magna, Lincolnshire. This was a newly constructed aerodrome that had opened just five months previously and became home to 101 Squadron as part of No. 1 Group, Bomber Command. Cyril and his crew undertook their first operation to Modane, France, on 10 November 1943. This provided the opportunity to experience flying against the enemy. It was no doubt like any first operation—tense and traumatic but nothing in comparison to the events that unfolded on the next raid into Berlin on 22 November 1943.

Flying in Lancaster LM369, they carried the huge 4,000-lb high capacity blast bomb along with other minor ordinance. The reputation of Berlin preceded any briefing, but the reliability built around the Avro Lancaster provided those same crews with optimism. Cyril experienced a relatively uneventful flight after departing from Ludford Magna at 5.10 p.m. on that darkening evening sky of 22 November 1943. This operation to Berlin would herald the last occasion on which the Stirling heavy bomber would be sent to Germany. Some 469 Lancasters, 234 Halifaxes, fifty Stirlings, and eleven Mosquitoes were engaged on this raid. It was a major operation and departure times were calculated to ensure that the Stirlings should arrive over the target and complete their bombing within a pre-set time period, essentially catering for the aircraft's differing capabilities.

Cyril knew from the briefing that they would be in the last numbers of Lancasters to bomb the target. Fuel consumption during the outward flight was as expected and Lancaster LM369 eventually arrived on time as it approached Berlin to commence the bombing run. LM369 was among many aircraft that were likewise trying to deal with the cloud conditions and comply with bombing upon the marking instructions. Unfortunately, Lancaster LM369 was singled out by searchlights, and then coned by others that saw them. The aircraft became an illuminated target for the anti-aircraft gunners. The intensity of the searchlights was monumental, with the cockpit area consumed in blindingly bright light. The flak gunners were well prepared, quickly assessing the aircraft height resulting in immediate damage being sustained to their aircraft. One engine burst into flames and was seriously damaged; however, the fire extinguishers worked effectively and the engine was shut down. White hot fragments from exploding flak shells were penetrating the cockpit area and the pilot received a serious wound to his arm. Having been committed on their bomb run, the bomb load fell onto the target marking flares. It then became imperative to escape the searchlights and only then deal with the complexities of returning back to base on just three engines.

Violent manoeuvres in a damaged heavy bomber could lead to a total loss of control. Many crews had to deal with such circumstances in evading searchlights, all being fraught with danger. Cyril himself had numerous tasks to ensure that primary mechanical functions were still operable; he assisted the injured pilot in gaining as much height as possible for the return flight. Aircraft that lose the power of their engines struggle to maintain altitude, so they drift down and attempt to stabilise at a lower height determined by their weight. The instructions to the flight engineer regarding damage by enemy action were to immediately check fuel content gauges and if any abnormal consumption was suspected on the tank the aircraft was running on, or should any of the other tanks show a loss of fuel, proceed with the following sequence of events:

(a) Cross-feed cock to the on position.

(b) Run all engines on the damaged tank, and switch on its booster pump. Thereby using as much of the valuable fuel as possible, before it leaks overboard. The fuel selector for the tanks on the other side of the aircraft should be off.

(c) When contents of damaged tank fall to 20 gallons, turn on fuel selector for the corresponding tank on the other side of the aircraft and turn off the cross-feed valve.

(d) Watch fuel pressure warning lights or fuel pressure gauge and change over to other tank as soon as pressure drops and switch off booster pump in empty tank. This will prevent a bad situation becoming worse, through the self-induced loss of serviceable engines from fuel starvation.

In the majority of circumstances, gaining height would be sought and maintained if at all possible. In this incident, the management of the three remaining engines was critical to ensure a safe return over occupied territory and the North Sea. The remaining engines were monitored with great scrutiny, assessing for other flak damage. A minor puncture hole in the engine coolant system alone would produce a gradual loss of coolant, creating an increase in operating temperatures. This would quickly become critical once the coolant started to boil. With any rapid temperature increase, any engine had the likelihood of eventually seizing. Coolant leaks also created potential for engine fires. A rapid increase in temperature in an engine and any atomised spray from boiling off coolant could itself be ignited. A large leak, caused by a large piece of flak through a cooler, would have resulted in an engine seizing within seconds. Despite the initial flak damage, no additional problems developed. The entire crew returned safely, successfully landing at Ludford Magna. Cyril had sat next to the injured pilot on the return, all too well aware of the injuries he had sustained. As he undertook the engine shut down procedure, the pilot collapsed, presumably the result of blood loss. As the aircraft was finally shutting down on the hardstanding, Cyril would have opened the bomb bay doors before ensuring he completed his flight engineer log. This would be needed for the engineer leader's scrutiny.

In December 1943, the entire crew (including the recovered pilot) were posted within No. 1 Group into 576 Squadron at Elsham Wolds, Lincolnshire. These movements between squadrons and groups were not uncommon events. No. 576 Squadron itself was a newly created squadron and between December 1943 and April 1944, Cyril flew as flight engineer on twenty-six heavy bomber operations. The Battle of Berlin took place within that period and Cyril returned to the German capital target on eight further occasions. Two of those were on two consecutive nights in January 1944. Without doubt, the events over Berlin would have included many moments of terror and thoughts of mortality prevalent. Bomber Command lost a total of 213 Lancaster heavy bombers during those particular Berlin operations. Accumulatively, 1,491 men never returned from the nine Berlin operations in which Cyril had partaken.

No. 576 Squadron carried an American staff correspondent, Sergeant Ben Frazier, within Lancaster ED888 to Berlin on 29 December 1943. His narrative report was written verbatim in the squadron operational records. This was an operation undertaken by Cyril and provides an excellent insight into the events endured by him and his crew when Berlin appeared on the operational orders:

At the airfield, V for Victor crew lounged around B Flight Office waiting to see if operations were on. They kept looking up into the sky as if trying to guess what the weather was going to be like. Some of the men chuckled. Papa Harris is so set on writing off the big city that he hardly even notices the weather, one of them said, the last time there were kites stooging around all over the place. The met boobed that one. It was a strange new language. What the airman was saying was that the last time out, the meteorological men had given a wrong steer on the weather, and the planes had been flying all over looking for the field, on the return trip. Papa Harris was Air Chief Marshal Harris Chief of Bomber Command.

V for Victor captain came back from operations with the news that there would be ops. That settled the discussion. You seemed to be aware, without noticing anything in particular, of a kind of tension that gripped the men, like they were pulling in their belts a notch or two to get set for the job ahead. And with the news, everybody got busy—the aircrews, the ground crews, the mechanics, the Waafs, the cooks. The ships already had a basic bomb and fuel load on board, and the additional loads were sent out in ammunition trailers and fuel trucks. The perimeter track lost its usually deserted appearance and looked like a well-travelled highway, with trucks and trailers, buses and bicycles hurrying out to the dispersal points. It was just like the preparations at any bomber base before taking off for enemy territory—but going over the big city was something different. These men had been there before. They knew what to expect.

In the equipment room, June, the pint sized Waaf in battledress, was an incongruous note. Over a counter as high as her chin, she flung parachutes, harnesses and Mae Wests. The crew grabbed them and lugged them out to the ships. You kept thinking they ought to be able to get somebody a little bigger for this job she was handling.

In the briefing room, the met officer gave the weather report and the forecast over enemy territory. There would be a considerable cloud over the target. The men grinned. An operations officer gave a talk on the trip. The route was outlined on a large map of Germany on the front wall. It looked ominously long on the large scale map. He pointed out where the ground defence were supposed to be strong, and where fighter opposition might be expected. He gave the time when the various phases should be over the target. He explained where the spoof attacks were to be made, and the time. He told the men what kinds of flares and other markers the Pathfinders would drop. There was the usual business of routine instructions, statistics and tactics to be used. The Group Captain gave a pep talk on the progress of the battle of Berlin. And all the while, that tape marking the route stared you in the face, and seemed to grow longer and longer.

In the evening some of the men tried to catch a few winks, most of them just sat around talking. The operational meal followed, it was only a snack, but it was the last solid food anyone would get until the fresh egg and bacon breakfast which has become a ritual for the proper ending of a successful mission. As there was still some time to wait before take-off, V for Victor crew sat around the ground crews hut near the dispersal point, warming themselves by the stove or chewing the rag with the ground crew. The Wingco came around to make last minute checks. The medical officer looked everyone over. The engineer officer checked the engines.

The minutes crept by until at last the time came to get into the planes. The deep stillness of the night was awakened by the motors revving up, one after another until each one was lost in the general roar. The crews scrambled into the planes and took their places. The great ships were guided out of their dispersal areas by the ground crew who gave a final wave as the Lancs moved off slowly down the perimeter track. One by one they turned into the runway and noisily vanished into the night. From now on until they return, the members of V for Victor crew were a little world in themselves, alone and yet not alone. For all around them were other similar little worlds, hundreds of them, each with a population of seven, hurtling through space, lightlessly huge animated ammunition dumps. For its safety, each little world depended utterly and completely on its members, and a large dash of luck.

There was not much conversation over the intercom. When you are flying without running lights on a definite course, and surrounded by several hundred other bombers, you have no time for any pleasantries. The Navigator was busy checking for air speed and any possible drift. Almost everyone else kept a look out for other aircraft, both friendly and foe. A friendly aircraft is almost as dangerous as an enemy plane, for if two block buster's meet in mid-air, the pieces that are left are very small indeed.

Occasionally the ship jolted from the slipstream of some unseen aircraft ahead, and frequently others overhauled V for Victor passing by to port and starboard, above and below…. Jocks Scotch accent came over the intercom. Taff we are eleven minutes late. Ok we will increase speed. The Flight Engineer pushed up the throttles…. Plane to starboard below, ok it's a Lanc. As V for Victor passed it you could see the bluish flames from the exhausts lighting the aircraft below in a weird ghostly manner. It was unpleasant to realise that our own exhausts made V for Victor just as obvious as the other plane. Away off to our port bow a glow became visible. It looked like the moon rising, but it was the first big German searchlight belt encompassing many cities…. another searchlight belt showed up to starboard. It was enormous, running for miles. It was all imprisoned under the cloud, but it was an evil looking sight just the same. The top of the clouds shone with millions of moving spots, like so many restless glow worms, but the impression was much more sinister, like some kind of luminous octopus. The tentacle like beams groped about seeking some hole in the cloud, some way of clutching at you as you passed by protected by the darkness. The continuous motion of the searchlights caused a rippling effect on the clouds, giving them an agitated, angry, frustrated appearance. Once in a while one found a rift and shot its light high into the sky. Flak came up sparkling and twinkling through this luminous blanket. V for Victor jolted violently from close burst, but was untouched. It passed another Lanc which was clearly silhouetted against the floodlit clouds.

Another leg of the trip was completed. The Navigator gave a new course over the intercom and added, seven minutes late. V for Victor passed plane after plane, and occasionally jolted in the slipstream of others. A third searchlight belt showed up, this one free of cloud. It was a huge wall of light and looked far more impenetrable that a mountain. It seemed inconceivable that any plane could pass through and reach the opposite side. You thanked your lucky stars that this was not the target. To fly out of the protecting darkness into that blaze of light would be a test of courage you would rather not have to face. Nevertheless, there were some facing it right now. The flak opened up and the searchlights waved madly about. It was a diversionary attack, the spoof. You watched in a detached, remote sort of way. It seemed very far away and did not seem to concern you at all. Until suddenly, one beam which had been vertical, slanted down and started to pursue V for Victor, and you realize that it did concern you very intimately. The seconds ticked by as the beam overtook the plane. But it passed harmlessly overhead and groped impotently in the darkness beyond. Four minutes late Jock called over the intercom.

The target itself, the Big City, came into view like a luminous patch dead ahead. It was largely hidden by cloud and showed few searchlights. It seemed so much less formidable than the mountain of light just behind that it came as a sort of anti-climax. Surely, you felt, this cannot be the Big City, the nerve centre of Europe's evil genius. It was quiet no flak as yet, no flares, and just the handful of searchlights. You tried to imagine what it was like on the ground there. The sirens would be about to sound, the ack ack batteries would be standing ready, the searchlights already manned…. Ever so slowly V for Victor crept up on the target…. Nevertheless, V for Victor was passing plane after plane and jolted in somebody's slip stream now and again. The other Lancs looked ominous bearing down on the target, breathing out blue flames as they approached.

The minute of the attack came and still the target was quiet. One more minute ticked by. Still quiet. The Flight Engineer opened up the throttles to maximum speed, and increased the oxygen supply. Still quiet. The whole attack was a minute or two late. Winds, probably. Suddenly the whole city opened up. The flak poured up through the clouds. It came in a myriad of little lights. It poured up in streams of red as if shaken from a hose. It went off in bright white puffs. The Pathfinders had arrived. In another moment they had dropped the target indicators, great shimmering Christmas trees of red and green lights. You couldn't miss. It would be impossible to miss such a brilliantly marked objective. Bright flashes started going off under the clouds. That would be the cookies of the planes ahead. V for Victor started the bombing run, the Bomb Aimer called the course now. Left left, steady now, right a bit, steady, steady cookie gone. V for Victor shot upwards slightly. Steady Incendiaries gone. V for Victor surged forward again ever so slightly. Standby Taff. It was the voice of Bob, the tail gunner. Fighter. Corkscrew starboard the tail gunner called. Instantly, the Pilot sent V for Victor over to starboard and rushed headlong downwards. A stream of red tracers whipped out of the dark, past the rear turret, and on past the wing tip, missing both by what seemed inches. A second later the fighter itself shot past after the tracers, a vague dark blur against the night sky. ME109, Bob said calmly.

V for Victor squirmed and corkscrewed over the sky of Berlin. You wondered how it could be possible to avoid all the other planes that were over the city. But the fighter was shaken off and V for Victor came back to a normal course again…. The dark black shapes of many Lancasters could be seen all over the sky, against the brilliant clouds below. They were like small insects crawling over a great glass window. It did not seem possible that these tiny black dots could be the cause of the destruction which was going on below. The insects crawled to the edge of the light and disappeared inti the darkness beyond. They had passed through the target. V for Victor followed close behind…and so the capital of Nazism dropped astern, obscuring the rising moon by its flames. The Government which came into power by deliberately setting fire to its chamber of representatives, the Government which first used wholesale bombing, and boasted of it, was now perishing in fires far more devastating than any it had devised. It was perishing to a fire music never dreamed of by Wagner … Standby JU88 starboard, corkscrew came Bob's voice. Again with lightning speed, the Pilot put V for Victor over and dived out of the way. The JU88s tracers missed us and shot down another Lanc which had not been so fortunate. After that the route home was uneventful. Crossing the North Sea, V for Victor went into a gentle incline towards home base, as if by a sort of homing instinct …

Cyril regularly flew in Lancaster ME586. The aircraft carried the unusual identification (UL B2) and was referred to as 'Baker Twice'. The confidence in consistently flying one particular aircraft and engaging with a regular ground crew was of utmost importance to any flight engineer. Cyril spent a great many hours flying in Baker Twice, attacking Leipzig, Stuttgart, Schweinfurt, Augsburg,

Frankfurt, Essen, Nuremburg, Düsseldorf, Karlsruhe, and Friedrichshafen among others. Those operations would have seen numerous events of concern and fear prevail and specifically for the flight engineer, endless hours of calculating fuel usage and engine monitoring.

As a crew, one final operation was required, their thirtieth, in order to achieve a tour of duty. Crews reaching such a milestone were not very common and all those sprog and mid-tour crews would have eagerly swapped places with them at the drop of a hat. A crew reaching an end of tour was of utmost importance to the moral of every squadron. Their thirtieth operation was to be against Mailly-le-Camp. The briefing exposed this target to be in France and the crew of Baker Twice would have gained great satisfaction, knowing it was not to be another long flight deep into Germany. The French targets were regarded as softer and it appeared Cyril had a final operation that would be no more than a short hop across the English Channel and then back home. His thoughts would have turned to celebrating the end of tour and leave with his wife.

On the night of 3 May 1944, Bomber Command undertook to attack a Wehrmacht training centre close to the village of Mailly-le-Camp. It was a large and substantial barrack complex originally built for the French Army in 1902. The initial marking by the Pathfinder Mosquitos was accurate, and that force was led by Wing Commander Cheshire. The master controller attempted to call in the 346 Lancaster bombers to begin the attack and bomb the markers. Devastatingly, an American Forces broadcast of band music appeared on the same frequency being used to control the events over the Wehrmacht barracks. At this most crucial time, the operation was thrown into turmoil with Lancasters holding on their initial destination, an assembly point above the French village of Germinon.

The two waves of Lancasters started to orbit, waiting for formal instructions. The raid planning required accuracy because of the proximity of a French village close to the military camp. In the maelstrom over the target, the marker leader for the Pathfinder Force was hit and went down just south of the target area. The deputy took over but the main force continued to hold until they responded to him; however, the Luftwaffe night fighters arrived and demonstrated their devastating efficiency. Tragically, 294 men went down within forty-two Lancasters. The bombing, however, had been very accurate and the Panzer troops, equipment, and a wealth of machinery were destroyed. Regardless, the losses to Bomber Command were exceptionally high and among them had been Cyril and his crew in Lancaster Baker Twice. They were never to celebrate the completion of that last and final operation to complete their tour. The 576 Squadron operations room blackboard simply had the chalked message 'MISSING' against Lancaster ME586.

Cyril and his crew had fallen victim while approaching Germinon and had no opportunity to attack the target. Their aircraft was shot down near Oeuilly despite the rear gunner's attempts to engage with a pursuing night fighter. Only two of the crew escaped, both by deploying their parachutes as they escaped out of the stricken Lancaster. Flight Engineer Cyril Van de Velde and the navigator, Sergeant Jack Ward, presumably escaped from the front emergency hatch. Cyril landed near Epernay and instinctively, but with little hope of actually achieving it, he commenced walking south, intent on reaching Spain. After two days of walking, he came across a couple of blacksmiths in a small village. They took him to a family who spoke English and who were in contact with the local Marquis. Cyril was hidden in the marshes near Mourmelon-le-Grand and provided with civilian clothing. The navigator Jack had likewise found refuge, but his fortune fell short when in Paris he was caught engaged in counterfeit money operations. He was subsequently imprisoned in Stalag Luft III.

Post-war, Raymond Crompton corresponded with Cyril Van de Velde and facilitated in the publication in 2013 with author, Oliver Clutton-Brock of *The Long Road* accounts of airmen prisoners of war in Stalag Luft VII:

[Cyril] joined [Maquis] raids on the Boche supply dumps of food, using a very large charcoal-burning car, which was later changed to a petrol car after the Marquis shot the collaborator who owned it … we were constantly on the move to evade capture. I was finally caught along with an American airman they had been sheltered by M. and Mme. Aubossu and their son in their farmhouse until 19 June, when they were captured. The Aubossus son was put on trial after the war as he was the prime suspect in giving them away. According to Cyril he protested his innocence, but I believe he did it, because the two Alsatian dogs they kept for alarm purposes were silent. No way could a stranger have approached that farmhouse without being detected.

Cyril was fortunate not to have suffered the fate of many of the French Resistance, for when captured he was wearing some civilian clothes and had lost his identification 'Dog Tags'. Accusing him of being a saboteur, the Gestapo locked him up for ten days or so in Chalona-sur-Marne prison, before he was sent to their large, central prison at Fresnes, Paris. The Gestapo had also picked up Monsieur Bouchem the senior Police Officer of Vertus, a large village twenty five kilometres south west of Chalons, who was working with the Marquis and was also brought to Chalons prison, as Cyril recalls:

'I saw him being tortured and blinded. He subsequently died soon afterwards'. There is now a monument in Vertus to M. Bouche and other Resistance members, along with a couple of French Farmers who were hiding us. The Boches killed them too'.

Cyril was interrogated in the infamous Fresnes prison, Paris. This prison was used by the Gestapo for holding and interrogating resistance and British SOE suspects, a repulsive place where terrible measures were taken to extort information from such brave men and women. Interrogations consisted of violent beatings and sadistic torture. The corridors were frequently filled with screams of personal agony and occasional single gun shots. Cyril's identity was eventually established as a British flight engineer; he was later transferred into the custody of the Luftwaffe at the Dulag Luft interrogation centre.

In 1945, Cyril was subject to a forced march away from a Stalag Luft camp to avoid the advancing Russian liberators. He was finally liberated by Allied forces as the war drew to a close and after his repatriation, he returned to the printing industry in Loughborough. During those immediate post-war years, he harboured the desire to return to France and pay his respects at the gravesides of his fellow crew members. This he did on several occasions, always placing flowers at the original temporary wooden grave markers and at the base of the subsequent permanent commemorative headstones which continue to stand in the Oeuilly cemetery near Epernay. All five casualties lie alongside each other in one immaculately tended grave.

16

Flight Engineer Rolfe DFM: Avro Lancaster

Reginald Stanley Rolfe was born in Aston near Birmingham, Warwickshire on 18 May 1914, just prior to the outbreak of the First World War. After his schooling, he moved to Hednesford, near Cannock in the West Midlands where he was eventually employed as a cellulose sprayer. Industrial cellulose spraying had developed significantly during the interwar years within the car manufacturing industry based around the Midlands of England.

Reginald was twenty-six years old when he enlisted into the Royal Air Force in 1940, volunteering no doubt for service as a fitter. His engineering background would have been of great assistance in his transition into that trade. We have seen the various routes available to the many ground trade volunteers who put their name forward to become flight engineers. It is unclear exactly the route taken by Reginald but following his training and promotion, he undertook operational flying duties five days prior to his twenty-ninth birthday, 13 May 1943.

The newly qualified, but slightly older than most, Flight Engineer Reginald Rolfe, had joined 460 Squadron. Operating from No. 1 Group and equipped with the Avro Lancaster heavy bomber, 460 Squadron was affiliated to Australian aircrews. The squadron suffered significant losses during the Second World War, losing 181 aircraft on operations and 1,018 fatal casualties, 589 of which were Australian. This was the highest number of casualties suffered by any of the four Australian-affiliated squadrons.

Reginald joined the squadron as it moved from Breighton, Yorkshire into the aerodrome at Binbrook, south-west of Grimsby, Lincolnshire. This was to become the permanent base for the squadron, where it remained for the duration of the war. Four high radio masts situated 8 miles distant from the aerodrome soon became the primary landmark for the aircraft to use when flying in daylight.

Reginald soon found himself in the dark skies high above miles of exposed sea and hostile enemy-occupied territories. The thundering roar of four powerful engines synchronised into reverberating equal pitches from the propellers surrounded the flight engineer at night. Only the dim orange glow of a lamp behind the navigator's curtain and the faintly green luminosity of the instruments in front and behind his right shoulder beckoned his constant attention. His chances of surviving a complete operational tour equated to the toss of a coin, odds of exactly one in two.

The 460 Squadron records show that he completed his tour of duty successfully—thirty operations over enemy held territory. Among those operations were two most notable and significant sorties that took place just five days apart. They were his eighteenth operation to Milan on 12 August 1943 and his nineteenth operation to the German rocket establishment on the Baltic coastline at Peenemunde on 17 August 1943.

Reginald was flight engineer for the Australian pilot, Flight Sergeant Daniel Rees. He was eight years younger than Reginald. The Australian pre-war civilian occupation was as clerk of courts with the Crown Law Department. He had volunteered for military service in Australia and trained under the Empire Air Training Scheme, successfully graduating as a sergeant pilot. In June 1942, Daniel was posted to Britain and trained on Lancasters at a heavy conversion unit before joining 460 Squadron at Binbrook. He captained a complete crew of both sergeant and flight sergeant-ranked men, three of whom were fellow Australians.

The crew rapidly commenced accruing operational sorties and Reginald had found an affinity towards Lancaster ED985. This Lancaster had become a regular aircraft to him and his crew and it proved to be a most reliable airframe. Lancaster ED985 had flown them to Essen, Wuppertal, Düsseldorf, Oberhausen, Gelsenkirchen twice, Cologne twice, Hamburg, Turin, Mannheim, and Nuremberg with no pressing mechanical issues. Gaining such reliability from any aircraft was always reassuring, creating as much confidence as possible for any flight engineer. This situation was no doubt also appreciated by the Australian pilot from Fremantle and his entire crew.

From early March 1943 until the end of March 1944, Bomber Command embarked on what are now frequently referenced to as battles—the 'Battle of the Ruhr', March to July 1943; the 'Battle of Hamburg', July to August 1943; and the 'Battle of Berlin', August 1943 to March 1944. There was hardly a major city within Germany during that time that did not feel the might of Bomber Command. Bomber streams of 200 aircraft were used for a small operation and upwards of 1,000 for a major attack. The heavy bombers of the Australian squadrons—460, 463, 466, and 467—all played an active part in those battles. They also went further afield and for Flight Engineer Reginald Rolfe, the operation to Italy on 12 August 1943 created numerous engineering incidents of significant magnitude. That particular operation required great skill and coordinated actions between himself and his pilot to affect an eventual safe return. They undertook a most hazardous crossing of the French Alps on three engines, one of which was unable to provide full power, a remarkable achievement. In the moonlight and unable to gain sufficient height, they wove through the snow-covered mountain peaks with Mont Blanc itself towering high above their Lancaster. The account is best described by reading the recommendation of the Distinguished Flying Medal to the flight engineer, dated 20 August 1943:

> Sergeant Rolfe is a Flight Engineer who has completed 18 successful operational sorties with Flight Sergeant Rees as Captain. On the night of 12 August 1943, this crew were detailed for an attack on Milan. Soon after crossing the French coast on the outward journey, the starboard outer engine commenced to emit sparks and overheat so, accordingly, the engine was cut and the airscrew feathered. This was restarted when it had cooled down sufficiently and kept running at half power. Afterwards, the starboard inner engine commenced to miss and the No. 3 stub on the port side of this engine burned away, allowing flames and sparks to shoot back over the mainplane. This engine was also throttled back but had to be kept running to enable the aircraft to climb over the Alps. On the return journey, the starboard outer engine was eventually feathered when crossing the French coast. It is considered that the skill with which the Flight Engineer manipulated the engines contributed to the successful completion of this operation. It is strongly recommended that the devotion to duty this N.C.O. has shown in the course of this operational tour merits the non-immediate award of the Distinguished Flying Medal.

The Station Commander remarked:

> Sergeant Rolfe is the Flight Engineer in a very successful crew which has brought back three photographs of the aiming point in recent weeks. He is a fine engineer who used his utmost ability to prevent an aborted sortie. He considers this a slur on his ability and on one occasion nursed two good engines and two doubtful engines to Italy and made it a highly successful mission. I strongly recommend him for the award of the Distinguished Flying Medal.

It appears unusual to see mention of aiming photographs for a flight engineer. Technical improvements in aerial photography helped to improve the accuracy of wartime bombing. Two important developments that helped to improve accuracy included the two-shutter master and slave camera, which helped to eliminate the frequent ruining of images caused by ground fires during a single prolonged exposure. Another later development was the H2S radar, which enabled bombing a target even when cloud was completely obscuring it. In these conditions, a photograph of the cathode ray tube radar image of the target was recorded at the moment the bomb load was released.

Three days before that recommendation for the Distinguished Flying Medal was composed and just five days following that epic operation, Reginald and his crew had experienced the events surrounding the secret briefing and planning to bomb Peenemunde. This operation was to lead to further recognition of the flight engineer capabilities of Reginald and the recommendation to award his pilot with the prestigious Conspicuous Gallantry Medal.

The preparations against Peenemunde saw several hundred aircraft at dispersals across the entire command being feverishly prepared. The significance of this operation has already been disclosed by the participation of other flight engineer accounts in previous chapters. An additional number of aircraft were nominated as a reserve to deal with last minute technical failures. The hundreds of dispersals were surrounded with activity, oxygen trailers, and fuel bowsers with bomb trailers delivering their vital supplies. Specialist fitters checked radios and instruments. Armourers attended to the Lancaster's enormous bomb bays, checking the bomb cradles or crutches that were to receive the allocated bombs. The flight engineer for every bomber visited his aircraft prior to the briefing process with the rest of the crew, which meant the day was already a long one before their allocated take-off time. The summer months inevitably dictated short nights with later departures. Crews were confined to their stations and no telephone calls were permitted from the facility, which was normally situated close to the guard house.

Peenemunde was attacked by a heavy force of bombers, among them Lancaster ED985 of 460 Squadron, piloted by Daniel Rees with Reginald sitting alongside him as flight engineer. The Lancaster had the unusual ability of housing the flight engineer in what most people would have assumed to have been a second pilot position. The flight engineer had a folding seat, which was necessary to allow access to the forward bomb aimer and front gunner positions. This seat was a rather unsubstantial fold down arrangement with a tubular footrest, which pulled out from under the raised floor section beneath the pilot seat. However, it was not uncommon for many flight engineers to fold up the seat and stand next to the pilot. The flight engineer had immediate access to the entire cockpit and his individual control panel of instruments alongside him. The view from that position was excellent looking across both wings and the Perspex bubble blister fitted on the cockpit canopy immediately next to his position allowed for a view which could be enhanced further.

The operational planning was a success, one factor being the diversion of the German night fighters towards Berlin by the spoof raid flown by 139 Squadron in their Mosquitoes. This worked well for the early stages of the attack. Inevitably, the absence of night fighters was temporary, and they were redirected to Peenemunde taking great vengeance upon the latter stages of the bomber stream downing forty bombers. Twin and single-engine fighters joined the bomber stream over Peenemunde. The Pathfinder marking had been most effective and the coloured markers were attacked by the main force with great efficiency. The night fighters were among the bombers that were suffering in the air with an alarming frequency. Coloured tracer bullets fired by the fighters were seen hammering into the wings and fuselages by many crews.

Reginald in Lancaster ED985 would have been scanning the sky to help with spotting the marauding fighters while periodically checking his instrument gauges. Their bombing run upon the nominated coloured marker was successful and no more than four minutes after having dropped their bombs, a fighter singled them out and attacked. The mid-upper gunner had sighted the attacker and screamed for a dive to port. The pilot immediately responded as he saw cannon shells stream past the starboard side of the fuselage between the inboard engine and the cockpit. So close were the shells to the aircraft that the Perspex blister, which was alongside the flight engineer position, was torn away in a violent torrent of exploding matter. Reginald was injured by the exploding splinters of Perspex and the cockpit filled with smoke. The smashed cockpit blister appeared to immediately suck the air away and with it was the trailing end of the navigator's curtain, which hung down separating the cockpit from his position.

The pilot executed an immediate dive to port, which ultimately saved their lives. As he did so, the rear gunner was able to open fire as did the mid-upper gunner. Both fired at the fighter as it broke away. It was no more than a passing moment, but both sets of guns struck home upon the fuselage and port wing of the fighter. The gunners saw the fighter roll away on its back and was last seen diving vertically.

Lancaster ED985 had also suffered cannon shell damage to one of the starboard fuel tanks and the starboard elevator had been shot away immediately, making the aircraft difficult to handle for the pilot. Reginald was no doubt preoccupied with his injuries and the immediate events of the attack when the starboard fuel tank registered as having been holed. No fire had broken out, but the hole was significant; within fifteen minutes of the attack, 500 gallons of fuel had been lost. Speedy manipulation of the fuel system minimised the loss from that point. By forcing all engines to draw fuel from the damaged tank, use was made of some of the fuel that would otherwise have been lost overboard. Around the seriously damaged Lancaster, heavy bombers were sustaining attacks; these continued as the stream of bombers made towards the Danish coast. The ferocity of some attacks was extraordinary as some bombers exploded in mid-air.

Flight Sergeant Daniel Rees in the cockpit called for more power from the engines in order to try and gain height; Reginald responded by acknowledging the request and set the throttles to a higher boost setting and the Lancaster gradually gained height. All possible measures were put in place with the pitch of the propellers and the balancing of power to the engines to obtain the most economical fuel consumption possible. Added to the mechanical problems, one engine had obviously sustained some damage and needed constant monitoring. Once they had crossed the Danish coast with the expected anti-aircraft flak below, Reginald was able to reduce the engine power. The speed was naturally reduced as was a loss in height resulting in precious fuel being preserved. Reginald had balanced the remaining fuel with the cross-feed system between the functioning fuel tanks. The fuel calculations, although evidencing a critical situation as they limped home, had been most accurately estimated. As they descended, the power was reduced further as Reginald pulled the throttles right back and virtually hung onto them to make sure they were off as the pilot manhandled Lancaster ED985 down onto the ground.

The remaining fuel in the aircraft was estimated to have been at a critical level and the starboard elevator had been shot away to such an extent that two crew members would easily stand in the damaged hole torn away by the night fighters cannon fire. The starboard wing root adjacent to the fuselage had suffered a gaping hole torn away by the same stream of shells which so nearly took the life of Flight Engineer Reginald Rolfe. Photographs were posed with the crew and later published; the exploits of this operation saw the pilot being recommended for the Conspicuous Gallantry Medal. The citation reads:

> One night in August 1943, this airman displayed superb skill when piloting an aircraft detailed for an operation against Milan. During the outward flight, two of the bombers engines became defective but Flight Sergeant Rees continued to his far distant target and bombed it, afterwards flying the disabled aircraft to base. One night in August 1943, Flight Sergeant Rees took part in an attack on Peenemunde. While over the target area, the aircraft was attacked by a fighter. The attacker was driven off but the bomber had been repeatedly hit. The starboard tail plane and the trimming tabs were shot away, one engine and the hydraulic system were damaged, while one of the petrol tanks was pierced and its contents lost. Despite this, Flight Sergeant Rees coolly and skilfully flew the damaged bomber to base. This airman, who has completed many sorties, has displayed courage and tenacity of a high degree.

The crew of Lancaster ED985 had been exceptionally lucky to have survived the Peenemunde operation, coupled with the skill and judgements by those on board. The following evening, 460 Squadron celebrated, having completed 1,000 bombing sorties. The Luftwaffe was likewise celebrating because Peenemunde had witnessed the deployment of their new *Schräge Musik* weapons. These were twin upward-firing cannons fitted in the cockpit of the Messerschmitt Bf 110, twin-engine heavy night fighter. This devastating weapon accounted for some of the visual displays witnessed by the bomber crews who saw many aircraft explode or burst into flames as cannon shells tore into them from attacks taking place directly underneath them. This devastating development by the Luftwaffe would ultimately develop into a lethal capability and thereafter claim significant number of Allied bombers.

Sergeant Reginald Rolfe had sustained minor injuries over Peenemunde and Lancaster ED985 was no longer airworthy. However, both would eventually return to operational status. Reginald continued his war with two consecutive operations to Berlin. As August 1943 rolled into September, Reginald would eventually be reunited with ED985 on 27 September 1943 with an operation to Hannover and other targets thereafter until his tour of duty was completed in October 1943. He had thirty operations recorded in his flying log book and was rested from operations with an instructional posting. He survived the war and died in December 1982, aged sixty-eight.

17

Flight Engineer Soames DFM: Handley Page Halifax

Stuart Leslie Soames was born in Oxfordshire in 1915, and for many years, lived on the South Coast in Dover, Kent. Educated at the prestigious Godwynhurst College in Dover, Stuart became a member of the college Sea Scouts and later became an assistant Scoutmaster to the group.

As the interwar years finally tipped towards another war with Germany, at the age of twenty-three, Stuart Soames married Eileen Till in 1939. He relocated to Reading with his wife and young son where he later volunteered for service in the Royal Air Force in June 1940. Serving as a ground-based engineer, he was later seconded to the Cowley works in Oxford. The Morris Motors factory at Cowley was by then manufacturing the Tiger Moth aircraft, a type extensively used within the Royal Air Force as a training aircraft.

With his engineer training, Leading Aircraftsman 1159268 Stuart Soames subsequently volunteered to become aircrew and applied with the desire to become a flight engineer. He wore the identifying white slip in his uniform side cap, displaying his status of having volunteered to serve as a member of aircrew. His previous affinity with the sea appears to have been superseded by his desire to fly. Stuart's initial training progression well, and he was the ideal volunteer, targeted by the Royal Air Force to serve on the large heavy bombers by virtue of his service engineering experience. He qualified as a flight engineer on the shortest training scheme and was promoted to sergeant rank. He had been selected for specific instruction on the Handley Page Halifax and was about to be posted to join a pool of recently qualified flight engineers at one of the heavy conversion units.

Sergeant Stuart Soames found his crew in July 1944 at the 1658 Heavy Conversion Unit at Riccall, North Yorkshire. His pilot was to be an Englishman, who, while resident in Australia in 1942, volunteered to serve in the Royal Australian Air Force. Ted McGindle sailed to England as a newly qualified sergeant pilot from the other side of the world and attended an operational training unit at Morton in Marsh where the nucleus of his crew came together and they in turn were posted into' 'C Flight at Riccall, where Stuart became their flight engineer.

This new heavy bomber crew had bonded from differing walks of life and continents. It was late July 1944 and the Allied invasion of France was still faltering in its efforts in breaking out of Normandy. Despite the crew having expectations of joining the night bombing campaigns endured by the Royal Air Force over the past years, they were unexpectedly thrust into undertaking daylight operations in support of the break out from Normandy. The flying time at Riccall consisted of twenty-two short sorties, accumulating just over thirty-seven hours in the air. Stuart would have experienced the sobering thought of becoming a prisoner of war when he received the personal issued Air Publication card 1548 titled 'The Responsibilities of a Prisoner of War'. The document was a folded card that opened out with guidance and instructions for all ranks in event of capture by the enemy. Among the many instructions was the need for every man to ensure that their pockets were emptied before flying. This ensured that no personal or other information fell into enemy hands.

The crew were posted to 640 Squadron at Leconfield in Yorkshire. The squadron had formed in January 1944, having extracted established aircrew from both 158 and 466 Squadrons, the latter being a nominated Royal Australian Air Force Squadron. No. 640 Squadron formed with two flights, of which the 'B' Flight held a contingent of Australian. 'B' Flight was commanded by Squadron Leader Woodhatch.

The presence of three Australians—Pilot Officer McGindle, Sergeant Boyle (the navigator), and Flight Sergeant Whelan (wireless operator)—in the crew explains the posting into 'B' Flight. Flight Engineer Stuart Soames was to be overseen in his general duties by the squadron engineer leader, Flight Lieutenant Coates. Harry Coates was a most experienced flight engineer, having previously completed a tour of duty in 76 Squadron Halifax aircraft. He had experienced the catastrophic failure of three engines on one occasion and survived the subsequent crash landing. Harry Coates would subsequently receive the Distinguished Flying Cross when serving as 640 Squadron engineer leader.

In early August 1944, Sergeant Soames was two months away from celebrating his thirtieth birthday. He was, in general terms, much older than others in any Bomber Command aircrew. He met the expectations of both his pilot and engineer leader, having brought with him a mature perspective, his wife having given birth to his second son in October 1943. His crew were to embark upon attacks in France, supporting the army operations and the subsequent offensive against the German rocket V1 flying bombs. These rockets became known as 'Doodlebugs'. They terrorised London and the south-east of England, simply dropping at random and exploding with great destructive might. German *Vergeltungswaffen* (vengeance weapons) were being launched from numerous ski ramp sites within France. These sites were particularly difficult for the Allies to locate and destroy.

The inexperienced Stuart Soames mixed with the experienced flight engineers on the squadron. However, regardless of experience, they were about to venture into France during daylight, very few of these men having undertaken such duties previously. On the morning of 9 August 1944, Stuart ventured into the aircraft that had been scheduled to be operated by his crew, the Mk III Halifax LW673. He performed his pre-flight tests and supervised the fuel oil and mechanical checks that were undertaken to ensure his first operational flight into France was well prepared for.

The 640 Squadron operational records provide detailed accounts of the operations against the V1 targets and no doubt the crew briefings were detailed in every respect. The Pathfinding target marking would be of imperative importance, Bomber Command was attacking seven individual V1 targets in the Pas-de-Calais area that day. Stuart, in his Halifax, would be joined by fourteen others from 640 Squadron flying to their target at Les Catelliers while four fellow crews were allocated the target of Les Landes-Vieilles-et-Neuve.

Having collected his parachute and other equipment, Stuart Soames and his crew boarded their Halifax. The pilot and flight engineer normally conducted a dispersal drill, ensuring the wheels were chocked and that the immediate area was clear of obstructions. The flight engineer checking that no external oil, fuel, or coolant leaks were visible. The four engines were started up and he monitored the instrument readings on his flight engineer panel. When all four engines were warmed up, Ted McGindle checked with the crew to ensure they were happy with their equipment and in particular that their oxygen and intercom systems were working. Applying additional power to the engines and releasing the brakes, they moved onto the perimeter track and awaited the signal to follow the preceding aircraft onto the runway. Stuart was beside the pilot, ready to assist him with the throttles, undercarriage, and flaps ensuring that the fully laden bomber got off the ground and monitored his instrument panel readings as they climbed to their allotted cruising height. On the right-hand side of the Halifax cockpit was a fold down seat that the flight engineer could use. The centre mounted throttles could be reached by both the pilot and flight engineer.

They took off from the aerodrome at 11.34 a.m. in good weather. The final weather briefing was predicted as good and a loose formation of Halifax formed up over the surrounding countryside below the Yorkshire terrain. Having reached the nominated cruising height, Stuart synchronised the propellers to minimise engine vibration and commenced to monitor and record fuel consumption. Great trepidation existed among the crew with attacks from enemy fighters, but these were later proved to be unwarranted—the deadly predicted flak would be the greatest threat to the bomber crews. Having crossed the enemy coast and progressed towards the target area, they experienced heavy calibre flak from various concentrated positions. Arriving onto the target area, which had been marked by the Pathfinders, Ted McGindle commenced the bombing run

VOLUNTEER FOR
FLYING DUTIES

AIR CREWS
IN THE
R.A.F.

In the drive to recruit aircrew, a recruitment pamphlet advised applicants they must be physically fit, intelligent, and have the desire to fight in the air. The Aviation Candidates Selection Board would ultimately decide whether their qualifications made them suitable for an aircrew trade. (*Author's collection*)

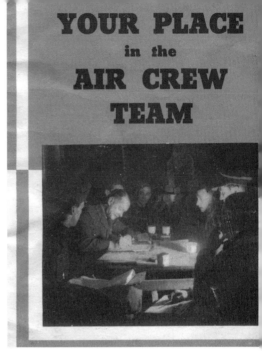

Above left: Air Ministry pamphlet given to candidates selected for training as a flight engineer, outlining the duties expected. (*Author's collection*)

Above right: This pamphlet was issued in 1944 to aircrew volunteers, including flight engineers. The cover illustration depicts the debriefing of a typical heavy bomber crew after their successful night operation to the squadron intelligence officer. (*Author's collection*)

Below: The intelligence officer, Flying Officer Dunbar, debriefing a crew after their return from Berlin. Far right with a cigarette is the crew's flight engineer, Sergeant Fletcher. Far left, the navigator with his flight map tracking the route taken to central Germany, 22 November 1943. (*Air Ministry photograph*)

Above and below: The proposed flight engineer brevet with the double lettering, which was neither approved nor officially worn. Subsequent approval was achieved for the award of the single 'E' brevet worn on the tunic of all qualified flight engineers from September 1942.

Left: Sergeant Cyril Van de Velde wearing his newly awarded 'E' Brevet. (*Author's collection*)

Below: Sergeant Cyril Van de Velde kneeling far left with his crew in front of Lancaster ME586 of 576 Squadron. Only two men would survive from this crew. (*Author's collection*)

Opposite: A Lancaster over the target of Mailly-le-Camp, 3 May 1944, where 1,924 tons of bombs were dropped. Lancaster ME586 fell to an attack by the Luftwaffe, east of the target near Montmort. Only the flight engineer, Sergeant Cyril Van de Velde, and one other survived. (*Author's collection*)

Above: Sergeant Cyril Van de Velde evaded capture for five weeks before becoming a prisoner of war. His photograph and thumb print identify him on his POW registration card. Post-war, Cyril would return to France to visit his fallen crew graves on numerous occasions. (*Author's collection*)

Below: Lancaster ED810 displaying oil streams from the inboard Merlin engine, which had cascaded back onto the tailplane. Flight engineer Sergeant Leslie Toal and his crew are making ready for a night operation to Stuttgart in April 1943. This crew later fell victim to a Luftwaffe night fighter on 15 June 1943. (*Air Ministry press release image*)

Above: Lancaster fuselages and wings at a factory where aircraft sections recovered from damaged aircraft were eventually returned to operational squadrons as complete aircraft. The Lancaster sections seen here carry identities from both 44 Squadron and 1661 Conversion Unit. (*Author's collection*)

Below: The Rolls-Royce Merlin engine was an important power source for the Royal Air Force. This 35 Squadron Halifax illustrates the exhaust trails over the wings from the engine manifolds. This aircraft with crew was lost in August 1942 while attacking Nuremburg. (*Air Ministry press release*)

The Halifax flight engineer station was positioned immediately behind the pilot, with fuel, oil, water pressure, and temperature gauges set within a panel on the rear partition bulkhead. The centre cross feed fuel cock to change fuel tanks was situated either side of the walkway.

Above the Halifax flight engineer station was a large Perspex window. The open aspect enabled a flight engineer to be in an ideal position to look for enemy night fighters. Many hours would be spent standing in this section, monitoring the engine and fuel performance.

A Halifax flight engineer on the steps that allowed access into the lower nose section where the wireless operator is sitting. To the right of the seated pilot is where the temporary seat could be positioned for the flight engineer.

A Halifax pilot looks back towards the flight engineer, who has a clear view into the nose section. The supports that provide the framework for the flight engineer's fold down seat are clearly illustrated.

The flight engineer seen sitting alongside the pilot in the Halifax cockpit. The temporary seat did not prevent access from or to the nose section, should it be required. This seat was reputedly uncomfortable and not generally occupied by the flight engineer over lengthy periods.

The Mk III Halifax-equipped Hercules engine variant came off the production line in mid-1943. This engine limitations card provided a quick reference for the later engines, which were regarded as less powerful than their predecessors. The guidance card instructions were instigated to avoid excessive engine wear.
(*Author's collection*)

HERCULES VI. XVI.
MAX. OPERATIONAL LIMITATIONS

		R.P.M.	BOOST LB.□″	TEMP. °C CYL.	TEMP. °C OIL INLET
TAKE-OFF 3 MINS. LIMIT		2800	+8¼		
CLIMBING ¼ HR. LIMIT	M	2400	+6	270	90
	S	2400	+6	270	90
CRUISING RICH MIXTURE	M	2400	+6	270	80
	S	2400	+6	270	80
CRUISING WEAK MIXTURE	M	2400	+2	270	80
	S	2400	+2	270	80
EMERGENCY 5 MINS. LIMIT	M	2800	+8¼	280	100
	S	2800	+8¼	280	100

OIL PRESSURE LB. /□″

NORMAL	80	EMERGENCY MINIMUM	70

GROUND SETTING   90 at 70° C.

Oil Temperature for TAKE-OFF

°C. MINIMUM   +5

FB.113569 C

Above: The Halifax wing bay ordinance is being winched up by the hand winches. It was one of these covers that flew off during an operational flight in 1942, causing Flight Engineer William Readhead some concern.

Left: On an operation to Düsseldorf on 10 September 1942, William Readhead of 76 Squadron and his crew were photographed and interviewed both before and after the event by representatives of *Life* magazine. (*Author's collection*)

BOMBER PILOT

By

**Squadron-Leader Leonard Cheshire,
D.S.O., D.F.C.**

*I'd be proud if I knew so
much about so many knobs as you
do.*

15th THOUSAND

*Leonard Cheshire
April 1943.*

**HUTCHINSON & CO. (Publishers), LTD.
LONDON :: NEW YORK :: MELBOURNE**

At the end of April 1943, Wing Commander Leonard Cheshire presented William Readhead with a copy of his book *Bomber Pilot* with the title page inscribed 'I'd be proud if I knew so much about so many knobs as you do'. (*Author's collection*)

Above: Flight Engineer Leader William Readhead, sitting third left, front row with the entire 462 Squadron contingent of flight engineers in 1945. (*Image supplied by Duke Newstead via Jamie Hibberd 462 Squadron*)

Below: Halifax NR271, emblazoned with artwork 'Nuts for Nazis'. Charles Lesesne regularly flew this aircraft. Lesesne died after capture while detained in a German prison cell. His flight engineer, John Tame, survived as a POW behind barbed wire. (*Photographed at Tholthorpe by John Rawbon, 1945*)

Right: Flight engineers on the Short Sunderland flying boat were provided with inspection platforms that folded out from the leading wing edge. The flight engineer precariously stands high above the water, wearing his Sidcot flying suit and boots. (*Author's collection*)

Below: The flight engineer foldout platforms can be seen clearly in this image taken at the Short Sunderland Factory. The woman working on the air-cooled radial Bristol Pegasus engines has her left hand resting on the interesting flame suppressors fitted to that engine type. (*Author's collection*)

Above: A Mk I Short Sunderland flying boat of 210 Squadron. The first operational Sunderland patrol for this squadron was flown on 3 September 1939 while detachment flights also operated patrols over the northern exits from the North Sea. (*Author's collection*)

Below: These boys were part of the Halton intake of 1937. Aircraft apprentice Paul Gees, aged sixteen, can be seen sitting second from right. Paul qualified as an engines and airframes fitter, later becoming a flight engineer with 210 Squadron. (*Author's collection*)

Despite only having two engines, the consolidated Catalina flying boat operated with a flight engineer station elevated within the wing pylon. This Mk IIIA example of a Catalina was a type in which Sergeant Paul Gees of 210 Squadron undertook flight engineer duties. (*Author's collection*)

The Guinea Pigs of Stirling LJ477. Far right, Flight Engineer Watkins, next to him, wireless operator Flight Sergeant Smith, who took over engineer duties after their aircraft had been struck by flak. (*Susan Watkins*)

Above: Reconstructive surgery conducted by Sir Archibald McIndoe entitled membership to the Guinea Pig Club. Many men from Bomber Command underwent surgery for serious burn injuries and received this badge. (*Author's collection*)

Below: Almost certainly, this is the panel belonging to the Battle of Britain Memorial Flight aeroplane PA474, which is technically a Mk 1 Lancaster. The oil pressure gauges at the top right of the panel are of a later design. The area formerly housing the oil dilution buttons, top left of the panel, now has a repositioned fuel booster pump ammeter. Below the ammeter gauge are four fuel low pressure lights and below that are the fuel booster pump switches. Each of the fuel booster pump switches has a test position, which brings the ammeter into that pump's motor circuit and displays the current it draws. (*Caption by Flight Sergeant Fellows MSc BSc MRAeS BBMF*)

A Lancaster flight engineer restrained by a simple wide back strap leaning back towards the fuel contents gauge switch situated just below and to the right of the two fuel tank selector cocks. The temporary seat arrangement allowed the flight engineer to provide vital support to the pilot; it was, however, restrictive in respect of viewing the gauges with accuracy. Some of the gauges and cocks are colour-coded to aid identification. (*Caption by Flight Sergeant Fellows MSc BSc MRAeS BBMF*)

The *Picture Post* was a weekly wartime news magazine. In 1943, 'The Last Hour in a Lancaster' article featured a heavy bomber crew making preparations prior to take-off. The flight engineer was Sergeant Sooley, 207 Squadron. The pilot, Sergeant MacIntosh, is shown indicating towards the flight engineer panel with his engineer operating the fuel contents gauge. (*Picture Post*)

Above: Flight engineer Sergeant Sooley photographed with both hands on the large fuel tank selector cocks. The wide back strap for his temporary seat arrangement can be seen as you view towards the cockpit area. The view beneath his outstretched arms is towards the bomb aimer's compartment. (*Picture Post*)

Below: The Lancaster flight engineer emergency escape route was through an escape hatch in the nose compartment. Ample opportunity existed for the bulky parachute and thick flying jacket to hinder any escape from what was effectively a fairly small hatchway. (*Picture Post*)

Moving around within the Lancaster fuselage was difficult. This 207 Squadron crew personalised their leather flying helmets with painted initials, probably to aid recognition. In the case of the flight engineer, his name had been painted in bold capitals. (*Picture Post*)

Right: The 2,500-gallon capacity AEC Matador fuel bowser. During refuelling, the bowser was required to be earthed to the aircraft in order to guard against static electricity, which had the potential to ignite fuel vapour. (*Author's collection*)

Below: The wartime construction of fuel tank cells used various rubber-based coverings to prevent puncturing. In 1944, Bostik Adhesives provided 1,400 tons of adhesive for use in creating self-sealing fuel tanks. The dope and fabric covering can be seen being applied to what in this case are small capacity fuel tanks.
(*Author's collection*)

THE GREATER "PRANGING" GREMLIN
Proved to be the source of all major "prangs".

Above: Gremlins were fictitious creatures frequently blamed for unexplained faults in aircraft, reputedly nibbling electrics and boring holes in pipes. Flight engineers coined the phrase of 'a gremlin in the works'. The author Roald Dahl, a pilot in the RAF, wrote a book about gremlins, published in 1943. (*Air Ministry image*)

Below: The 'Glycol' gremlin. Ethylene glycol was used as an engine coolant and featured in the development of the Rolls-Royce liquid-cooled engines. The pressurised cooling system was vulnerable to damage by anti-aircraft flak and gunfire. Any loss of glycol in any circumstances was a serious matter for flight engineers. (*Air Ministry image*)

THE GREAT "Glycol" GREMLIN
PIPE NIBBLING TYPE.

Above: Sergeant Rolfe, kneeling at the wing root section inspecting the damage inflicted when the enemy ordinance tore into the aircraft and subsequently smashed the Perspex observation window. His Australian pilot, Flight Sergeant Rees, looks on, aware that his flight engineer had also dealt with a ruptured fuel tank in the attack. (*Air Ministry press release image*)

Below: Sergeant Rolfe won an immediate award for his duties as flight engineer in bringing back to base his seriously damaged Lancaster. Flight Sergeant Venning and Sergeant Harris from his crew are standing within the shredded hole of the tail plane destroyed by the Luftwaffe night fighter. (*Air Ministry press release image*)

The large and complicated landing gear of the Short Stirling situated immediately beneath the two inner Hercules engines. The cooling gills were operated by the flight engineer to control engine temperature. This aircraft was flown by 149 Squadron and failed to return from operations on 8 December 1942. The flight engineer was thirty-year-old Haydyn Williams from Alton Hampshire. (*Air Ministry press release image*)

Above: A Stirling in preparation for a raid deep into Germany. A maximum fuel load of 2,254 gallons would be required to ensure a safe return. Ground crew are filling the wing fuel tanks from the bowser and it was the responsibility of the flight engineer to ensure the fuel load was sufficient. (*Author's collection*)

Below: The Stirling flight engineer station. In the far section is the electrical distribution panel. Several primary functions on the aircraft were electrically driven. Immediately right of the panel are the fuel tank cock controls and the adjacent large round turning valve is the fuel jettison control.

Sergeant Gunn, Stirling flight engineer, in 1944. In May 1945, flying from 1651 Heavy Conversion Unit, Woolfox Lodge, Sergeant Gunn in Lancaster ED631 was undertaking instruction on three-engine practice landings. The loss of an engine induced a forced landing, crashing through a hedge on the airfield boundary and bursting into flames. Two crew members were killed. The remaining seven crewmembers suffered injuries, including Sergeant Gunn.

A Stirling flight engineer in a late model Stirling, wearing a 'B' Type flying helmet with the larger zipped ear pieces; he is no doubt in the process of taking gauge readings on engine performance for his log.

The Halton Barrington-Kennett Trophy Medal and Distinguished Flying Medal awarded to William Watson. Only 249 apprentices were awarded a Distinguished Flying Medal. He later lost his life as a flight engineer instructor. (*Author's collection*)

The Bomber Command sculptured figure of a flight engineer in clay by Philip Jackson CVO DL MA FRBS. This sculpture is one of seven incredibly detailed aircrew sculptures that were later cast in bronze to form the heart of the Bomber Command Memorial in London. The flight engineer is wearing a typical Irvin flying jacket of the period, supporting the observer parachute harness. (*Philip Jackson image*)

Flight Sergeant Fellows MSc BSc MRAeS, flight engineer, Battle of Britain Memorial Flight, on board Lancaster PA474 prior to taxying to the runway. Flight Sergeant Fellows is seen reaching for his pen to record the engine performance. (*Photograph released by Coningsby Media Communications Officer, September 2012*)

onto the red target indicators burning below. Opening the bomb doors, they jammed, causing the crew to orbit the target on a port circuit. Stuart no doubt experienced immense pressure to resolve the technical malfunction as the enemy flak continued to explode among the bombers and their particular vulnerability to flak increased immensely. One problem occasionally associated to bomb door malfunctions was the presence of icing. The doors were hydraulically operated by pumps, which were completely independent of the aircraft engines. Their Halifax circled and at 1.50 a.m., after successfully opening the bomb bay doors, the bomb load was dropped from 12,000 feet onto the illuminated red markers. Once more exposed to deadly flak on the predicted bombing run, Ted was forced to take immediate evasive action, which prevented the camera securing their aiming point photograph. Halifax LW673 had been fairly well peppered by flak splinters and the entire sortie had been a rather traumatic introduction to operational flying for the entire crew.

This first operation for the novice flight engineer saw him report issues with the bomb door mechanism to both ground crew and engineer leader. The Halifax effectively operated four individual door sections—two large and two small, which cantilevered open in an overlapping manner. Stuart reported to the ground crew using what was known as 'Form Seven Hundred' and additionally submitted his four-page flight engineer log for review and signature by Harry Coates, the engineer leader. Each aircraft received a routine daily inspection from the Squadron maintenance engineers, sometimes known as the daily servicing section and according to the hours flown, an aircraft would undergo a thorough periodical inspection. This was also termed a minor inspection and a full major operation was undertaken on every eighth periodical by which time the particular aircraft would have accumulated 400 flying hours. That extensive service was undertaken by what was often recognised as the base major servicing section.

The debriefing process after this operation to Les Catelliers revealed seven aircraft had sustained flak damage to differing degrees. MZ344, flown by Warrant Officer Spencer, only managed to limp home to the Sussex coast and force-landed at Tangmere. That aircraft was particularly damaged with flak and the flight engineer standing at his control panel had a remarkable escape from death when his control panel shattered apart as it was torn into by metal flak fragments. The difference between life, death, or serious injury was often no more than bending down, adjusting your position, or looking at a crew mate.

The next day at Leconfield, Sergeant Stuart Soames observed the ground staff work upon Halifax LW673. Holes were patched and the bomb door mechanism was examined in detail. He and his crew were required to crew the same aircraft and attack the important French railway and marshalling yards in Dijon that evening. The operation was to directly support the Allied invasion forces on the ground by disrupting the enemy communication and supply system. No. 640

Squadron were required to provide fourteen aircraft to support the raid upon Dijon in the late evening on 10 August 1944. The aircraft took off at 9.01 p.m. using the summer darkness as a cloak in the hope of protecting themselves from the vicious flak they had experienced the previous day. This operation concluded with Stuart noting in his log book that it had been 'a good prang on the target' and only negligible light flak had been encountered. That said, two Halifax from Leconfield aerodrome never returned. No. 640 Squadron lost Halifax NA563 and LW654—fourteen men lost to an unknown fate.

Operational orders and briefings were coming thick and fast with the next raid scheduled for 12 August 1944. The briefing disclosed Rüsselheim near Frankfurt as the target. It was not going to be an easy run, the exact target being the Opel motor factory. Bomber Command was sending nearly 300 aircraft to attack the Pathfinders' markings dropped upon what was a relatively small target. No. 640 Squadron had twelve crews adding to the operation but everyone across the Command knew that the enemy night fighter stations at St Trond and Florennes in Belgium posed a serious threat to the briefing flight path they had been allocated. Within the stream of bombers, the 640 Squadron aircraft were expected to arrive over the target between 12.19 a.m. and 12.22 a.m. That four-minute window would have seemed a long way away when Stuart assisted Ted McGindle in lifting off the runway at 9 p.m. The Luftwaffe night fighters made an appearance long before they were expected and commenced to lay claim to their selected prey. Among the losses were two 640 Squadron Halifax, MZ855 and MZ345. Included in those men lost was Wing Commander Maw, who commanded the squadron. Stuart and his crew survived unscathed, commenting in official documentation that there was 'bags of fighter activity'. This was only Stuart's third operation; a predicted twenty plus would follow—a daunting prospect with little respite available.

On 14 August 1944, the Army once again required assistance in Normandy. Another daylight operation took place to support the Canadian Division at Falaise. Stuart and his crew were selected alongside four other crews for this operation. They were supporting 800 other bomber crews being briefed for the same operation across the Command. They successfully dropped their bomb load upon the target markers, having arrived in their allotted two minutes of time over target at 2 p.m. to 2.02 p.m. Briefing instructions required a dive down to 7,000 feet in height and they hoped that they had destroyed both panzer tanks and troops. The next day, 15 August 1944, an opportunity presented itself to seek retribution upon the Luftwaffe night fighter bases across Belgium. Another daylight operation was ordered to attack Eindhoven. Stuart and Ted McGindle gained a panoramic view from the flight deck and witnessed their bombs dropping upon the Luftwaffe airfield. A significant explosion occurred; they surmised at having hit a munitions or combustible stores. Their onboard camera captured good aiming point evidence at 12.02 p.m. In the distance, similar targets were being attacked by the plethora of Bomber Command aircraft engaged in the operations against the night fighter bases. The extraordinary sight of Spitfires and other fighter aircraft adding to the attacks was viewed by Stuart as he stood at his flight engineer station, which allowed him an unobstructed view looking past the pilot. Immediately above the engineer station was a large Perspex astrodome fitted within a larger Perspex section. In daylight, this created a light and airy environment. At night, the astrodome allowed for good overall observation for spotting marauding night fighters. The flight back to Leconfield was uneventful, but following their debriefing, they were greeted with the knowledge that the following night they were assigned to another operation into Germany. That late evening operation was to bomb the German port at Kiel on 16 August 1944. Not only did the operation add a further five hours into the individual accumulation of operational hours flown by the crew, but more importantly, it was another raid added to their respective tour of required operations.

It was not uncommon for flight engineers to have an aircraft of preference. Each Halifax on station had their own characteristics despite being identical in the vast majority of respects. Stuart had thus far experienced no continuity, having flown in numerous differing aircraft; however, Halifax MZ544 carrying the identity letter 'Z' was about to become an aircraft regularly scheduled for use by him and his crew. In all probability, flight engineers more than anybody appreciated the need to keep an aircraft clean and tidy. In an emergency situation requiring dynamic flying, anything on the floor of the aircraft was likely to be thrown up into the air with capabilities of traveling significant distances. Debris could easily become trapped in mechanical linkages or other mechanisms capable of creating flying difficulties. Having a dedicated aircraft assisted in reducing that risk; the flight engineer was also capable of instilling extra discipline with ground crew.

On 18 August 1944, the target Sterkrade appeared at briefing. At the time, it was simply another target. Sterkrade was creating synthetic oil for the German machines of war. However, any target in the Ruhr of Germany was a dangerous one to attack. The Ruhr Valley was intensely defended with anti-aircraft artillery, which had been distributed in a geographical grid pattern. Accurate radar-controlled searchlights produced high intensity beams, which were capable of penetrating to the height and beyond that Allied aircraft were flying. These primary searchlight beams, which were sometimes blue in appearance, attempted to locate and provide other searchlights the ability to pool onto individual bombers. Known as being coned by searchlights, those aircraft would be subjected to accurate anti-aircraft flak. Once coned, a bomber's only escape was to deploy violent evasive flying among the bursting flak fired from numerous gun batteries consisting of heavy and medium flak guns.

Sterkrade and other similar oil production plants were consistent targets of priority in 1944. At a later date, Sterkrade would become associated with life changing events for Flight Engineer Stuart Soames, Pilot Ted McGindle, Bomb Aimer Cecil Baldwin, and Wireless Operator Edward Whelan. However, this particular attack against Sterkrade passed with no real significance, other than the endeavours of a particular Luftwaffe night fighter who attempted to shoot them down with a diving pass. The mid-upper and rear gunners, Sergeant Offley and Smith respectively, did sufficient to thwart the attack and the pilot managed to escape into the darkness. It must be said that these two air gunners would likewise undergo traumatic experiences over that same target but differing significantly to their remaining crew members previously mentioned. Returning home, the entire crew welcomed a break of five days without operational flying, which gave them time to gain some respite. Operational crews within Bomber Command should have received five days of leave within every six-week period.

Australian and commonwealth personnel benefited greatly from what became known as the Nuffield Aircrew Leave Scheme. This provided operational aircrew, mainly from Bomber Command, with a subsidy or free accommodation at numerous hotels throughout the country. The vast majority of men elected to take the five shillings (twenty-five pence) a day provided by the scheme. Lord Nuffield greatly admired the willingness of these men and decided to make life more comfortable for them. He immediately set aside 1 million ordinary Morris Motors stock units, representing a huge financial gift to create the Trust for the Forces of the Crown on 14 October 1939.

Halifax MZ544 'Z' was air tested by Stuart and Ted McGindle on 23 August 1944. Preparations were in hand for what turned out to be four consecutive daylight operations between then and the end of the month. Good fortune favoured the newly appointed regular crew of that aircraft, and in particular, Stuart, who experience no mechanical failures whatsoever:

Brest—shipping was bombed on 24 August, operational, five hours and ten minutes.

Watten—V2 rocket site bombed on 25 August, operational, three hours fifteen minutes.

Homberg—synthetic oil refinery on 27 August, operational, four hours and twenty-five minutes.

La Pourchinte—V2 rocket storage site on 31 August, operational, three hours and fifteen minutes.

After the final operation against the flying bomb site at La Pourchinte, Squadron Leader Woodhatch, the 'B' Flight Commander, signed the individual log books of the crew. He inscribed declarations that they had completed eleven operational sorties under his command. He did so knowing that Ted McGindle and his crew were leaving 640 Squadron, having been posted to 462 Squadron at Driffield, an aerodrome that was just ten miles north of Leconfield. It was a short move between bases, most probably sanctioned to consolidate the Australian contingent in

462 Squadron Royal Australian Air Force. Both Leconfield and Driffield aerodromes had been established in 1936 and the facilities were not significantly dissimilar. Each had a distribution of thirty-six aircraft hardstandings for their Halifax aircraft and the crew accommodation benefited from the pre-war standards that were constructed at that time. The contingent of Australian personal would be noticeably increased as 466 Squadron Royal Australian Air Force was also at Driffield.

On 3 September 1944, as part of 'A' Flight 462 Squadron, the daylight bombing operations continued for the crew. The briefing formula was identical and the entire process continued with great continuity. The Luftwaffe airfield Soesterberg in Holland was their first target to be attacked from Driffield. The briefing described the target as a night fighter station, which must have resonated with any bomber crew who would have personally witnessed a horrendous loss of aircraft and crew during the bombing campaign over occupied Europe. Soesterberg had been consistently targeted by Bomber Command and this operation was to hopefully finally render it unusable. The Command was deploying nearly 700 bombers across southern Holland, attacking six enemy airfields. Once again, Stuart Soames suffered no mechanical issues with his Halifax. He annotated that the enemy flak, both light and heavy calibre, was present, but no damage was caused to Halifax LL598. The relatively short sortie of three hours and fifty-five minutes was terminated with a diversion landing at Mildenhall because of bad weather. The crew were then able to return to Driffield at 11 a.m. on 4 September.

Operation Astonia was the codename for the Allied plan to capture the important French Channel port of Le Havre. During early September 1944, the Allies sought to secure an operable deep-water port to facilitate a direct supply route for the advance into enemy occupied territories. Bomber Command was charged with disabling the heavy gun positions protecting the extensive port facility. Halifax LL600 was allocated to Stuart and his crew for six consecutive daylight operations that month. The first three operations were to Le Havre on 9, 10, and 11 September. It only proved possible to bomb on the Pathfinder target indicators on two occasions, the first operation having been abandoned due to weather conditions, which resulted in Halifax LL600 carrying the bomb load back to Driffield. Ted McGindle's bomb aimer, Sergeant Baldwin, was ultimately responsible for the dropping of their bomb loads.

The operation to Le Havre on 11 September was noted as 'Cadillac' in Ted's log book. This reference is explained by selected bombing areas being allocated code names. 'Cadillac' was the harbour installations, 'Alvis' were exterior wire defences and anti-personnel targets, and 'Bentley' and 'Buick' both related to barracks and depots.

After the liberation of Le Havre, Air Chief Marshal Harris of Bomber Command received a congratulatory message from the commanding army officer who had led the Allied forces. Many cases of great accuracy were evident against the German garrison ordered by Hitler to fight to the last man. Le Havre had been exposed to a tremendous amount of allied bombing. The French civilian casualties were, by September 1944, estimated to have been several thousand. Flight Lieutenant Delderfield, a public relations officer, entered Le Havre tasked with gather intelligence of the bombing strategy and accuracy. During the first eleven days of September, Le Havre had been targeted by Bomber Command on six occasions. A total of 2,507 aircraft had carried bomb loads to that target but the weather conditions prevented many sorties from being completed. No. 35 Squadron undertook many Pathfinder marking duties at Le Havre. Flight Sergeant Peter Varty was one flight engineer who visited that target on four consecutive dates—an unusual occurrence to enter in any flying log book. Peter Varty survived the war and became a Territorial Officer in the Army. Very rarely if ever did a Territorial Army officer wear the flight engineer brevet on his uniform.

Within 462 Squadron, synthetic oil became the subject of conversation once again when Ted saw Halifax LL600 allocated to a daylight operation to Gelsenkirchen. This was the aircraft he had previously flown on his trio of Le Havre raids. No doubt Stuart would have gained some satisfaction at that news because LL600 had been exceptionally reliable and from a flight engineer perspective, this provided some pre-raid assurances.

It transpired that two consecutive operations to Gelsenkirchen were undertaken by his crew on 12 September at the refinery, Scholven Power Station, and on 13 September, at Nordstern coal mine at Gelsenkirchen. Both operations were successful with a reference in Stuart's flying log book to the effect that both venues were robustly defended by intense heavy flak. No. 462 Squadron dispatched twelve Halifax to the Nordstern objective and eight returned with various degrees of damage inflicted by flak. The squadron records after debriefing disclosed that smoke had risen to 2,000 feet in the sky. These daylight operations provided the crew with ample opportunity to see the results of their efforts against these important targets and moreover, they were not subjected to any enemy fighter activity. The rear gunner in Halifax LL600 was Joseph Alexander Smith, who benefited from the best view possible as they turned away from the target area. Both operations were survived unscathed and allowed the crew to register their growing total of operations, which had now reached seventeen.

The German naval facility in Kiel was a target that had been consistently attacked by Bomber Command during the war. The battle order or roster list of aircraft and crews nominated for a night operation was normally posted at about 9.30 a.m. The target at that time was a closely guarded secret, but as a result of the close working relationships with the ground crew, the fuel load would be known to the flight engineer. That fuel load would have dictated fairly obviously if it was an operation into France, Belgium, or deep into Germany. On the afternoon of 15 September 1944, the briefing disclosed that Stuart and his crew would add to their operational tour total by flying in Halifax LL600 to attack the Krupp Armaments Works at Kiel. Some 490 heavy bombers would take part in the night assault bombing led by pathfinder markers.

Once again, Halifax LL600 provided a safe haven for her crew. The normal pre-operation engineering maintenance was overseen by Stuart and he would have witnessed the high explosive bomb and incendiaries being loaded into the bomb bays. The armourers would stand on the wings and winch the smaller loads into the wing bomb bays while the primary load was held in the fuselage bay. Leaving Driffield at 10.33 p.m., the crew returned after seven hours and two minutes, unmolested and undamaged. However, in common with the vast majority of Bomber Command sorties, there were casualties. Four Halifax and two Lancaster crews never returned, adding to the ever-increasing losses assumed to have been caused by flak gunners.

It had been approximately seven weeks since the target of Sterkrade on the north-western edge of the Ruhr had been first mentioned to Ted McGindle and his crew. Since then, other synthetic oil targets had been attacked with little differentiation between any other targets. All had been heavily defended. However, the nineteenth operation for Stuart was to revisit Sterkrade in an operation scheduled for an afternoon take off on 6 October 1944.

The reassurance of flying in Halifax LL600 was denied to Stuart, who noted that Halifax NP990 was rostered as the aircraft they would fly in. Stuart checked the aircraft and upon walking around it, he would have paid little attention to the unusual squadron code letters of 642 Squadron, Z5 painted on the fuselage. The aircraft's identity letter following the code was 'L' and it was commonplace for crews to simply identify their aircraft by the code, making this aircraft 'L' for Love. The entire crew had completed a practice bombing exercise in Z5 L and some satisfaction was gained in the flight engineers' notes knowing that no mechanical fault had been reported.

Seventeen crews formed the contingent of 462 Squadron who undertook the morning briefing for the Sterkrade operation. The flight leaders for navigation, bomb aimers, and flight engineers all provided the specific technical information relative to the attack. The preparation and execution of this operation was nothing other than normal for any daylight operation into the Ruhr, but for Ted McGindle and his crew, it was going to be far from normal. At 2.09 p.m. on 6 October 1944, pilot Ted McGindle and Flight Engineer Stuart Soames ensured that NP990 took off safely. Within the bomb bays, was a combined weight of 8,000 pounds of high explosives. They formed up in a loose collection of aircraft. The Australian navigator, Sergeant Boyle, commenced the calculations to navigate to the Ruhr Valley, which was sarcastically referred to as 'The Happy Valley' by many Allied bomber crews. Stuart commenced his physical checks on the flight engineer instrumentation and undertook the flight duties of recording oil temperatures and fuel consumptions.

The Bristol Hercules engines with their two-speed centrifugal supercharger and simple air-cooled system on the Mk III Halifax had proved to be very reliable. The supercharger system provided two speeds at which it was driven. When carrying out long range operations, engines could be run on high boost to reduce the engine workload, providing the best air speed for maximum air miles per gallon. At higher altitudes, the superchargers were reduced to slow in order to obtain the same air miles per gallon as was capable of being achieved in the other setting. Flight engineers were frequently exposed to the motto. 'Reduce the revs and boost the boost, you'll have enough petrol to get home to roost'.

In theory, liquid-cooled engines had greater vulnerability. Rolls-Royce, the manufacturer of the Merlin engine, was aware of that theory. Rolls-Royce instigated inspections of their engines where enemy action had damaged cooling systems and in many cases, extensive and detailed examinations took place to establish if anything could be done to reduce that perceived vulnerability.

Inevitably, some mechanical failures did occur with the Bristol engines. One 462 Squadron crew was forced to leave the stream of aircraft bound for Sterkrade with engine problems, resulting in an early return to Driffield. The Australian pilot, Flying Officer Hourigan, had suffered a catastrophic oil loss from the port outer engine, but he was able to manage a safe return. A previous harrowing experience with this pilot flying with 466 Squadron took place in Halifax LV943 over Forges le-Eaux on 7 May 1944. Luftwaffe fighters had attacked his aircraft, raking the fuselage with cannon fire, which caused a fire in the cockpit. Forced to abandon the aircraft, the flight engineer who had already donned his parachute assisted the pilot into his and all seven crew members successfully parachuted out at around 11,000 feet. By that time, the port engines were also ablaze, and the inner engine was falling away from its mounting and tumbling downwards followed by the Halifax.

There were four escape positions in the Halifax. In the cockpit, there was a small hatch above the pilot seat with a second escape hatch in the form of a trap door, which lifted out in the section between the flight engineer and navigator's area. The third exit was the main fuselage door located behind the main wing. The rear gunner had the fourth optional exit, one where he could climb out of his turret, strap on his parachute, re-enter the turret, fully rotate it, and then fall clear from the aircraft.

Six of the crew in Halifax LV943 were Australian and one was British. Four men were immediately captured while three, including Edward Hourigan, evaded and no doubt assisted by an escape line network, which resulted in him managing to return to England. It deserves mention that following his escape, the 462 Squadron flight engineer leader, Tam Readhead flew with this pilot on three operations—30 September 1944 to Bottrop, Germany, 30 November 1944 to Cologne, and 2 November 1944 to Düsseldorf.

Returning to 6 October, Stuart reported no concern over any engineering matters as they progressed to Sterkrade. The fuel flow from both port and starboard tanks was being equally distributed and as fuel was consumed, each tank and its content was calculated accordingly. Those calculations were written in the fuel log as were any manipulations of the cross-feed cock if used. The weather was very clear with little if any cloud present. As they approached the target area, the sky was completely clear with just a slight haze. The pathfinder red, green, and yellow markers were easily identified as were the deadly black puffs of exploding flak shells. The flak was intense and concentrated as they commenced their bombing run onto the target, which was becoming covered in grey smoke. Despite the smoke, the coloured markers were easily seen and the bomb aimer, Sergeant Baldwin, was able to pick out physical target recognition to ensure an accurate delivery of their bomb load. The enemy flak concentrated itself within an 11,000 feet deep sector of sky, exploding between 15,000 to 21,000 feet above the target area. This caused the formation of bombers to break up, with a large percentage of the 462 Squadron aircraft damaged. Pilot Officer Hancock flying over the target had his knee torn open by flak. Warrant Officer Taylor suffered some serious damage to his aircraft as did Pilot Officer James. Ted McGindle, however, suffered terribly. He was at 18,000 feet with his bomb bay doors open and committed to the bombing run. The predicted flak was bursting in a concentrating barrage which appeared to track him in the sky and so ahead of him were random flak explosions at his exact height. At that time, the rear gunner, Sergeant Joseph Alexander Smith, called on the intercom reporting a predicted barrage of flak was progressing closely towards them. Almost immediately, Halifax NP990 shuddered as it absorbed a direct hit. Fire erupted in the mid fuselage above the bomb bay. The flak had actually struck at a point just behind the flight engineer station setting the bulkhead on fire. Unimaginable terror would have existed at that moment. The pilot called for the crew to abandon the aircraft and so instinctively, Sergeant Baldwin instigated to drop the bomb load; however, his bomb sight had been damaged, resulting in him having to drop the load visually.

As the flight engineer, Stuart had already commenced to fight the fire while the wireless operator, Flight Sergeant Whelan stepped up onto the flight deck. Both air gunners—Sergeants Smith and Offley—were in the furthest positions away from the flight deck and responded to the emergency call to bail out. A second flak shell exploded, creating a gaping hole where the wireless operator had just been positioned at his station and the navigator, Sergeant Boyle, screamed out in pain as white-hot flak shell fragments tore into his body. An immediate assessment by Ted made him realise that the navigator would not be able to bail out. The Halifax was terribly damaged, instruments were broken, and the fire was still burning. The bomb aimer had also sustained injuries, but he saw no reason to report them at that time, especially as the injuries of the navigator were so serious. He was bleeding profusely and still confined in the nose of the aircraft. The wireless operator applied tourniquets in an attempt to stem the bleeding while Stuart went to the aft section behind the main bulkhead to quell the fire with a small extinguisher, his own bare hands protected only by his flying gloves. Having successfully put out the fire after repeated attempts, he then returned to his station and checked the engines. Stuart reported to the pilot that three were fully serviceable, but the port inner was suffering from a loss of oil. Despite the aircraft still being at a height where oxygen was required, Stuart, without the support of oxygen, returned along the fuselage to collect what first aid wound dressings he could find. Unable to find sufficient, together with the wireless operator, they improvised by seeking permission of the pilot to use an intact parachute silk canopy as dressings. This selfless act added to the fact that fire damage had already rendered the crew to having insufficient parachutes available for any additional emergency. The wounds were bandaged as best possible, releasing the bomb aimer to attempt the navigation duties and calculate a route to fly. He would not disclose his own leg injuries until sometime later.

Stuart monitored the port engine, which had suffered some damage but had continued to work at a much-reduced efficiency. The air speed indicators were inoperable rendering most calculations as best-case estimates. In normal circumstances, the flight engineer would feather a damaged engine, but these circumstances were extraordinary and it was decided to leave the engine working until such time that it completely failed. This was a calculated risk because it could have sheared the propeller or burst into flames.

The inevitable failure of the port inner engine took place at an estimated 10 miles short from crossing the enemy coast line. With great fortune, the engine responded to being feathered successfully. They were at that time over occupied Holland in broad daylight, alone in the sky and at a low altitude. Everything was stacked against them reaching England. The navigator was fighting for his life, having sustained shocking injuries to his abdomen and legs, which had caused a significant loss of blood. Cold air was ripping through the damaged nose section of the Halifax. Their vulnerability from any enemy aircraft or further anti-aircraft artillery was exceptionally high as the aircraft was incapable of taking any evasive action. Ted was flying an aircraft capable of little else other than maintaining a straight and level flight. Ahead of them, the sight of what appeared to be light anti-aircraft fire emanating from a small built up area brought immediate fears of tragedy. Ted then caught sight of a fighter appearing above and forward of their position. Fate had played a part because it was a Spitfire from 610 Squadron. In a remarkable coincidence, the Spitfire pilot was also Australian, the greatly experienced Squadron Leader Gaze who had often flown as Douglas Bader's wingman and was himself an 'Ace' pilot. Since July 1944, he had been leading Spitfire Mk XIVs on long-range bomber escorts and by chance, he had come across the distressed Halifax limping home over Holland. Leading a flight of four Spitfires, the Australian Spitfire pilot engaged with the light flak unit quelling that particular threat.

In the damaged Halifax, an assessment of their position and ability to reach the emergency landing facility at Woodbridge was undertaken. Flight Engineer Stuart Soames advised from his fuel calculations that it was more than feasible and in the knowledge that the facilities at Woodbridge could not be surpassed, the route was calculated. Woodbridge had been opened on 15 November 1943, and was situated just east of Ipswich. It was no more than one extensive runway encompassing a width of three normal runways and extending in length for some 3,000 yards. Aircraft that were unable to land in any conventional way or that had simply crashed onto the runway were attended to immediately with the primary intention to save crew lives. Once any life-saving measures had been accomplished, seriously damaged aircraft were simply bulldozed off the runway. The width of the runway was such that other aircraft were able to land despite the presence of a crashed bomber, but efforts were always made to clear the runways as soon as possible. At night, the runway was illuminated by three sets of lights, creating three individual runways, with the most southerly runway prioritised. Pilots required no communication or authority to use it, in effect, making it a non-regulated facility. The main runway had extensive grass run-off and approach areas situated at each end, an additional safety facility for aircraft falling short, or running long on their approach and landings, a facility of great importance to those aircraft that had failed brakes and damaged flaps.

Halifax NP990 eventually reached Woodbridge and to the great credit of the pilot and flight engineer, they were able to land safely at 6.30 p.m. Greeted with a vehicle signed 'Follow Me' to clear the runway as quickly as possible, Ted was allocated a safe standing for his aircraft. The emergency services immediately extracted the seriously injured Australian navigator Sergeant Boyle, who was rushed to hospital along with Sergeant Baldwin who received attention to his leg injuries. 'L' for Love sat on the runway at Woodbridge with the port inner wing blackened with the engine oil fluids strewn backwards in a thick band. The Perspex nose section was smashed open and flak penetration with fire damage was obvious to see. Rather grimly, the significant loss of blood in the nose section surrendered to the effects of gravity finding its way to the runway, but these and far worse sights were commonly seen at the emergency landing facility at Woodfield.

The 635 Squadron, Lancaster III ND453 from Downham Market also desperately tried to reach Woodbridge. Itself badly damaged by Flak at Sterkrade, the Lancaster crashed at 6.30 p.m., 4 miles south-east of Woodbridge after overshooting the runway. Both aircraft had been over Woodbridge at exactly the same time. Thoughts would have turned to the two missing crew members, Sergeants Offley and Smith, the air gunners who had bailed out over the Ruhr. All that was known was that other crews had reported seeing that both parachutes had operated properly and it was hoped they had descended into safe circumstances. Unfortunately, that was not the case for the rear gunner, Smith, who was the subject of civilian retribution against what they termed 'Royal Air Force terror flyers'. He was beaten up to such an extent that he suffered a partly severed tongue. He later fell into the custody of the Luftwaffe, becoming prisoner 1045 at Bankau. Likewise, the mid-upper gunner, Offley, was prisoner 1035, also held at Bankau until 1945.

On 9 October 1944, Ted McGindle, unaware of the fate of his gunners, sought to locate the home details of his missing crew and personally write to their families. It was three days after the harrowing operation and he was back at Driffield. Stuart, along with the wireless operator, was also on station but without bomb aimer Baldwin, who was still recovering. He was, however, soon to return to the squadron and so was passed as fit for operational flying. With swift efficiency, replacement crew members were posted to fill the vacant positions, all being officers. They were an experienced navigator, Flying Officer William Watt from Southern Ireland; mid-upper air gunner, Pilot Officer Robert Nicholls; and rear gunner, Flying Officer Medway. Both air gunners were Australian.

On 17 October 1944, the wing commander, who commanded 462 Squadron at Driffield, submitted recommendations for Immediate Gallantry Awards to the crew of Halifax NP990. Seven weeks later, within a joint citation, the prestigious immediate awards were published in the London Gazette, the pilot receiving the Distinguished Flying Cross, with his three non-commissioned crew members each receiving the Distinguished Flying Medal. Worthy of recognition, the original recommendation to Flight Engineer Stuart Soames reads:

SOAMES Stuart Leslie 1159268 Sergeant (IMMEDIATE) Sorties 18 Flying Hours 79.25 FLIGHT ENGINEER. Air 2/9646.

On 6 October 1944, the crew with whom Sergeant Soames flew as Flight Engineer was ordered to attack the synthetic oil plant at Sterkrade in daylight. On the approach to the target, the aircraft was hit by heavy anti-aircraft fire and fire broke out in the fuselage behind the main bulkhead. Sergeant Soames went aft to deal with the fire and did not hear the order to abandon the aircraft which was acted on by the two gunners. Almost immediately the aircraft was hit again and the navigator and bomb aimer were wounded, the former seriously. The captain decided to attempt to fly home. Having extinguished the flames after repeated attempts and with complete disregard to his own safety Sergeant Soames checked the engines and reported to the captain that three were serviceable, but the port inner had been damaged and owing to loss of oil could be used only for a short while. He then inspected the aft part of the aircraft for damage and having satisfied himself that he could leave his own duties temporarily collected all the field dressings from the aircraft for the navigator who was bleeding profusely and later helped to make bandages out of a parachute. The outstanding coolness, initiative, indifference to personal safety and fine spirit of crew co-operation displayed by Sergeant Soames, together with the sound technical advice he gave, played a vital part in bringing the seriously damaged aircraft back to base and contributed in no small measure to the saving of the navigator's life. The immediate award to Sergeant Soames of the distinguished flying medal is strongly recommended.

As 1944 drew to a close, 462 Squadron moved in its entirety to Foulsham, where it became part of 100 Group, Special Duties, to undertake 'Window' operations. Within a matter of weeks, in January 1945, twelve wireless operators, all Australian flight sergeants, were posted into the squadron. These men were specifically required to undertake the duties of dispensing 'Window' and relieve flight engineers on the squadron who had initially taken on those additional duties. A second contingent of Australian wireless operators bolstered the numbers of crew dispensing 'Window' in April 1945.

Stuart supported Ted as flight engineer on several operations, creating feint or spoof illusions of Bomber Command activity. The crew were engaged in dropping combinations of target marking flares, incendiary bombs, and radar-confusing 'Window' foil. These activities were diverting Luftwaffe capabilities away from the primary mainstream bombing operations and proved to be most effective. On 22 January, Stuart attended a briefing for the allocated early evening operation to create two feint attacks into Sterkrade, Germany. The four crew members—McGindle, Soames, Whelan, and Baldwin—would no doubt have considered if fate was playing a hard hand against their survival. Fortunately, on this operation to Sterkrade, they escaped unscathed in Halifax MZ429.

During February 1945, five operations were undertaken into the Ruhr area of Germany. Flying at various departure times, both early and late evening sorties, these added an accumulated twenty-four hours and fifty minutes to their personal operational statistics. On 3 March 1945, the Dortmund Ems Canal became the next target entered into Stuart Soames flying log book. This vital target had been the subject of many operations to render it incapable for carrying immense quantities of cargo between Dortmund and the port of Emden. It was effectively an industrial water highway for the German war campaign. No. 462 Squadron was charged with sending eight aircraft to create a feint attack upon the canal while bombers from the command earnestly targeted another section of canal, the Ladbergen aqueduct. Stuart was flying in Halifax MZ429 which was tasked to lead the operation and drop a load of ten illuminated flares emanating or feigning pathfinder marking.

Unfortunately, these were not the only flares deployed. The night fighter Luftwaffe aircraft were dropping flares above them and initiating attacks. Stuart and his crew brushed alongside the Luftwaffe hunters again when they reached what they thought was the safety of Foulsham aerodrome. The log book entry made by the crew, 'Intruders over base' is a rather inert statement when the facts reveal that the eight 462 Squadron Halifax aircraft landed safely while other bombers waiting in the circuit were attacked by enemy Ju 88 intruders. The operational record for

462 Squadron records that three aircraft were shot down in close proximity to the aerodrome, but no further information was provided. The Luftwaffe tactic of attacking Allied bombers as they approached the safety of their aerodromes was one that accounted for many unexpected casualties. The Royal Air Force likewise sought to do the same, stalking the night sky around Luftwaffe bases.

For Ted McGindle and his crew, an additional three spoof raids were completed satisfactory in March 1945. However, on 16 March near Frankfurt, while imitating a raid with incendiaries, their Halifax sustained the loss of the entire port bomb bay doors. At the end of March, the total number of operations for the crew had reached thirty. That accumulated figure of thirty was inevitably regarded as having completed a full tour of duty. Several instances of completing a figure under thirty had been recognised as a full tour on many other squadrons. Statistically, every additional operation flown was likely to be the last and stories of crews not returning on their very last operation abounded among the various aerodromes. Statistics for reaching thirty operations in Bomber Command were heavily stacked against all and any crew. Regardless to the circumstances, 'A' Flight of 462 Squadron continued to post Ted McGindle's crew on the crew list for operations into April 1945.

On 2 April, the crew carried target indicators and general-purpose bombs to Stade where searchlights prodded the sky in attempts to assist the flak gunners, a relatively uneventful operation for Stuart. Remarkably, Berlin had never been a city visited by Stuart up to this time. On 4 April 1945, he entered Berlin as the target in his log book but in fact he was being tasked to create a feint attack over Magdeburg, situated just south east of Berlin. 462 Squadron engaged twelve Halifax carrying Window, Incendiaries and Target marking flares. His crew was to deposit twenty-one flares over their target. It was a late evening departure at 18.51 hours but at around 22.00 hours as Stuart peered into the dark sky from his engineer station, he saw the extraordinary sight of what he reported to have been a Messerschmitt Me 262 jet fighter.

The development of the Messerschmitt Me 262 had taken many years. It was complimentary to the engineering and development of rocket research that resulted in the V1 and V2 bombs. The jet fighter was available to the Luftwaffe in limited numbers from mid-1944. However, establishing jet fighter training with faltering supplies of experienced pilots capable of flying the challenging jet was limited. It was not until a select unit of Luftwaffe pilots began flying the Me 262 in February 1945 that it truly represented a serious threat to Allied heavy bombers. The debriefing intelligence officers were sceptical about the number of Me 262 sightings being reported and concluded after analysis that what the crews may well have been seeing were rocket or jet-powered projectiles, used to visually signal the position and course of the Allied bomber stream. Such signals were certainly fired from the ground and may have also been fired from the air; they had no connection to the manned jet fighter aircraft.

Supporting aircraft feigning the attack on Magdeburg subsequently flew on towards Berlin to bomb the capital city. The primary raids upon the oil targets of Harburg and Leuna had achieved good results. However, the Luftwaffe night fighters had actively destroyed several Allied aircraft that night.

It was not just the enemy that caused fatalities. Technical issues with heavy bombers were always serious matters. The flight engineer in Flying Officer O'Sullivan's Halifax advised an early return to Foulsham. Returning on three engines, other mechanical issues also may well have been present. The Halifax overshot the end of the runway, indicating brake or flap malfunctions. The normal landing distance for the Halifax was 1,100 yards and the primary runway at Foulsham was 800 yards longer than that figure. This was undoubtedly a serious incident because the squadron record book advised that the Halifax was in need of repairs beyond the engineering staff capacity, and likely to be repaired on site or removed by contractor. Fortunately, the entire crew had survived uninjured.

On 9 April 1945, Stuart was briefed prior to completing his operational tour of duty. He and his crew were required to enhance a spoof attack to protect the Bomber Command force of nearly 700 heavy bombers intent on thwarting any additional submarine capability from Deutsche Werke boatyards in Kiel. It was to be his thirty-third operational sortie and the mature and now experienced flight engineer realised that on his safe return, he would play no further part in waging war against Germany.

The operation, which he recorded as target Hamburg, took four hours and ten minutes to complete. The early post-war years saw the Operational Research Section within Bomber Command describe the feint attack on 9 April 1945 upon Hamburg and Stade as one of the most successful diversions ever achieved. In all probability, Stuart Soames will never have known of the accolade. His 'A' Flight Commander signed off as correct that his tour of duty was completed officially on 11 April 1945. He had completed nineteen operations at night and fourteen in daylight, all of which entailed flying against the enemy as a flight engineer for 154 hours and twenty-seven minutes.

18

Escaping the Flames

The civilian-based academics working within the Operational Research Section were engaged with Bomber Command in providing scientific and technical advice on numerous matters. One matter of importance was the analysis of intelligence provided by heavy bomber crews who survived emergency escapes. Fires on board aircraft induced many emergencies, but inevitably they were only reported upon by third parties who had witnessed the assumed demise of both crew and aircraft. Exceptional and unequivocal intelligence was, however, available to investigators from repatriated prisoners of war and evaders. Prisoner of war exchanges were conducted between Germany and Britain from 1943 onwards. These were an exchange of prisoners predominantly with injured men, many of which would have been survivors from within Bomber Command.

The accumulation of statistics for heavy bomber crew losses within Lancaster, Stirling, and Halifax crews commenced in January 1943. These statistics were significant, revealing that between January to June 1943, 6,498 men from Bomber Command had failed to return from operational duties. The Red Cross prisoner of war notifications communicated through Switzerland were no doubt responsible for establishing that there were 1,203 survivors from within that six-month period of loss data. The Operational Research Section concluded from the gathered intelligence that the respective heavy bomber aircraft designs appeared to have had a direct connection to survivability in emergency escapes. Moreover, they deduced that the differing crew positions also had correlated survivability statistics and these were directly connected to the escape locations used within the heavy bombers.

Survivors provided evidence of explosions occurring, fires originating from fuel tanks, and oil leaking from hydraulic lines in exceptionally high percentages. The emergency evacuation procedure in the Lancaster specified that the bomb aimer, flight engineer, navigator, and wireless operator should escape through the front hatch and that they escaped in that sequence. The mid-upper air gunner and rear gunner had instructions to leave through the rear starboard door and that they escaped in that sequence. The pilot was inevitably the last member of the crew to leave the aircraft via the front hatch. It was possible for the pilot and other crew members to use the escape panel above the cockpit as an auxiliary emergency exit but this was primarily used after having ditched into the sea or in a forced landing situation where the aircraft collapsed onto runways or other terrain.

The Lancaster had a front emergency escape hatch in the bomb aimers compartment, which would be released by retaining catches, then simply lifted up and jettisoned into the open hatch void. The hatch was only 22 inches wide and 26 inches deep, the barest minimum dimensions for escaping through. It was not unknown for the hatch cover to jam into the void as it was discarded. The force of air rushing through the opening was intense and all too often, it needed to be kicked free. Using this escape while wearing full flying gear and a chest-mounted parachute must have been daunting, with men mentally assessing if they were able to get through the opening safely while avoiding all of the equipment fitted within the enclosed area. The urgency of saving your life evidences that it was possible and many lives were saved in that way.

The rear escape route at the rear starboard door was simpler in that the doorway was a large opening. The slipstream of air, however, made it difficult to open and frequently, men who used this escape suffered traumatic injuries sustained when they were deflected by the slipstream into the tail plane configuration that was immediately behind the doorway.

Any emergency evacuation undertaken at above oxygen height added another specific element of danger to the crew. If a jammed hatch or other reason delayed their exit after removing their oxygen supply, anoxia was most likely to create disorientation followed by being rendered unconscious. At high altitude, movement was further complicated by the need to carry the portable oxygen bottle when moving around. The flight engineer in particular had to overcome handicaps when moving through the aircraft regardless of circumstances.

The construction of the Halifax installed two large metal wing spares crossing the fuselage at a height of about 2 feet above floor level and 12 feet apart. These had to be climbed over to reach the deep step in the floor at the rear of the bomb bays. This area also had the mid-upper gun turret, which hung down and was prime for collision with their heads. At night, all of these features had to be negotiated in almost complete darkness, as was the task of operating the Halifax fuel supply control valves mounted on the front wing spar some 8 feet behind the engineer compartment.

In an effort to reduce injuries, additional training was undertaken whereby the method of escaping from the two primary escape routes was enforced on station and reiterated on training exercises. In respect of the rear starboard door opening, crews were instructed to hold the outer sides of the doorway with closed hands. It was important to not separate thumb from fingers. The jump was made with simultaneous outwards and downwards movement while turning your back into the slipstream, then falling into a crouch position with the head tucked into the chest as one hand moved in preparation to pull the parachute rip cord. These instructions were designed to avoid contact with the tail section, effectively inducing a fall immediately below the structure and into open air. The front escape hatch required a roll into the opening, keeping the head and knees tucked in. The slipstream would be taken upon the back as you fell away and opened the parachute.

Falling from a stricken aircraft with nothing more than an eventual billowing piece of silk cloth to prevent almost certain death would have taken great courage. The word 'Parachute' is formed from the French—the prefix '*para-*' meaning shield or guard against (from the Latin *parare*) and '*chute*', which equates to fall. Thus, parachute literally means, 'To defend from a fall'. During the Second World War, parachute safety was a primary objective of the Royal Air Force. It is thought that Irvin, the primary parachute manufacturers, based themselves at Letchworth because it was in close proximity to the aerodrome at Henlow where parachute safety was developed. In 1940, Henlow employed between 250 and 300 men and women in the parachute repair and packing sections.

Many differing circumstances existed during the Second World War where men leapt from an aircraft and entrusted their lives to the parachute. Concerns over the significant loss of pilots and crew in circumstances where it may well have been possible to escape from a stricken aircraft sooner were officially expressed. Pilots were required to assess a situation and not attempt to force land an aircraft unless there was a 75 per cent chance of succeeding, and in addition, the pilot should not retain his crew on board an aircraft unless it was assessed as being 99 per cent certain of being successful. Clearly, this last statistic indicates that aircrew personnel were more likely to be ordered to jump from aircraft far more frequently than had been previously experienced.

There were two primary reasons to abandon an aircraft—the first resulting from catastrophic damage caused by anti-aircraft flak and the second, a culmination of events, possibly as a result of mechanical failures, fuel shortage, or battle damage, which then rendered the aircraft unsafe to attempt to return back to base in England. In many instances, the requirement to cross the North Sea brought forward a decision to use parachutes when the certainty of landing on the ground still existed.

The parachute was without question the saviour of countless lives, but it was not, however, infallible. The device operated with a sequence of events that would normally lead to the successful parachute deployment. The inability to operate the rip cord as a result of injury or incapacity of the wearer inevitably caused fatalities. The deployment of the parachute canopy in circumstances where the device was prevented from inflating properly by severely tangled lines was also most likely to prove fatal, as were the circumstances where the canopy fabric was on fire or badly damages as a result of fire. Twenty-year-old flight engineer Sergeant George Motts, who flew with 76 Squadron over Nuremburg on 30 March 1944, suffered such a tragedy. The starboard wing of his Halifax LK795 suffered ruptured fuel lines and an eruption of flames. It was the second occasion that fire had broken out in the aircraft during that flight. The final night fighter attack induced a critical situation, forcing an emergency escape for the entire crew. Sergeant Motts's parachute had apparently failed to escape damage from the flames and it malfunctioned as he dropped to earth. Three days later, his body was found entangled in a tree. The burnt remains of his parachute were draped about his lifeless body.

Parachute failures after initial deployment were frequently referred to as 'Roman candles'. It is thought that the uninflated silken canopy streaming in the air looked like a candle flame. The importance of parachute construction and its packing never left the minds of the predominantly female WAAF staff employed within that department. Each parachute was packed and checked with the utmost care possible. It was then allocated on a daily basis with the crews frequently making light-hearted quips about bringing it back if it did not work.

Tragedy could still strike once the silk canopy had deployed. Sergeant Chaffey was the flight engineer in Halifax JD160 of 78 Squadron, which was attacking Dortmund in the early hours of 24 May 1943. Flak defences struck the aircraft, sending it plummeting to the earth over Germany. The entire crew of seven men escaped and deployed parachutes safely. The flight engineer, however, was killed while suspended by his silk canopy when a deadly flak splinter struck his body. This was a surprisingly rare occurrence. Sergeant Chaffey was a married man, thirty-three years of age, and the only casualty from his crew. The remaining men survived as prisoners of war.

Leslie Irvin of the Irvin Air Chute company agreed to give a gold pin to every person whose life was saved by one of his parachutes. In order to gain membership to his 'Caterpillar Club', prospective members had to produce documentation to verify the incident to the parachute manufacturer. In many applications, the parachutes were identified by serial numbers and types and then checked against the factories production information. Letters to the parachute company were in some instances very detailed. The requirements for receiving a gold pin and membership were stringent with all personnel applying to the club needing to evidence that their life had been saved by the emergency use of an Irvin parachute. In addition to the membership pin, a membership card with at least two variants was issued to demonstrate that each recipient of the Caterpillar pin was a living testimony to the lifesaving ability of the Irvin air chute. Applications to join the Caterpillar Club consistently increased throughout the Second World War, a great many of which were from crew members within Bomber Command. Many applications originated from prisoner of war camps with the majority of allied airmen captured across Europe being imprisoned in the Stalag Luft camps. In early 1945, the combined camp registration undertaken by the Germans indicated that approximately 169,000 officers and men of the British Dominion, and other allied forces were imprisoned across European camps.

The Operational Research Section data created statistics from collated aircraft type survivability. Despite the lack of polarity between the numbers of each aircraft missing, they provide an insight in respect of the survivability of flight engineers in those instances:

Lancaster	365 missing	Forty-five flight engineer survivors	12.4 per cent
Stirling	161 missing	Thirty-one flight engineer survivors	19.2 per cent
Halifax	274 missing	Ninety-three flight engineer survivors	34.0 per cent

The academics concluded that aircraft design had the capability of impeding the escape in emergencies. Statistically, it becomes obvious that in respect of the heavy bombers, the Halifax created the best option of survivability for all aircrew in emergency escapes. The larger escape hatches and space to access the forward hatch within the Halifax was undoubtedly responsible for creating such statistics.

The Lancaster parachute exit hatch in the floor of the nose section was originally released by securing clips which when lifted inwards allowed the hatch to be jettisoned. A later modification, no doubt undertaken as a result of recommendations (Mod. 1336) resulted in the hatch being modified and subsequently enlarged. The hatch was refined and opened by a handle arrangement fitted at the port side. The hatch opened inwards and was secured by a clip that held the hatch open on the starboard side. This modification was a most important improvement to the later aircraft and will have assisted in emergency escapes for the crew who were forced to use them.

Within the Avro Lancaster, hand-operated fire extinguishers were available at several positions—in the nose on the right side of the bomb aimer's compartment; within the cockpit situated on the left side of the pilot's seat; on the right side forward of the front spar; further down the fuselage, aft of mid-upper turret; and at the left side of the rear turret. The Handley Page Halifax was equipped with additional fire extinguisher stations to the Lancaster, with one positioned in the navigator's station; one on the lower panel of the flight engineer station; one within the reach of the pilot; three at positions within the fuselage; and the final position accessible to the rear gunner. The locations indicated tended to be consistent regardless of the various mark or type of production aircraft. The Stirling had extinguishers at the bomb aimer's position; under the top step between the cockpit seats; another in the cockpit, behind the starboard pilot's seat; one in the flight engineers position adjacent to the instrument panel; and the wireless operator had an extinguisher fixed behind the radio equipment framing.

Another was positioned on the starboard side of the fuselage just forward of the mid-upper gunner's turret and the rear gunner was able to access the final extinguisher on the port side forward of the turret.

No common denominators appeared to exist in relation to the predictability of where fire was likely to break out in these heavy bombers. Each individual engine was facilitated with extinguishing capabilities, but the entirety of the fuselage had the capability of sustaining fire despite the lack of readily combustible material. Of utmost concern would be a fire in the bomb bay, particularly when still carrying a bomb load. The bomb bay was 33 feet long and 5 feet wide and in an emergency, the only physical access to that area while in flight would be by cutting into the area with a crash axe from inside the fuselage. Small viewing portals were present, which provided limited visual inspection for the flight engineer along the length of the bomb bay.

Lancaster ME787 of 619 Squadron was attacking the heavy gun emplacements at Flushing in daylight on 23 October 1944 when they were struck in the under fuselage by flak. Immediately, the bomb bay burst into flames and in an effort to save the aircraft, the bomb load was quickly dropped. The flight engineer on board was twenty-six-year-old Kenneth Pearson. He had been a motor mechanic in Northampton who had immediately volunteered to serve when war was declared. Kenneth was a commissioned officer by the time of the Flushing operation. His crew were all of similar rank and likewise experienced apart from the rear gunner. Unfortunately, further flak caused another fire within the actual fuselage, which was immediately fought by two of the crew who sustained burn injuries. The pilot, Squadron Leader Purnell, ordered the crew to bail out, having assessed that the aircraft was about to be completely consumed by fire. The rear gunner simply turned his turret and gathering his parachute; he fell away into the sky. He was followed by three officers escaping from the forward emergency exit, one of which was the flight engineer. All four men successfully parachuted to safety but were surprised to see no sightings of the three remaining crew members falling away from the Lancaster. It appears that the perilous situation of the fires subsided sufficiently for the pilot to attempt a return flight across the North Sea. In normal circumstances, opening any emergency escape hatch increased the flow of oxygen and fanned the flames, but in this instance, there appears to have been an extinguishing of the fire by unknown means. The desperate return flight over the sea was achieved safely and once over England, the pilot instructed the two remaining crewmembers to bail out while he attempted an emergency landing at Woodbridge. Lancaster ME787 finally reached Woodbridge, where a successful crash landing took place.

The flight engineer and his fellow crew members who took to the silk while over enemy held territory became prisoners of war for the remaining seven months of conflict. Kenneth Pearson applied to become a Caterpillar Club member from the Bellaria camp, Stalag Luft III. Irvin later sent him his small pin welcoming him as another flight engineer who had saved his life by parachute.

Luck and misfortune mixed together to create circumstances that shaped many flight engineers' lives, none more so than the events over Germersheim on 14 April 1943. Halifax HR678 from 35 Squadron was outbound to attack Stuttgart and the flight engineer on board was an ex-Halton apprentice, Flight Sergeant T. L. Brown. A Luftwaffe night fighter raked the Halifax, causing a fire to break out in the fuselage. The flight engineer endeavoured to fight the fire, no doubt taking his extinguisher from his instrument panel to do so. As he fought the fire, a photoflash bomb exploded. These small bombs were designed to explode with an amazingly bright illumination at a pre-determined height to allow onboard cameras to photograph the bomb load reaching the target. The intensity of the light was immensely bright and sustained for many seconds. The fate of Halifax HR 678 was sealed at that moment. The flight engineer, although initially completely blinded by the intensity of the photoflash bomb, was one of three crew members fortunate enough to escape by parachute. His descent was uneventful but with great misfortune—he landed in a town area and outside an occupied *Orpo* police station. The *Orpo* (*Ordnumgspolizei*, meaning ordinary police), were the uniformed police force of Germany. Under the command of the SS, Himmler reorganised the *Orpo* so that their responsibilities included the management of traffic and public transport, the organising of air raid precautions, fire safety, and emergency response. A number of the *Orpo* divisions were trained to act as a reservist military force and home guard.

Escaping arrest was inevitably difficult for the men who fell into enemy territory, regardless of the theatre in which they operated. Sergeant John MacFarlane, an ex-Halton apprentice, flew as the flight engineer with 10 Squadron over Germany and the Mediterranean. Flying with a well-established crew, they undertook an operation to bomb the Heraklion aerodrome on the island of Crete. Flak caused terrible damage to Halifax W7679, which burst into flames and vents spiralled out of control very quickly. Only three men were able to escape by parachute, the flight engineer being one of them. His account of survival is explained in the joint recommendation which led to the significantly rare award of a Military Medal to a flight engineer. Only 121 Military Medals were awarded to members of the Royal Air Force during the Second World War:

These airmen Sergeant J. Bradley and Sergeant J.W. MacFarlane were Wireless Operator and Flight Engineer, respectively, of a bomber which was shot down over Heraklion on 5 September 1942. Three of the crew being killed and a fourth member was taken prisoner. Sergeants Bradley and MacFarlane evaded the enemy, and a fortnight later, linked up with certain British organisers but were not content merely to remain passive and inactive until arrangements could be made for them to be evacuated. From October 1942, until he was actually evacuated on 14 February 1943, Sergeant Bradley operated a hitherto disused wireless set and made contact with Headquarters, Middle East, sending much valuable information. During the period he remained cheerful in all difficulties and shared, with other members of the organisation, in the trials of hurried night moves and constant hiding necessitated by the activities of German field troops and counter-espionage agents. He also proved invaluable in making friendly contacts with local inhabitants. Sergeant Bradley assisted the organisation in every way and voluntarily became an active and enthusiastic agent. Sergeant MacFarlane proved himself equally valuable, not only assisting Sergeant Bradley but giving continual and encouraging assistance to other wireless operators.

At the end of the Second World War, the number of applicants who joined the Caterpillar Club had grown to over 34,000, although the total of people saved by Irvin parachutes was estimated to be 100,000. There were other parachute manufacturers who issued an insignia for successful jumps. GQ Parachutes formed their Gold Club in 1940, and issued a lapel pin. The Switlik Parachute Company of Trenton, New Jersey issued both gold and silver caterpillar pins and the Pioneer Parachute Co. in Skokie, Illinois, presented plaques to people who packed the parachutes that were known to have saved lives.

19

Wireless Operator Smith DFM: Short Stirling, Guinea Pig Club

The account of Thomas Smith, who volunteered for aircrew duties in 1940 and trained as a wireless operator, explains the relevance of heavy bomber crew members having the ability to undertake additional specialist duties. That said, in all probability, he had little if any flight engineer training of any substance.

Thomas had previously served in 149 Squadron, flying as the wireless operator in the Vickers Wellington Bomber. His first operation on 23 April 1941 had been to Brest, France. He subsequently completed an additional thirty operations before he was rested from operational flying. He was later posted to No. 1651 Heavy Conversion Unit to undergo conversion training onto the heavy Short Stirling in March 1944. Thomas was the only operationally experienced member in the newly formed crew. On 11 March 1944, Thomas witnessed a dramatic accident on the airfield. Stirling LK520 was being refuelled for a training flight when it caught fire and became engulfed in flames. Two refuelling vehicles and a David Brown tractor were parked alongside, adding to the inferno that consumed them. It was a chilling example of how combustible the large bombers were.

In April 1944, Thomas's crew were posted and by sheer coincidence, Thomas would return to 149 Squadron. Stirling LJ477 was allocated to the crew and carried the identification letter M which was responsible for the aircraft nickname of 'Red Hot Momma'. Embarking on his second tour of duty, ironically, their first operation was to plant sea mines in the harbour at Brest, the same target written in his log book three years previously. It was not a problem-free experience—their first run to drop the mine was thwarted when the bomb doors failed to open properly; a second run was hampered by searchlights; and the final run resulted in sustaining flak damage to both fuselage and wings.

The crew later engaged on several low-level supply-dropping operations to the Resistance over France. A briefing on 5 July 1944 for a further drop, assumed to be another which would pass without any great significance was not to be. Ten supply drops to the Resistance had been scheduled within the Péronne, Marle, Le Mans, and Rouen areas. No. 149 Squadron were dropping containers and packages containing arms and supplies. The crew captain, Pilot Officer Holmes, was flying Stirling LJ477 to the Haute-Savoie area close to the Swiss frontier with the Australian bomb aimer, Flying Officer Stannus, next to him. The navigator, Flight Sergeant White, was sitting behind the pilot, facing sideways at the map table with the screen between the navigator's table and the pilot. The flight engineer and wireless operator were both further back in the fuselage.

Having reached the dropping site and circling the area in bright moonlight, no signal from the ground was seen with no reception party evident by the resistance and so, in following normal procedures, the load would be returned to the aerodrome. As they climbed in height away from the drop area, Stirling LJ477 was suddenly struck by flak and sustained serious damage. This may well have been the result of having strayed over an enemy aerodrome. The port wing fuel tanks were ruptured resulting in fuel flooding into the wing and fuselage. One port engine was completely disabled through damage. The second engine on the same wing was also damaged and a fire broke out in the port wing root section. The starboard outer engine also began over running. The intensity of such situations is difficult to appreciate, but the flight engineer would have been under great duress to address and assess multiple problems. As dangerous situations escalated in an aircraft, other crew members would assist wherever possible. In 2016, the Australian bomb aimer Harold Stannus provided further details of what was taking place in Stirling LJ477:

> With one engine out and the second on the same side disabled, the Pilot was forced to fly in a crablike attitude. I advised the pilot to feather the disabled engine to prevent drag. We flew that way for some time and then the load was jettisoned in the English Channel. I had opened the canopy hatch above the pilot while still in flight and let it loose so the opening was free in case we ditched.
>
> The aircraft was damaged by flak the tanks were holed and fire broke out in the port wing root, Flight Sergeant Smith displaying great present of mind, chopped through the fuselage with an axe, thus enabling him to reach the flames with extinguishers, thereby putting out the fire. He then assisted the Flight Engineer in an attempt to repair the damage sustained to throttle and pitch linkages. The Flight Engineer subsequently became overcome by petrol fumes. Flight Sergeant Smith not only carried out his duties as Wireless Operator, but also those of the Flight Engineer and gave frequent petrol and engine checks. Throughout the whole of the trip, Flight Sergeant Smith remained calm and extremely helpful and played a large part in getting the aircraft back to this country. He advised that all of the fuel tanks were registering as empty and that a ditching was highly probable.

Despite the lack of apparent fuel, the crew managed to reach Thorney Island aerodrome where they crashed landed at around 4.52 a.m. on 6 July. Harold Stannus recalled:

The Wireless Operator contacted Thorney Island which was closed and dark for an emergency landing. The base lit their runway lights. As the landing gear was not working, the Pilot aimed for the grass and successfully landed missing concrete pylons and structures in that area but unfortunately the plane skidded across the runway and this created sparks and ignited the fuel. The open escape hatch created a flue for the flames which rushed forward toward the cockpit. The Pilot climbed out first but was sideways and his hips got stuck so I had to help him turn sideways to get out. I then followed the drop from the top of the plane to ground was about 8–10 feet. The navigator lost his life in the ensuing fire while the remaining crew all escaped with burns.

Flying Officer Stannus was the last survivor to escape the flames due to the pilot getting stuck in the cockpit escape hatch. This delay was sufficient for his burns to be more severe than the other survivors. He had used his left arm to cover his eyes as he sustained burns on his left hand, his left cheek, nose, mouth, chin, and neck. His upper left arm suffered somewhat more minor burns as he was protected by a long-sleeved jacket and short-sleeved shirt underneath. The main fuselage doorway was used by the other crew survivors. Thomas Smith had suffered significant burns to his hands, no doubt inflicted as he fought the initial fire. That gallant action and acting as the flight engineer saved the crew. The recommendation for the award of a Distinguished Flying Medal appeared in the *London Gazette* on 10 January 1945. The recommendation stated:

> As a wireless operator this NCO has completed a total of 47 operations of which 12 have been his second tour. His first tour was entirely against main targets but his second has also consisted of mining and special operations. On one special operation, the aircraft in which he was flying was severely damaged by light flak, resulting in a large amount of petrol entering the fuselage. Flight Sergeant Smith immediately stood by to start the distress procedure as the Captain considered it necessary and continued to do so until the aircraft reached the English Coast. The Flight Engineer became affected by the petrol fumes, turning on petrol tanks that had already been emptied and was quite incapable of keeping his log or intelligently watching his instruments. Flight sergeant Smith manipulated the fuel cocks correctly and watched the engineers panel in addition to his own duties. The aircraft landed wheels up and caught fire, Flight Sergeant Smith being slightly burnt. After some time in hospital he re-joined the Squadron with his enthusiasm for operations undaunted in any way. This NCO enthusiasm and devotion to duty merit very high praise and I strongly recommend that the DFM be awarded to Flight Sergeant Smith.

The flight engineer, Pilot Officer Charles Watkins, had suffered intoxication by the high-octane fuel resulting in his incapacity to control and manage the remaining fuel. Following the forced landing and explosion of fuel, he suffered burns to his face and both hands while escaping from the burning aircraft. The surviving crew members all suffered burns of varying intensity and they received initial medical treatment at the nearest local hospital to Thorney Island, St Richards, in Chichester. The following day, those men with more serious burns were taken to the Queen Victoria Hospital burn unit in East Grinstead.

During the Second World War, not even a handful of entire Bomber Crews jointly became members of the Guinea Pig Club. Thomas Smith and his crew of Flying Officer Stannus, Flight Sergeant Bacon, Pilot Officer Watkins, Pilot Officer Holmes, and Sergeant Marjoram had all suffered burn injuries and became members of Sir Archibald McIndoe's Guinea Pig Club. The remaining member of this crew, Flight Sergeant White, became a casualty to the flames and lost his life. He was later laid to rest in Brookwood Military Cemetery, Surrey.

20

Flight Engineers on Operation Chastise

The great hydroelectric dams of the Ruhr and Eder valleys were assessed as possible targets early in the war. Disabling those structures would disrupt the powerful industrial heartlands of the Third Reich. Several studies were undertaken, but these exceptionally difficult targets thwarted conventional options. However, the proposal to target the dams gathered momentum with the engineer Barnes Wallis developing the bouncing bomb concept, which was successfully tested over Chesil Beach, Weymouth, on 4 December 1942 when a bouncing bomb was dropped from a Lancaster.

On 16 May 1943, an attack finally took place against the Ruhr dams. Codenamed Operation Chastise, this operation has now become embedded in Royal Air Force history. Guy Gibson would receive the Victoria Cross for this operation and his entire crew would be individually decorated. His flight engineer, Sergeant Pulford, received an immediate Distinguished Flying Medal, and was the only flight engineer to be directly decorated during Operation Chastise. The participating flight engineers consisted of an unusually high proportion of non-commissioned men, seven of whom lost their lives that day. Many of the nineteen flight engineers who engaged in this historical operation had enlisted as boy apprentices who then subsequently volunteered to become flight engineers.

Recorded in this chapter are the flight engineers who took part in the audacious attack on the important hydroelectric dams, using a spinning bomb dropped onto water in the most remarkable and testing of circumstances:

Sergeant J. Pulford

John Pulford was born in Hull, a motor mechanic by trade who joined the Royal Air Force just before the outbreak of war as ground crew. He volunteered for retraining as a flight engineer in 1942. After being decorated for the Dams Raid, he was killed in a flying accident on 13 February 1944. His brother, Thomas, was also a flight engineer and likewise did not survive the war.

Sergeant J. Kinnear

John Kinnear was born in 1922 in Fife. He was another young motor mechanic before joining the Royal Air Force in 1939. After more than three years of work as ground crew, John volunteered for flight engineer training and qualified late in the summer of 1942. He lost his life on the Dams Raid with his crew, after his pilot, Flight Lieutenant Bill Astell, hit a high-voltage cable near Marbeck, Germany, and crashed before reaching the target area.

Sergeant R. J. Henderson

Robert Henderson was Scottish and born in Ayr. He joined the Royal Air Force in 1937, and was serving as ground crew when the war started. He was quick to take up the opportunity to volunteer to fly when selected for flight engineer duties. He qualified in early 1942 and survived the war.

Sergeant E. C. Smith

Edward Clarence Smith was born in 1919 at Easthampstead, Berkshire, and joined the Royal Air Force in 1937, serving as ground crew until 1942. He retrained at St Athan to become a flight engineer and was later posted to Scampton in December 1942. He arrived on the same day as several other men who would later fly with him on the Dams Raid. While flying with 617 Squadron, he was killed on 20 December 1943.

Sergeant R. Marsden, DFM

Ronald Marsden was born in 1920 at Redcar, North Yorkshire, and joined the Royal Air Force in 1935 as an apprentice at the School of Technical Training in Halton. He then served in ground crews in a number of establishments. In 1942, he was quick to apply for the role of flight engineer, qualifying in September 1942. He lost his life flying on the Dams Raid.

Sergeant J. Marriott, DFM

Jack Marriott was born on 19 January 1920 at Buxton, Derbyshire, and was employed as a factory worker before the war. After the outbreak of war, he joined the Royal Air Force and worked as ground crew. As soon as the opportunity arose for experienced mechanics to retrain as flight engineers, Jack volunteered and served with distinction. He was recommended for the Distinguished Flying Medal in April 1943 while flying with 50 Squadron, but lost his life attacking the Dams before he received the award.

Sergeant W. Radcliffe

William Radcliffe was born in British Columbia, Canada. In March 1939, he travelled to England and volunteered to join the Royal Air Force, where he served for three years as a ground crew mechanic. In 1942, he trained at St Athans and qualified as a flight engineer. He completed a tour of operations prior to the Dams Raid and was later recognised for his service, receiving the Distinguished Flying Cross in June 1944. He survived and returned to Canada in February 1945.

Sergeant R. C. Paterson

Robert Paterson was born in 1907 in Edinburgh and joined the Royal Air Force to serve as ground crew. He volunteered to train as a flight engineer and qualified in 1942. Following the Dams Raid in September 1943, he failed to return from an attack on Mannheim on 23 September 1943, his aircraft having been shot down by a night fighter near Offenbach.

Sergeant D. T. Horsfall

David Taylor Horsfall was born in 1929 in Hove, East Sussex, and joined the Royal Air Force as a boy entrant at Halton. He had been among the large 1936 Halton expansion entry and served in ground crew duties until 1942. He then retrained as a flight engineer and was posted operational in late 1942. The Dams Raid was only his third operation; he did not survive, having been shot down when returning from the operation.

Sergeant R. E. Grayston

Raymond Grayston worked as a motor mechanic before the war. Initially, he served as ground crew and volunteered to become a flight engineer. He was posted operational in October 1942. After surviving the Dams Raid, he attacked the important Dortmund-Ems Canal, joining the Ruhr to the North Sea. His Lancaster struck some trees, badly damaging two engines; despite valiant efforts, he was forced to parachute into enemy-held territory to become a prisoner of war on 16 September 1943. Raymond was sent to Stalag Luft III. He eventually returned home on 27 May 1945.

Flight Sergeant W. Hatton

William Hatton joined the Royal Air Force at the outbreak of war and worked in ground crew duties. After qualifying as a flight engineer in late 1942, he served in Bomber Command. Four months after participating in the Dams Raid, his entire crew were killed on 14 September 1943. Having been recalled from a proposed attack on the Dortmund-Ems Canal, his Lancaster hit the sea with a wing tip and crashed. William has no known grave and his life is commemorated on the Runnymede Memorial.

Sergeant D. J. D. Powell

Dennis John Dean Powell was born in 1922, in Sidcup, Kent. He was a boy entrant before the outbreak of the war and served in ground crew. In 1942, he eagerly took the opportunity to train as a flight engineer. Returning from the Dams Raid on three engines, he was mentioned in despatches in June 1943. Four months later, he attacked the Dortmund-Ems Canal. The crew failed to return.

Sergeant A. J. Taylor

Alastair James Taylor was born in 1923 at Alves, Moray. He joined as an apprentice at Halton in January 1939. He served in ground crew duties until training for flight engineer duties, joining Bomber Command in the summer of 1942. The Dams Raid took his life when his aircraft was shot down by flak from the heavily defended island of Texel, killing all on board before reaching the target.

Sergeant H. B. Feneron

Harry Basil Feneron joined the Royal Air Force in 1940 and served in ground crew. He qualified in October 1942 as a flight engineer, surviving the Dams Raid and the war. His Canadian pilot, Flight Sergeant Ken Brown, received the Conspicuous Gallantry Medal for the Dams Raid. He made nine runs over the Sorpe Dam, which was covered by mist; he eventually dropped his bomb, causing significant damage. On his way to the Sorpe Dam, their aircraft had sustained flak damage to the fuselage.

Sergeant C. Brennan

Charles Brennan was born in Alberta, Canada. He moved to England and joined the Royal Air Force in 1939 as ground crew. He later qualified to become a flight engineer at St Athan in the summer of 1942. The Dams Raid took his life. While flying over the primary target, his Lancaster was struck by flak and crashed on the far side of the dam.

Sergeant F. E. Appleby

Frank Ernest Appleby volunteered to serve in the Royal Air Force just a few weeks before the outbreak of war. He was assigned to ground duties and took advantage of the chance to volunteer as a flight engineer at St Athan in late 1942. His Lancaster suffered electrical failure after being struck by flak as they crossed over the Dutch coast. Forced to return from the operation, he later received the Distinguished Flying Medal and survived the war.

Sergeant G. Pegler

Guy Pegler was born in 1921 in Bath, Somerset. He joined as a Halton apprentice in 1938 and later served in ground crew in the early part of the war, mainly servicing aircraft in Fighter Command. In 1942, he trained as a flight engineer in Bomber Command. On the Dams Raid, his Lancaster was shot down flying close to the heavily defended Gilze-Rijen Air Base and the crew perished in a ball of flame.

Pilot Officer I. Whittaker

Ivan Whittaker joined the Royal Air Force as an apprentice at Halton in 1938. He spent the first three years of the war serving as ground crew. In 1942, he retrained as a flight engineer and was soon posted into Bomber Command, surviving both the Dams Raid and the war.

Pilot Officer S. L. Whillis

Samuel Leslie Whillis originated from Newcastle-on-Tyne and joined the Royal Air Force shortly after the outbreak of war, serving as ground crew until 1942. He volunteered to become a flight engineer and the Dams Raid took his life. Flying low, his Lancaster collided with a high-tension electric pylon. When the Luftwaffe found the crashed aircraft, it provided them with an intact bomb, which was defused and revealed the Barnes Wallis concept to their experts.

Operation Chastise Summation

Nineteen crews, encompassing 133 men, participated in Operation Chastise. Eight crews were lost, resulting in fifty-three men losing their lives and three being taken prisoner. Twenty-seven of the men who died on Operation Chastise are buried in the Reichswald Forest War Cemetery.

Many of those men who returned from the Dams Raid subsequently received later awards or were killed serving with 617 and other squadrons. By example, the Halton apprentice Ivan Whittaker witnessed the celebrations of success that fell upon 617 Squadron and the surviving crews from the Dams Raid. Eventually, his service would be recognised in a recommendation for the Distinguished Flying Cross in November 1943 and that was followed by a second award in March 1944. The recommendation made reference to the Dams and his flight engineer duties:

> During a long and strenuous tour Flying Officer Whittaker has taken part in many missions of a daring and hazardous character including the attack on the German Dams. In September 1943, he flew as a Flight Engineer in an aircraft detailed for a low level night operation. His sortie was completed in the face of adverse weather and heavy opposition from enemy defences. This officer's skilful manipulation of the throttles while the aircraft was flying in low level formation contributed largely to the outstanding performance of the crew. He has always displayed high devotion to duty and courage. It was overdue recognition for his courage and devotion to duty in the raid on the Dams and other dangerous operations on which he has flown with 617 Squadron that year.
>
> In February 1944 this officer was the Flight Engineer of an aircraft detailed to attack a target in Southern France. While over the target his aircraft was repeatedly hit and sustained much damage. Flight Lieutenant Whittaker was wounded in both legs but, in spite of this he coolly made a detailed examination of the aircraft and gave his captain a full report of the damage sustained. He displayed great fortitude and devotion to duty and his efforts were of much assistance to his captain who flew the damaged bomber to an airfield where a safe landing was affected.

From among all of the men who had participated in the iconic Dams Raid operation, only forty-eight actually survived the war. Among them were just a handful of flight engineers who were entitled to call themselves 'Dambusters'.

21

Flight Engineer Tame: Handley Page Halifax, Prisoner of War (Caterpillar Club)

Fate itself dictated many factors in the lives of flight engineers. These men inevitably only took to the air at the heavy conversion unit, joining a crew who had gained in confidence during their air experience whist flying at the Operational Training Units.

John Tame from Teddington in Middlesex completed his Royal Air Force flight engineer course in December 1944. Being able to sew sergeant stripes onto his flight tunics combined with the engineers' brevet would have no doubt been accompanied by some apprehension as John arrived at the 1664 Heavy Conversion Unit. The unit was at that time operating at Dishforth, training Halifax heavy bomber crews destined for No. 6 Group, Royal Canadian Air Force Squadrons. Dishforth was a well-equipped pre-war aerodrome and as such, it provided good accommodation. In common with the Canadian practice adopted with their naming of units and squadrons, the conversion unit was given the title 'Caribou'. It should be reiterated that the Canadians did not have any formal training program for flight engineers for most of the war; therefore, the usual crew formation at Dishforth frequently consisted of six Canadian crew members and one British flight engineer. Aware that he had no flying experience whatsoever and that he was to be among a Canadian crew, John embarked on practicing the skills he had acquired at St Athan. The engineer leader on base would have been well-versed in the process of integrating British flight engineers into well-bonded Canadian crews.

Unlike operational training units, heavy conversion units were less frequently called upon to support Bomber Command operations, presumably because the courses were not very long and the crews were in constant distribution onto their various operational squadrons. However, in the latter period of the war, these units were called upon to take part in diversionary sweeps. These were operations designed to entice the Luftwaffe into the air in an attempt to make them use precious fuel that was in short supply. This tactic was to reduce opportunities of attacks upon the main bomber forces. These operations were known as 'Sweepstakes' and John benefited from flying on two such operations while on station at Dishforth. Before he had the opportunity to operationally fly on a 'Sweepstake', John witnessed a contingent of aircraft from Dishforth add its contribution to the night of 3 March 1945. A diversionary force of ninety-five aircraft was supplied to act as diversion protection for the main bomber forces. These aircraft were pulled mainly from crews serving with the heavy conversion units, which included Dishforth.

That same night, the Luftwaffe undertook Operation Gisela, which would be their last large-scale night fighter intrusion over Great Britain. A significant strength of night fighter Junkers Ju 88 aircraft had been instructed to follow the returning bombers back to their bases. Over twenty aerodromes were targeted by the Luftwaffe. The weather predictions were favourable and the operation provided good pickings for them to locate the heavy bombers as they returned to their home stations, having attacked the Dortmund-Ems Canal near Ladbergen as well as a synthetic oil production plant at Kamen. It was not unusual for several aircraft to be circling the aerodrome, awaiting instructions from the airfield control with their navigation lights switched on by pilots, further adding to the opportunities that were presented to the Luftwaffe pilots. Twenty Allied bomber aircraft were shot down, among them one conversion unit Halifax returning to Dishforth. Halifax NA612 was nearing the aerodrome when it was attacked by a Junkers Ju 88. The crew of six Canadian along with twenty-one-year-old British flight engineer, Sergeant Sidney Forster, were all killed. A stone memorial to these men now stands in Brafferton, near Thirsk, close to the scene of the crash site.

John had personally witnessed the tragedy that had taken place on the night of 3 March 1945. It was, in fact, the 2,000th day of the war against Germany and that day would eventually commemorate the last occasion when a Luftwaffe aircraft fell onto English soil. Three night fighters had crashed during Operation Gisela, apparently through unintentionally flying into the ground.

The inevitable loss of men and aircraft during crew training continued into 1945. One such incident involved Halifax MZ481 at Dishforth on 15 March 1945 and is deserving of mention. The Canadian crew—together with their English flight engineer, twenty-one-year-old Sergeant Kenneth Parrish—had, in exactly the same fashion as John Tame and his crew, received briefing instructions to embark on a cross-country training flight. The briefing details were uncomplicated and in all probability, some thoughts were no doubt being applied to their imminent operational posting where cross-country flying exercises would be replaced by perilous sorties into Germany. Although the seven young men in Halifax MZ481 successfully took off from Dishforth, they simply disappeared without trace. A subsequent search for wreckage or survivors was undertaken with no success. To this day, the circumstances and whereabouts of the aircraft and crew remain unknown. Their names are not forgotten and are inscribed on the memorial at

Runnymede. It is there where the names of over 20,000 airmen who have no known graves and were lost in the Second World War flying from bases in the United Kingdom and north and western Europe are commemorated.

On 17 March 1945, John Tame took control of flight engineer duties on a 'Sweepstake' operation over northern France. Taking off from Dishforth at 6.35 p.m., in company with twenty-eight other Halifax aircraft from training units, their briefing was to entice Luftwaffe fighters into the sky. Foremost in his mind would have been his flight engineer responsibilities to respect the engine limitations. The majority of aircraft held at heavy conversion units had old airframes and he would have needed to monitor all of his gauges and calculations with great care. The sortie proved uneventful and they returned safely.

Three days later, another 'Sweepstake' over France saw John take to the sky, this time departing Dishforth at 11.30 p.m. With gaining confidence, John assisted in warming up the engines and ensured the aircraft would be able to safely achieve maximum power for the take-off. As the flight engineer, John was responsible for several matters including the monitoring of all pressure and temperature gauges and the booster coil switches. The engines were started, primed first, then he instigated the starters and booster coil buttons. Only when the engine was running satisfactorily did John remove his finger off the booster coil button. Once the engine was warm, the supercharger was tested and preparations continued to taxying onto the runway. The safe return to Dishforth after his second uneventful sortie saw the conclusion of flying at the heavy conversion unit training for John.

John Tame and his crew were posted to join the Canadian 425 'Alouette' Squadron at Tholthorpe, North Yorkshire. The name 'Alouette' denoted the connections with the French-Canadian contingent of men within that particular squadron. As a young flight engineer from Middlesex, John would have found himself surrounded by countless French-Canadian accents. One pilot, Charles Lesesne, stood apart; he was a mature American volunteer from South Carolina serving with the Royal Canadian Air Force. He was aged thirty-four, highly experienced, and in need of a replacement flight engineer and navigator for his next daylight operation to Hamburg on 31 March 1945. This was to be a particularly large attack at the Blohm & Voss shipyards and Sergeant John Tame would fly on what he regarded as his first operational sortie into Germany. The young flight engineer from England soon found himself among a crew consisting of five Canadians and one American. He was about to venture deep into enemy-held territory on what was probably the longest flight he had ever undertaken.

Alouette Squadron, in keeping with several other Canadian-based squadrons, painted murals and individual pieces of artwork onto their Halifax aircraft. John's Canadian rear gunner, Sergeant Fred King, was an artist of some considerable skill and would regularly fly with his pilot, Charles Lesesne, in Halifax NR271 emblazoned with splendid artwork painted on the cockpit section by him.

The crew chose the name 'Nuts for Nazis' with artwork that featured a monkey wearing flying gear and spitting out engineering nuts.

For reasons unknown, possibly due to servicing schedules, NR271 was not available for the Blohm & Voss shipyards attack. Orders for the squadron revealed that Halifax MZ418 had been allocated to John's crew, an unfamiliar Halifax to them, on the morning of 31 March 1945. The briefing later revealed that the Canadian bombers drawn from within No. 6 Group were to be in the last wave of many bombers flying over the shipyards. This was an unenviable position because any Luftwaffe fighter capability would most probably be present and the anti-aircraft gunners will have been well versed by then on their direction and height.

Tholthorpe aerodrome had three large hangars and thirty-six aircraft dispersals distributed around the perimeter access road. Collecting his parachute and making for the muster point to be taken to their Halifax, John would have been aware that the aircraft would be fully fuelled and bombed up. Arriving at the dispersal, in common with all the flight engineers, John checked with their reliable ground crews that all was as it should be. Wearing the full flying gear combined with carrying out initial preparations made everyone hot and uncomfortable. With the last ground checks completed, John climbed aboard the Halifax. The normal crew access door to enter or depart the Halifax was smaller than that of the Lancaster or Stirling. The Halifax door was an opening that included a section of both the side fuselage and floor panel. The actual door lifted and folded upwards into the aircraft. Even while wearing full flying kit, it was an easy procedure to lift oneself into the fuselage from the ground, the parachute having been thrown into the aircraft prior to climbing in.

The parachute issued to John would have been an observer parachute manufactured by the Irvin Company. The personal harness was worn at all times while in the air but with no actual parachute attached. The parachute itself would be stowed and accessible when needed. Fitted with metal loops, it was a simple requirement to clip the parachute pack onto the harness hooks. The Irvin assembly was well liked by the vast majority of aircrews and in emergency situations, the parachute could be attached with no regard to its position. Either way up, the 'D' ring or rip cord could be pulled by the left or right hand. The Observer parachute assembly became the most commonly used harness used by aircrews across all commands of the Royal Air Force. The key to that success was the method of simply attaching the parachute pack onto the two chest-mounted fasteners. Once attached, the parachute sat upon the chest but when deployed, the harness strapping became detached by the stitching, effectively ripping upwards to rise above the shoulders as the parachute opened.

The take-off at 6.27 a.m. and the subsequent altitude climb took place without complications. John had assisted with the throttles and on reaching 10,000 feet, the crew put on their oxygen masks as they climbed as high as possible over

Yorkshire. The throttle controls had three primary positions, which were marked with luminous paint and these were locked into position by a friction lever that ensured vibrations were not able to influence the settings. The navigation tasks were set and the route to Germany commenced. Having calculated how much fuel had been used in the warm up and long climb for altitude, John set about his monitoring of other essential engineering tasks. He viewed the propellers, assessing if any balancing adjustments were needed. Fine adjustments to the pitch were made, ensuring that all four airscrews were synchronised properly.

According to the official reports, the target area was covered in cloud and little is recorded on the events that befell Halifax MZ418 as it approached the target. It is likely that flak or possibly the most unexpected Luftwaffe contingent of Me 262 jet fighters that appeared had attacked them during brief but intense action, which saw several heavy bombers destroyed. Post-war research has established that the entire crew of Halifax MZ418 successfully manage to escape their doomed airframe by parachute. The time would have been around 9.15 a.m. and no doubt every parachute would have been seen as the crew fell towards the ground beneath their billowing canopies. The seven men would have landed over a relatively large geographical area. John Tame was quickly rounded up, as were his fellow Canadian crew members. The pilot, Charles Lesenes, no doubt having been the last to leave the aircraft, landed safely but by great misfortune ended up quite close to one of the many flak battery units defending Hamburg.

During the latter part of the war, it became common practice for the anti-aircraft flak guns, along with their radar stations, to be generally operated by female Luftwaffe auxiliaries, known as the *Flakhelferinnen*. Due to the deteriorating war situation for Germany, the *Reichsjugendführung* (National youth leadership) in collaboration with the *Reichsluftfahrtministerium* (National aviation ministry) began the formation of the *Kriegshilfeinsatz der Deutschen Jugend bei der Luftwaffe* (War assistance action of the German youth within the Air Force), which became active in 1943. The German regulations stipulated that personnel who had reached the age of fifteen were to immediately volunteer for auxiliary service in the Luftwaffe. Although the auxiliary service could be performed in any branch of the Luftwaffe, the most common branch of service for these individuals was with the air-raid defence units.

The flak unit where Charles found himself sought retribution for the bombing by setting upon him, inflicting injuries through a seriously intensive beating. He was eventually taken into protected custody and taken to a central holding cell where he was unceremoniously reunited with his crew. In a letter published in *Air Force Magazine* (Winter 2008), Francois Guy Savard, a navigator from 425 Squadron, described his recollections of Charles Lesenes and what he had been told by his crew:

> I sat across the table from him (Lesesne) in the Mess for the pre-op meal before the
> Hamburg operation. Lesesne was in a very jovial mood, laughing and cracking jokes

as if he did not have a care in the world ... Upon landing, he felt really exhausted and decided to lie down and rest a bit. Unbeknownst to him, he had come down near a flak battery operated by women. They saw him lying there and proceeded to beat him quite severely. Sometime later, his battered body was thrown in the same cell as some of his crewmates. He was clearly near death so they called the guards and demanded medical help for their skipper. The reply they received was that every doctor in Hamburg had his hands full that night. Lesesne told the story to his crewmates before he died in the cell.

Flight Lieutenant Charles Lesesne was the last member of 425 Squadron to die on operations in the Second World War. The Commonwealth War Graves Commission now tends his grave in the Hamburg Ohlsdorf Cemetery. In the adjacent grave, the headstone simply states that within it lays an 'Unknown Airman', exemplifying the fate that befell so many.

John Tame and the rest of the crew were later transported to Stalag Luft 1. All six men were held within the camps west compound. John was given the prisoner of war number 8103. No doubt he and his crew will have harboured great bitterness, having witnessed the death of their pilot. Back at Tholthorpe, instructions had been given for John's personal belongings to be sent to the central depository, as his fate and that of his crew was at that time unknown. His flying log book was examined and endorsed with the comment of no operations having been completed. John may well have been the only flight engineer to officially have completed no operations and to have served one of the shortest periods of imprisonment by the Luftwaffe. His time held behind barbed wire was just thirty days.

On his repatriation to England, John Tame commemorated his survival over Hamburg by becoming a member of the Irvin Caterpillar Club. He owed his life to the silk canopy that successfully cascaded out from his parachute, which he had collected from the stores on 31 March 1945.

In February 1945, Irvin Air Chute had published a special request to all of its members:

> The Caterpillar Club is a properly constituted organisation open to all who save their lives in emergency with an airchute of Irvin design, regardless of the manufacture. There is no entrance fee or charge of any kind. Those who qualify are enrolled as soon as authenticated applications have been scrutinised. A membership card is sent immediately to a newly elected member and, shortly afterwards, follows the Club badge, the little golden caterpillar with his name engraved on the back. This genuine gold pin is the only approved badge of the Club.

John Tame proudly wore his Caterpillar pin, celebrating his exceptionally short operational service as a flight engineer.

22

Flight Engineer Jackson VC: Avro Lancaster

In the archives of history associated to flight engineers, Norman Cyril Jackson sits at the pinnacle of recognised gallantry during the Second World War. Born in Ealing, London, in 1919, and having been adopted as a small child, he was educated at Archdeacon Cambridge and Twickenham Grammar School. Norman developed an interest in general engineering and became an engine fitter after he left school. He was successful in that trade, gaining in skill, and had married his wife Alma by the time war broke out against Germany.

Norman volunteered and enlisted into the Royal Air Force in October 1939. He received training at Halton and Hednesford where he qualified as an engine fitter II, following which he was posted into Coastal Command and sent overseas to Freetown in Sierra Leone. Norman joined the Short Sunderland-equipped 95 Squadron in January 1941. No. 95 Squadron at that time was engaged in anti-submarine patrols and reconnaissance over the South Atlantic. Inevitably, opportunities arose to experience test flights and the Air Ministry Order in March 1941 enabled an opportunity for Norman to volunteer for duties as a flight engineer. Having been successful in his application, he was posted to England for training in September 1942. After interim duties, in March 1943, Norman attended the school of technical training at St Athan. His previous work experience saw him pass through the shortened training syllabus and on 14 June 1943, he successfully qualified as a flight engineer.

Immediately promoted to the rank of sergeant, Norman was posted to become the flight engineer to a Lancaster crew forming at the 1645 Heavy Conversion Unit, Wigsley, Lincolnshire. On 18 June 1943, Norman met the man who would become his regular pilot—the Canadian Flight Sergeant Frederick Manuel Mifflin. This Canadian pilot was two years younger than Norman but had already experienced a rather unusual service life. Having initially trained as a fighter pilot in Canada, Frederick Mifflin had arrived in England only to be shipped out to Singapore. The war in the Far East had taken a most unexpected development before he arrived at that British stronghold. It was overrun and following the surrender to the Japanese, Frederick was diverted to Africa where he flew Hurricanes in the North African Campaign, eventually returning to England in 1943. He then re-trained as a bomber pilot, which explained his presence at the heavy bomber conversion unit.

Norman accompanied Flight Sergeant Mifflin and his crew to Syerston, where they joined Bomber Command and 106 Squadron. Wing Commander Guy Gibson had recently left 106 Squadron, which was by then regarded as a premier Lancaster squadron. Norman and his crew embedded themselves well into the squadron and commenced operations at a time when Bomber Command was undertaking concentrated sorties into Germany. Operations commenced in a flurry of activity to various targets. Flight Sergeant Mifflin gained a reputation as being rather heavy handed when landing his Lancaster, but his crew accepted this regular trademark despite it being of concern to others who watched such events from afar. During their initial period of operations, Norman accrued an additional operation to his crew when he had volunteered to replace a fellow flight engineer (who had been unable to fly) on another crew at the last minute.

No. 106 Squadron moved into the newly constructed Metheringham aerodrome in early November 1943; here, Lancaster JB612 became the regular aircraft that Norman and his crew would continue their tour of operations within. This aircraft had the identity letter 'U' displayed on the fuselage and was normally referred to as 'Uncle'.

Between November 1943 and March 1944, Berlin became the target for Bomber Command no fewer than sixteen times. During that period, 595 heavy bombers were lost while attacking that prime target. The intensity of the campaign was very significant to aircrews and ground staff, who mounted more than 9,000 operational sorties in those short winter months. On the night of 22 November 1943, Norman flew on what was his fourth operation to the German capital. Twenty-six heavy bomber crews were never to return that night. These and more significant casualty statistics were repeated on many returning operations.

Fuelled to capacity, Lancaster JB612 took off again for Berlin on the night of 2 December 1943. The Squadron Operational Record Book states that Lancaster JB612 was: 'Attacked by fighter aircraft, extensively damaged ... Also hit by heavy flak and the whole of the return journey was made on three engines.' This was another Berlin operation that cost the command thirty-nine heavy bomber crews. Lancaster JB612 was very nearly added to that statistic. Norman had experienced many events while flying over several heavily defended German targets, but this particular operation required all of his experience to prevail. The combat report held in the National Archives (AIR50/208/395) allows for further understanding of events. Lancaster JB612 was hit by flak over Berlin as they turned away from the bombing run resulting in the starboard engine being set on fire thus acting as a beacon of despair. Intent on inflicting the final throes of death, the Lancaster was strafed by a Luftwaffe night fighter causing more fire to break out in the fuselage. Both the rear and mid-upper gun turrets were disabled in the attack adding to the vulnerability of the Lancaster. It is difficult to have any understanding of the intensity of such desperate conditions, but Flight Engineer Norman Jackson worked valiantly in efforts to save himself and his crew. The internal fires were fought successfully as was the engine fire which presumably responded to feathering and the nacelle fire extinguisher. Great scrutiny would have been paid to potential fuel loss in the starboard tanks. A hydraulic leak, which would affect the undercarriage and flaps, also needed to be resolved before the crew's thoughts of safely reaching home could materialise. Communications between the crew had been reduced to hand signals at any distance due to the intercom not working. It was remarkable that given the danger, the crew remained intact without anyone bailing out. A presumption must be that the pilot had managed to control the Lancaster, which provided the reassurance of survivability, borne out by Lancaster JB612 and the crew reaching home albeit on three engines. It had been a most collaborative success by the entire crew. Although Lancaster JB612 had been torn by flak and struck by the night fighter, repairs took place, which enabled Norman and his crew to fly within it once again.

The new year saw the accumulation of further operational sorties being entered into Norman's flying log book. Norman was to achieve his all-important thirtieth operation on 26 April 1944 when he flew to attack Munich in Lancaster JB664. Successfully completing that operation meant that Norman was regarded as officially tour expired. As he had previously carried out an additional operation with another crew, there was one further operation for his own crew to complete in order for them to also become tour expired. It appears that Norman's crew, captained by Frederick Mifflin, were so bonded that they all agreed to volunteer for an immediate continuance of duty within the Pathfinder Force of No. 8 Group. Norman understandably volunteered to fly with his crew on their final operation before taking leave.

On 26 April 1944, Norman was to accompany his crew to the target of Schweinfurt, having just been informed that his wife, Alma, had given birth to their first child. Undoubtedly, he would have been excited to complete the operation and commence his leave with the expectation of being able to see his wife and son. Schweinfurt was an important target, the home of the German ball bearing industry. At 9.35 p.m., recently commissioned Flying Officer Mifflin and his crew took off from Metheringham in Lancaster ME669. His long standing and reliable crew consisted of navigator Flying Officer Frank Higgins, wireless operator Flight Sergeant Ernie Sandelands, bomb aimer Sergeant Maurice Toft, mid-upper gunner Sergeant W. Smith, Flight Engineer Sergeant Norman Jackson alongside the pilot, and guarding the rear was Flight Sergeant Hugh Johnson in his turret. They were just one of 215 Lancasters making for Schweinfurt that night.

The weather predictions at the operational briefing proved to be woefully wrong. Unexpected strong headwinds delayed the main bomber force quite significantly. This provided the German night fighters more time to locate and eventually infiltrate the bomber stream. Lancaster ME669 was in the unenviable position of arriving late, if not last, over the target. Aerial combats took place sporadically during the period of the raid. No. 106 Squadron itself experienced a most tragic evening when five Lancasters failed to return; among them was Lancaster ME669. At that time, no one was aware of the events that had taken place on board that aircraft or the gallantry undertaken by their flight engineer. Mrs Jackson would now be faced with not knowing if her baby son would ever see his father. No. 106 Squadron dealt with five missing crews that fateful night while other squadrons would deal with identical matters involving a further sixteen missing crews.

Eventually, news filtered back from the Red Cross to confirm that Lancaster ME669 crew's navigator, bomb aimer, wireless operator, and mid-upper air gunner had survived and were being held as prisoners of war. Flight Engineer Norman Jackson had also survived despite severe injuries and was likewise later reported as a prisoner of war. Tragically, the pilot and rear gunner had both died in the remains of the aircraft wreckage. Both would have no doubt witnessed an immensely brave scenario prior to the crash from two differing perspectives relative to their crew positions. Both men would have died presuming their brave flight engineer had perished. The details of those events that had taken place on board Lancaster ME669 would remain unknown for more than a year and were only revealed after the repatriation of the crew members held as POWs who all survived to see the end of hostilities.

The official and moving account of the brave flight engineer is best explained by reading the citation for the Victoria Cross that was awarded to Norman Jackson for his actions in trying to save his crew:

905192 Sergeant (Now Warrant Officer) Norman Cyril Jackson R.A.F.V.R., 106 Squadron.

This airman was the Flight Engineer in a Lancaster detailed to attack Schweinfurt on the night of 26 April 1944. Bombs were dropped successfully and the aircraft was climbing out of the target area. Suddenly it was attacked by a fighter at about 20,000 feet. The captain took evading action at once, but the enemy secured many hits. A fire started near a petrol tank on the upper surface of the starboard wing, between the fuselage and the inner engine.

Sergeant Jackson was thrown to the floor during the engagement. Wounds which he received from shell splinters in the right leg and shoulder were probably sustained at that time. Recovering himself, he remarked that he could deal with the fire on the wing and obtained his captain's permission to try to put out the flames.

Pushing a hand fire-extinguisher into the top of his life-saving jacket and clipping on his parachute pack, Sergeant Jackson jettisoned the escape hatch above the pilot's head. He then started to climb out of the cockpit and back along the top of the fuselage to the starboard wing. Before he could leave the fuselage, his parachute pack opened and the whole canopy and rigging lines spilled into the cockpit.

Undeterred, Sergeant Jackson continued. The pilot (Tony Mifflin), bomb aimer (Maurice Toft) and navigator (Frank Higgins) gathered the parachute together and held on to the rigging lines, paying them out as the airman crawled aft. Eventually he slipped and, falling from the fuselage to the starboard wing, grasped an air intake on the leading edge of the wing. He succeeded in clinging on but lost the extinguisher, which was blown away.

By this time, the fire had spread rapidly and Sergeant Jackson was involved. His face, hands and clothing were severely burnt. Unable to retain his hold he was swept through the flames and over the trailing edge of the wing, dragging his parachute behind. When last seen it was only partly inflated and was burning in a number of places.

Realising that the fire could not be controlled, the captain gave the order to abandon aircraft. Four of the remaining members of the crew landed safely. The captain and rear gunner have not been accounted for.

Sergeant Jackson was unable to control his descent and landed heavily. He sustained a broken ankle, his right eye was closed through burns and his hands were useless. These injuries, together with the wounds received earlier, reduced him to a pitiable state. At daybreak he crawled to the nearest village, where he was taken prisoner. He bore the intense pain and discomfort of the journey to Dulag Luft with magnificent fortitude. After ten months in hospital he made a good recovery, though his hands require further treatment and are only of limited use.

This airman's attempt to extinguish the fire and save the aircraft and crew from falling into enemy hands was an act of outstanding gallantry. To venture outside, when travelling at 200 miles an hour, at a great height and in intense cold, was an almost incredible feat. Had he succeeded in subduing the flames, there was little or no prospect of his regaining the cockpit. The spilling of his parachute and the risk of grave damage to its canopy reduced his chances of survival to a minimum. By his ready willingness to face these dangers he set an example of self-sacrifice which will ever be remembered

Since the publication of the original *London Gazette* citation, some additional clarity of information became available. Norman had climbed onto the navigation table to access the escape hatch and deliberately opened his parachute inside the aircraft, while Higgins and Toft sorted out the rigging lines and chute to prepare themselves as 'anchor-men'. Once out of the aircraft and into the blasting wind stream, he laid flat along the top of the fuselage and lowered himself until his feet met the wing root below. He managed to grasp the leading-edge air intake and directed the contents of the extinguisher into an engine cowling opening. The flames died down momentarily. Mifflin was forced to bank the Lancaster to port, taking evasive action against the returning German fighter that raked the aircraft with cannon fire once again and wounded Jackson for the second time.

The flames once again erupted, blowing over Norman as he retained his perilous grip. He lost his grip and was swept off the wing, to be held in the slipstream by the smouldering rigging lines and canopy furiously being played out by Toft and Higgins before they released the parachute. Breaking free from the stricken Lancaster, Norman fell rapidly. His hands, with shrivelled skin burnt by the flames, were mercifully numb. The parachute canopy was slashed and torn, but, more ominously, it had smouldering holes in it that were getting larger as he fell towards and landed on the ground. Barely conscious, Norman lay in the darkness until daybreak.

Following his capture and hospitalisation, Norman was transferred into the Allied prisoner of war camp structure. His burn injuries were debilitating but fully healed. He was repatriated to Britain in early May 1945 when he at last had the opportunity to meet his young son who had just celebrated his first birthday.

On 26 October 1945, the Victoria Cross was gazetted and Norman was invested with the Cross at Buckingham Palace on 13 November 1945. Allowed to have two guests at the investiture, Norman, in addition to his wife, invited Gertrude Johnson to be present, mother to his rear gunner, Norman Hugh Johnson, who had failed to escape from the fated aircraft. His friend, known as Hugh to his crew, in his own final moments of life would have undoubtedly assumed his flight engineer had fallen to his own death.

Norman left the Royal Air Force with a disability pension of £2 a week. In the post-war years, he repeatedly stated: 'It was my job as flight engineer to get the rest of the crew out of trouble.' Climbing out of Lancaster ME669 during such perilous circumstances, knowing any return into the aircraft was futile, was an act beyond comprehension. Clearly, his personal responsibilities as flight engineer to his crew were—without question—remarkable, as was his survival.

In early 1948, news reached him that his friend Hugh Johnson had been formally identified following the exhumation conducted by the Missing Research and Enquiry Section. His body and that of the pilot, Flying Officer Mifflin, were removed and commemorated in a British Military Cemetery. In early 1955, at the Durnbach War Cemetery, a final and permanent memorial headstone was placed at the grave of Hugh Johnson. The words inscribed read 'Duty was his watchword, the beloved and loving son of Harris and Gertrude'.

Norman Jackson, Victoria Cross recipient, died in March 1994 and is buried in the Percy Road Cemetery, Twickenham, Middlesex.

23

Coastal Command

The Short Sunderland flying boat operated throughout the entire period of the Second World War. The imposing dimensions of the Sunderland were a symbol of the ability of the Royal Air Force to reach out over Allied convoy routes. Among other aircraft, they protected the vital Atlantic supply routes and hunted the enemy forces that sought to sink the convoys on the sea routes to Britain.

The Sunderland was an exceptionally large aircraft. The initial versions were powered by four Bristol Pegasus air-cooled radial engines set within a broad wingspan of 112 feet. Such was the depth of the wings that flight engineers within the aircraft fuselage could access the ominously dark interior of each wing. When in the air, the wing voids were filled with reverberations from the four engines set within them. The height from the lower keel to the top of the tail was 34 feet and it had an overall length of 85 feet. The later Mark 'V' Sunderland had four American-made Pratt and Whitney radial engines, but regardless of engine type, a total of 2,034 gallons of fuel was carried within six fuel tanks. Three fuel tanks were built into each wing—the first tank inboard of the inner engine, another between the two engines, and finally one outboard of the outer engine. Four smaller fuel tanks holding 516 gallons were subsequently incorporated behind the rear wing spars. These additional tanks provided a total fuel capacity of 2,550 gallons, enough for an extended fifteen-hour patrol.

Fuel consumption was initially very high with an average of 400 gallons consumed by the Sunderland in the first hour of flight. Taking off from the water was at times problematical. Often, a calm sea had the ability to pull or suck the hull into the water, requiring great power to break that connection and then lift the huge aircraft away from the water. Once in the air and having gained height with the supercharger, which maintained a constant boost pressure from ground level to the rated altitude of around 13,000 feet, the fuel consumption fell towards the figure of 100 gallons an hour. In normal conditions, the flight route to a convoy would be at below 10,000 feet, descending to a much lesser height when patrolling along a convoy of shipping. Endurance in the air inevitably incorporated lengthy return flights, which had the potential of being affected by adverse headwinds. Safety factors calculated by the flight engineer were imperative; assessing additional fuel consumption on any return flight was vital to survival.

The flight deck on the Sunderland was reached either by the forward entrance door or internally by a ladder in the galley just aft of the wardroom. The flight deck accommodated two pilots, the flight engineer, a navigator, and a wireless operator. Sitting at his engineer station, the flight engineer had a sloped writing desk that was ideal for maintaining the records. Directly in front and on a bank to his left were the collection of gauges and controls, all clearly visible and easy to access. The four starter switches for the engines were positioned at the top of the instrument panel. The flight engineer commenced take-off proceedings by priming and starting the engines—normally the outer port engine first, followed by the starboard outer. These engines allowed for the moorings to be slipped and once free, both inners would be started. The flight engineer would check the engines at full power and operate the propeller controls to ensure that the fine to coarse pitch mechanism was functioning. Running the engines at full take-off power would clear any oiled plugs on a lean fuel mixture and the pilot would be able to undertake the navigation towards a safe take off.

Once airborne, the flight engineer synchronised the propellers (the inner pair first followed by the outer pair). This task was done with the accessory gearbox, which was a complex unit mounted on the rear of the engine. The gearbox drove all of the engine accessories and oil pumps. These include the oil pressure pump; the oil scavenge pump; the oil filtration system; the dual magneto ignition system; the engine starter; the interrupter gear to synchronise the propeller; and the electrical generator.

The oil tanks fitted to each engine held 23 gallons. In an emergency situation, it was possible for flight engineers to crawl into the confined wing and reach the rear engine components. This was, however, a dark, claustrophobic, and intensely noisy environment, which required both bravery and great body flexibility, especially as no possibility of an emergency escape existed. The Sunderland flight engineer had to be a rather dexterous man who prior to taking off had the task to climb out onto the wings to dip the tanks to check the fuel. The walk along the wings provided no hand holds and was precariously high above the water. Roosting seagull matter deposited on the wings inevitably added to the slippery nature of this task. Maintenance could be performed on the main engines by opening panels in the leading edge of the wing either side of the actual engine. These openings created small platforms and a plank could be fitted across the front of the engine on the leading edges of the open panels.

Within the starboard inner wing, aft of its leading edge, was a small auxiliary petrol engine and dynamotor. This engine operated a bilge and fuel pump for clearing water and other fluids from within the fuselage bilges. The dynamotor was an electric motor for transforming direct current into alternating current. The entire unit was built into a fireproof compartment and was an important engine to maintain; however, it was inaccessible to the flight engineer while the aircraft was in the air. When moored, the flight engineer would climb out onto the wing and lower a section of the leading wing edge. This provided a platform to stand on. Using a rope pull starter, the auxiliary power unit provided 24 V power to the aircraft.

The substantial hull of the Sunderland was constructed with a skeleton framework which consisted of channel section and vertical frames, interconnected by section bearers. The frames were numbered in sequence, with frames number forty-two and forty-six joining across the flight deck. Between these frames was the flight engineer's instrument panel. Frames forty-two and forty-six were attached to the wing roots by four steel bolts. It was necessary to climb over the number forty-two cross member to get into the flight engineer's compartment. This frame was approximately 3 feet high and the girder across number forty-six frame was the separation walling between the flight deck and the bomb bay. The flight engineer station consisted of the instrument panel operating the petrol tank cocks, and a primary main lever that shut off all tanks. The panel had dials or gauges indicating the contents of each tank, a row of four warning lights for each engine, dials giving the boost to each engine, and a set of dials giving engine revolutions. Below the floor, at the junction of the galley and the bomb bay, were similar cross beams. Every crew position had a connection plug for the intercom, but often orders would be passed verbally within the flight deck or called down to whoever was in the galley floor below them.

The Sunderland had two decks. Crew bunks were provided on the lower deck including a galley with a kerosene pressure stove and a flushing toilet which was an additional responsibility of the flight engineer to ensure sufficient sea water was held in the flushing header tank. The flight engineer was also provided with a small machine workshop for undertaking inflight repairs. The crew compliment fluctuated between nine to eleven men capacity—two pilots, a radio operator, a navigator, a flight engineer, a bomb aimer, and three to five air gunners. Armaments included eight 250-lb depth charges suspended on racks that were rolled out of the fuselage extending under the wings. Flares that were essential for illuminating the sea on possible contacts with enemy submarines were ejected from a chute near the rear of the aircraft.

Daily maintenance was performed while the aircraft was moored on the water. A minimum of two men were required to be on board during the night. During predicted bad weather, a pilot and flight engineer had to be on board because the engines were inevitably used to turn the aircraft into the wind. The bilges had to be pumped out regularly utilising both a manual pump and the auxiliary power unit. It was not uncommon for crews to remain in residence between flights.

24

Flight Engineer Riddell DFC: Short Sunderland Flying Boat

Warrant Officer William Allen Riddell was a flight engineer who had left school and pursued a career in engineering, initially as an apprentice mechanic at Barnehurst Garage in Essex. At the earliest opportunity, he joined the Royal Air Force to serve as a mechanic. He was posted to Singapore as an aircraftsman first class where in June 1939, he witnessed the second Short Sunderland to be lost while in service. Shortly after taking off, Sunderland L5801 stalled and crashed in the Johore Strait. The 230 Squadron aircraft was destroyed, two men drowned, and another later died from his injuries. However, worse was to follow when the Japanese made a declaration of war, waging an offensive onslaught across the Pacific. Those events eventually resulted in a withdrawal of the squadron's flying boats. The evacuation was by no means easy for William Riddell. He was lucky to survive additional unsavoury experiences in the Mediterranean where he became involved in the evacuation of Greek dignitaries escaping the Italian military forces. Once safely back in Britain, he volunteered to become a flight engineer.

In January 1942, William Riddell commenced flying with Coastal Command in the United Kingdom. He served with 422 Squadron equipped with Sunderland flying boats. The squadron operated from Castle Archdale, on the banks of Lough Erne, Northern Ireland, and the most westerly flying boat station in the United Kingdom. This was an important flying boat base for Coastal Command due its close proximity to the Atlantic, which was approximately 30 miles due west. Unfortunately, those thirty miles lay across County Donegal, a part of neutral Eire. A secret deal was struck between Britain and the Irish Republic, which allowed their Sunderland aircraft to overfly Donegal along a controlled narrow corridor to reach the Atlantic. This concession provided an additional 100 miles range to the Flying Boats something which was crucial to the protection of the North Atlantic convoys.

The men in Coastal Command were required to fly operationally for eighteen months or have undertaken 800 operational hours in the air (whichever was attained first) before being entitled to be rested or screened from further operations.

William Riddell was an experienced mechanic and qualified flight engineer operating in a crew that was equally experienced. Their wireless operator, Morris Annely, was a pre-war Halton apprentice, and 422 Squadron being a Canadian squadron, unsurprisingly, the crew had three Canadian members. The Canadian pilot was known to them all as 'Bud'. His family name was Rothschild and he captained the eleven-man crew with great compassion and friendship. The unusual environment of the Sunderland flying boat had the ability of creating crews that were particularly well bonded.

In March 1944, the endless hours of patrol over the Western Approaches had reached a total where the twenty-five-year-old flight engineer was about to be tour expired. He had accumulated 1,445 hours flying within his flying log book and seventy-four operational patrols had consumed 800 of those hours. His pre-war experience of having been a motor mechanic combined with his in-service flight engineer training was brought to bear in two notable incidents. Both were almost identical in respect that they involved crawling into the confined spaces of the Sunderland wings, and attending to engine fires and oil leaks in two inner mounted Bristol Pegasus air-cooled radial engines. The last of those incidents resulted in him sustaining burn injuries inflicted by boiling hot oil while he was entombed inside the wing. The intensity of those injuries resulted in William being hospitalised for six weeks. Wing Commander Frizzle subsequently submitted a recommendation for the award of a Distinguished Flying Medal. Air Ministry Bulletin 14172/AL823 refers to this citation, which appears to identify the sortie as being on 30 March 1944:

Flight Lieutenant M.J. Rothschild, captain:

This Warrant Officer is an exceptional Flight Engineer who has completed arduous flying duties in several theatres of war, including the Far East, Middle East, Malta, Crete, Greece and the United Kingdom. In all his operational flying he has displayed the highest qualities of leadership and efficiency. On a number of occasions his skill has probably saved the lives of his crew. Recently he crawled out in the wing to the starboard outer engine of his aircraft, and in an attempt to repair a broken oil pipe, worked for nearly an hour with hot oil spraying over him. On this occasion his efficiency and advice to his captain probably saved the aircraft.

Public Record Office Air 2/9627 has the original recommendation dated 10 April 1944. The award was consequently presented to William Riddell at the Pembroke docks. His subsequent commission ultimately saw him being awarded a Distinguished Flying Cross.

William later served as a flying boat instructor, where he experienced the trauma of an emergency ditching when two of the crew perished, drowning inside the submerged hull. He survived the experience by the use of his life jacket and he became a member of the Goldfish Club.

25

Flight Engineer Galliford DFM: Short Sunderland Flying Boat

The Short Sunderland served across the entire global conflict of the Second World War. No. 209 Squadron had a long association to flying boat service and it commenced operations with the Sunderland over the Indian Ocean in February 1945. In July 1945, the squadron moved to Ceylon with a detachment at Rangoon to provide constant patrols against Japanese shipping along the long narrow southern part of Burma, the Kra Isthmus, and the Tenasserim, the narrow coastal region of south-eastern Burma, bordered to the east by Thailand and to the west by the Andaman Sea with its useful ports and airfields of Mergui. The Japanese were adept at camouflaging small vessels to look like native boats, even though they were in fact well-defended military vessels.

Flight Sergeant Thomas William Galliford most likely joined 209 Squadron in the July and transported out to the Far East during the delivery of their new Mk 'V' Sunderland Flying Boats. He was another flight engineer who demonstrated the ability of crawling into the wing voids of the Sunderland to undertake repairs to save his crew and aircraft. In keeping with the vast majority of Sunderland crew members, he was also trained as an air gunner. The Mk 'V' Sunderland, in addition to the firepower in the rear turret, had the capability of providing four fixed forward-firing guns and two hatches in the aft fuselage for additional beam gun positions.

Flight Sergeant Galliford was flying on 9 August 1945 when two suspected enemy-operated vessels were sighted. To assess such targets, the Sunderland was required to approach at a low level with every gun position manned. Inevitably, when approached in that way, the enemy always held the element of surprise. In this instance, the vessels opened fire and anti-aircraft fire immediately damaged the Sunderland. The aileron controls in one wing were lost to the pilot, rendering the control surfaces attached to the back of the wing inoperable. The pilot's control column had no effect upon the ailerons, effectively preventing the aircraft from being turned in flight. The subsequent recommendation written by the 209

Squadron commanding officer explains the hotly contested action against the brace of armed enemy vessels:

> During a low-level attack on two armed enemy vessels on 9 August 1945, this N.C.O. was manning the beam gun of a Sunderland. He used this with considerable effect. The aircraft was damaged by anti-aircraft fire and aileron control lost. In his capacity as Flight Engineer, Flight Sergeant Galliford discovered fractures in the control cables. He crawled inside the wing to the point of the fracture and working in a cramped and confined space directly behind the fire wall, he affected a temporary repair. Had the aircraft crashed owing to lack of control, he would have had no chance of survival. Despite this he worked for nearly an hour at the task, thereby enabling the aircraft to return safely to base. He has shown throughout his operational tour a high standard of technical ability, a capacity for hard work and a consistent devotion to duty.

At the time of this recommendation, Flight Sergeant Galliford had completed over eighty hours of operational flying. The Distinguished Flying Medal was duly awarded and was officially published in the *London Gazette* on 4 June 1946.

26

Flight Engineer Lenson DFM: B-24 Liberator

No. 224 Squadron, Coastal Command operated the American-built B-24 Liberator on extended patrol duties hunting submarines over the Atlantic. In 1942, operating out of Beaulieu, as part of 19 Group of Coastal Command, Hampshire's large four-engine Liberators endured long patrols over the Eastern Atlantic and Bay of Biscay, supporting the many convoys moving to North Africa. Also, anti-submarine patrols were carried out over vast, open expanses of water. Frequent fifteen-hour duties often revealed no enemy activity. However, on 20 October 1942, events revealed a German submarine on the surface and Liberator FL910 would engage combat on the small target sighted in the distance.

The day had commenced at 7 a.m. when the crew of Liberator FL910 were advised that low cloud over their aerodrome at Beaulieu would frustrate and postpone their intended departure. At 9.30 a.m., the weather provided an opportunity to depart, but conditions were predicted to worsen during their long flight and they were to anticipate foretold instructions to return to a different aerodrome. Extraordinary endeavours took place in Coastal Command to combat the submarine menace that prowled the western approaches. The pilot of Liberator FL910, Flying Officer Sleep, and his flight engineer, Sergeant Lenson, would ultimately combine their skills to save Liberator FL910 from fatal disaster that day.

Having reached the Isles of Scilly at approximately 11 a.m. and started a patrol, the weather had cleared revealing ideal visibility and a constant sturdy breeze from the north-west. These were ideal conditions which remained for an eight-hour period of flying. The patrol had extended for 650 miles without incident. As they turned south, the rear gunner sighted a large four-engine German bomber, which he identified as a Fw 200 Condor about 3 miles away. The German crew appeared to avoid engaging with the Liberator as it sought to disappear in the cloud formations. The Condors were used to report Allied shipping movements and to guide their submarines to the convoys as they shadowed them overhead, transmitting direction finding signals as indirect communication with the submarines. The Fw 200 crews were instructed not to engage in offensive action and to evade all combat unless unavoidable. The Liberator was estimated to be 100 miles out on their last navigation plot and approximately 550 miles from land when the flight engineer reported seeing what appeared to be a white smudge on the sea, about 5 miles ahead and a little to the right of the Liberator. The sighting was confirmed to be a submarine making at full speed for the French coast. The pilot immediately started a shallow dive on the sighting and the flight engineer opened the bomb doors. The flight engineer went into the nose section to gain the best possible view of the submarine despite the possibility of flak coming up as they got closer. As they rapidly approached at low level, six depth charges were selected to be dropped in a stick pattern. The Liberator passed over the submarine at approximately 20 feet above the conning tower. The pilot had the job of pressing the bomb release, which he did, but as he did so, an explosion erupted beneath them. Unsure if they had been hit by the submarine, the explosion thrusted them violently upwards. The pilot instigated an instinctive climb but as the flight engineer made his way out of the nose section, the aircraft then commenced to drop. The nose going down was the result of the pilot attempting to increase flying speed and prevent a stall that would have been fatal at that altitude. The rear gunner on the intercom reported that he was jammed in the turret and that he could see both elevators had been destroyed. The elevators sat either side of the rear gunner's turret; it appeared that the blast from beneath the aircraft had torn them away and dislodged the turret fixings. The wing, stabilisers, and fins on the Liberator were all metal but the ailerons, elevators, and rudders were fabric-covered. In all probability, the fabric covering on the elevators had been stripped away in the blast from the depth charge explosions. In theory, the aircraft should not have been able to fly without both elevators. The wireless operator sent an immediate SOS to provide a positional fix of their aircraft. The bomb bay doors were still open but an oil line had fractured, squirting oil over the access walkway. This was reported by the rear gunner who had managed to hack his way out of the jammed turret and make his way to the front of the aircraft. The pilot managed to gain height and stability with an intention to try and reach Predannack, the nearest possible aerodrome from their position on the Cornish Lizard peninsula. Due to the missing elevators, four crew members moved forward to weigh the nose down for stability while the flight engineer went to the rear bomb bay to extract the remaining bombs and tackle the oil leak. The electrical circuit had broken, which prevented the bombs from being dropped through the open doors and so they needed to be released manually. The oil made the walkway treacherous and so the flight engineer took off his footwear and socks in order to gain as much grip as possible. Stretching out over the open void was dangerous work and certain death if he should fall.

The Liberator had unique roller shutter-type bomb doors that rose upwards and the bomb bay had a catwalk that provided access through the fuselage. However, it was restrictive—less than 1 foot wide and with vertical stabilising rods supporting the gangway. The flight engineer was unable to wear a parachute or life jacket as he worked to remove the bombs. The pilot continued to increase height gently as Sergeant Lenson worked in the bomb bay. It took more than an hour to deal with the releasing of the bombs, which eventually fell from the aircraft. The dangerous situation with the bomb load had been averted but it was replaced by the failure of the radio and intercom system no doubt caused by electrical faults. The navigator was immensely restricted with the occupancy of the forward area with four men wearing Mae Wests in a space designed for one. The crew knew from the morning briefing that expected weather conditions over south-west England were likely to be exceptionally poor and the loss of the radio simply added to the anxiety being experienced. Sergeant Lenson returned from the bomb bay covered in oil, which he tried to wipe away as much as possible as he checked his station gauges and attempted the fuel consumption calculations.

The pilot was under immense strain dealing with the damage and trying to maintain stability. His feet were positioned up on the instrument panel to help with the force required to push the column forward with his hands and knees. Eventually, the crew sighted the Isles of Scilly, approximately 3 miles south of their position. The weather was holding with just a few patches of cloud at about 4,000 feet and therefore the chances of a successful landing increased dramatically. The crew agreed that a forced landing at Predannack was the best option, so they adopted a most unorthodox crash position with the whole crew in the front compartment all lying on top of each other. The escape hatch had been opened and discarded to allow for best escape options as the Liberator lost height. Flight Engineer Lenson was the only crew member other than the pilot with any view of what was happening while holding on as best possible on top of the pile of men. Committed to landing, when only a short distance from the runway, the pilot suddenly and most unexpectedly lost all tension upon the control column. The control column had lost all connectivity and was flopping around uselessly as the runway rapidly approached. The Liberator struck the runway and commenced to buck and slide but most importantly, the nose wheel held firm and took the strain without collapsing. One of the port engines caught fire and the flames illuminated the scene as daylight faded. The air inside the aircraft was full of a combination of smoke and dust, which severely restricted visibility. The noise was deafening but at last, the aircraft came to rest. The fuselage had split apart just aft of the bomb bay, leaving the tail section behind. Everybody got out pretty quickly, except the flight engineer and navigator who had both ended up entangled among the debris. The navigator had sustained a shocking gash to his left leg, which was also trapped. With no regard for his own safety and despite a nasty injury to his right hand, Sergeant Lenson removed the navigator's flying boot to allow the extraction of the injured leg and assisted him down and through the escape hatch. The navigator's leg was also badly broken and was therefore unable to support any of his weight. The pilot and flight engineer together carried the navigator away from the burning aircraft to await the rescue party. The crew realised that had the controls been lost no more than ten to twenty seconds earlier, they most probably would have all been killed. It was quite remarkable that the controls had held strong for nearly three hours before finally giving way when they did.

The pilot, David Mackie Sleep, was awarded the Distinguished Flying Cross, and the flight engineer, George Thomas Lenson, received the Distinguished Flying Medal. Their joint recommendation reads:

One day in October, 1942, Flying Officer Sleep and Flight Sergeant Lenson were captain and Flight Engineer respectively of an aircraft which engaged a U boat far out in the Atlantic. During the attack an explosion, caused by what appeared to be a hit on the submarine, severely damaged the aircraft. It went into an almost vertical climb but, with a great effort, Flying Officer Sleep recovered control and manoeuvred to observe the result of his attack. It became necessary to jettison the remaining bombs but, to accomplish this they had to be manhandled. Regardless of his own safety, Flight Sergeant Lenson performed the task and, for one and a half hours, he worked on the narrow catwalk with the bomb doors open in order to release the bombs, the catwalk was extremely slippery and Flight Sergeant Lenson had to shed his boots and socks to enable him to obtain a firm grip. On reaching this country Flying Officer Sleep executed an emergency crash landing at night with great skill. On impact, however, the aircraft caught fire, but Flight Sergeant Lenson succeeded in extricating an injured comrade from the burning aircraft. In most trying circumstances, both these members of air crew displayed great courage and devotion to duty.

Liberator FL910 had attacked the submarine *U-216*, a type VIID boat commanded by Karl-Otto Schults of the Ninth Flotilla based in France. This submarine had previously attacked and sank the steam ship the *Boston* in a convoy bound for England in the North Atlantic on 25 September 1942. The submarine was responding to orders to return to the U-boat pens in Brest when it was catastrophically damaged by the accurate drop of depth charges. The entire compliment of forty-five crewmen on board were lost.

27

Flight Engineer Gees:
Catalina Flying Boat, Evader

The Catalina flying boat was another prominent aircraft operated by Coastal Command. The flying boat was rather unique in many respects. Primarily, the most significant difference was that this aircraft had a flight engineer despite only having two engines. The entire principle of flight engineers being required was because of multiple engines, yet this was absent with the Catalina. This aircraft was technically described as a high-wing monoplane flying boat. The wing was 104-feet long and had two twin wasp engines fitted. The high-wing design saw the aircraft fuselage sitting significantly lower than the wing and the physical connection between the two housed the flight engineer station. The dimensions and physical shape of this aircraft created a unique engineer station where the occupant was sitting higher than any other crew member and almost shrouded by both engines. Technically, the structure, which housed the flight engineer was known as the pylon, with two small observation windows providing a view to both engines. They also provided a view to the wing-tip floats, which were mounted on pivoted frames and could be retracted electrically. During flight, they effectively reduced drag and formed an extended wingtip.

The Catalina flight engineer was a most important member of crew as the aircraft flew very long endurance operations which were capable of covering 2,520 miles. The Pratt & Whitney R-1830 fourteen-cylinder radial engines were among the most produced aviation engines ever built. Among others, they were also used on the B-24 Liberator and the Douglas DC-3 Dakota. The Catalina was normally operated by a crew of seven men. Two air gunners occupied the large open blisters situated aft of the wings. The flight engineer was trained as an air gunner and capable of occupying one of those positions in any emergency.

Paul Stanley Gees joined the Royal Air Force as a sixteen-year-old engineering apprentice within the 1937 intake at Halton. He would be destined to eventually serve as a flight engineer in a Catalina.

The apprentices were given the opportunity to state their preference of trade. Choices were aero-engine fitter, airframe fitter, armourer, instrument maker, or wireless operator mechanic. Kitted out with uniforms and equipment, all civilian clothing was packed and later sent to their homes. When called on parade, the intake was told which trade they would be taking. Those selected in the trade of instrument maker or wireless operator mechanic would be sent to the Electrical and Wireless School at Cranwell, while the remainder formed up in their respective trades. Not everyone was given the trade of their choice; however, Paul had elected for engines and airframes, which he secured.

In September 1939, aged eighteen, Paul Gees passed as an aircraftsman fitter, aircraft engines, and airframes. The Second World War brought a foreshortening of the course duration. Aircraftsman Gees later volunteered for aircrew duties and was unsurprisingly selected for training as a flight engineer. He passed out from the School of Technical Training at St Athan on 28 November 1942.

Paul was posted to No. 4 (Coastal) Operational Training Unit at Invergordon. This training unit formed within 17 Group, provided flying boat crews for Coastal Command, which had been previously designated as the flying boat training squadron. Sergeant Paul Gees actually gained his first air experience flying in Catalina flying boat AH551 on circuits and landings on 1 January 1943. He became the flight engineer to a crew captained by the high-ranking Squadron Leader John Lobley. They would jointly be posted into 210 Squadron on 3 April 1943 for operational flying Coastal Command duties. From October 1942, 210 Squadron had been operational from Pembroke Dock with a detachment serving in Gibraltar, covering the landings in North Africa. In early 1943, 210 Squadron were responding to suggestions made by operational research developments to increase opportunities of locating surfaced enemy submarines. This involved homing onto targets with the impressive Leigh Lights illuminators, effectively a search light mounted on the aircraft.

In preparation for a concerted offensive in the Bay of Biscay, the squadron moved to Hamworthy, in Pool Harbour, Dorset, in April 1943. Squadron Leader Lobley flew to that location on 16 April, but without his regular flight engineer. That day, Flight Sergeant Alderson was short of a flight engineer and Paul was loaned to fly with him on an operational sortie against enemy submarines in the Bay of Biscay. This was his first operational submarine hunt, and it was to be with an unknown pilot and crew. Allocated Catalina FP271, they left the station at 8 p.m., making for the Gulf of Biscay. It was to be an eventful operation.

The crew of FP271 consisted of Flight Sergeant William Alderson (pilot), Flying Officer George Aldanson (navigator), Pilot Officer Alfred Isaac (co-pilot), Sergeant Paul Gees (flight engineer), Sergeant Frank Hobson (observer air gunner), Sergeant Claud Pottinger (observer air gunner), Flight Sergeant Charles Carson (observer air gunner), Flight Sergeant Alan Allen (observer air gunner), Sergeant William McDonald, and Leading Aircraftsman Thomas Bouvier. Paul manoeuvred himself up and into his unique engineer station. From his prominent position, the aircraft galley was behind and beneath him while the navigator's and wireless operator's positions were below and to the front of his position. He was elevated above them but effectively, his position was open and accessible with his back shielded by the armoured plating, which provided some protection. The flight engineer panel was constructed to fit within the oddly pylon-shaped compartment, narrowing at the top section where the fuel content gauges were fitted as two vertical bars, which provided readings against scale gradients. Beneath those were the fuel flow meters and then the two fuel mixture levers. The panel widened with the hand fuel pump levers sitting above the line of switching lamps, which enabled the pilot and engineer to signal each other. The instructions to each light related to raising the wing floats, lower floats, three fuel mixture instructions, and among others, stop engines. The carburettor air intake controls, oil tank gauges, and temperature gauges were displayed along with the main fuel tank control cocks. The two fuel tanks, one in each wing, held 725 gallons each and each engine held an oil tank capacity of 54 gallons. Immediately in front of the flight engineer at knee height was the two-engine cowl grill controls. Independently, these enabled greater or lesser air flow into the engines and were frequently adjusted to control engine temperatures. The flight engineer station in a Catalina was a most unusual location to occupy and gaining access into and out of the position was an acquired skill. Two handhold bars were fitted towards the narrowing top section, which, once in reach, enabled the flight engineer to haul himself into position.

Five hours into the patrol, Paul was monitoring fuel consumption when he detected a fuel problem at 1.43 a.m. It is unknown if Catalina FP271 was carrying the auxiliary or additional fuel tanks. Paul assessed the fuel loss situation when they were approximately 150 miles west of the Spanish coast. Calculations revealed that it would be impossible to return to their station on the Dorset coast, and so the pilot made as best possible for north-eastwards before they would be forced to make an emergency landing in the sea. The communication between the flight engineer and pilot would have been crucial in relation to managing the fuel in this scenario. The navigator needed to ascertain exactly their position along the Portuguese Spanish coastline.

Eventually, with fuel almost exhausted and only sufficient remaining to negotiate a safe landing, they made a decision to land on the water. This was dangerous in the darkness, but at 4 a.m., they successfully landed on the water at a position estimated to have been 12 miles west of Cape Torinana, in the province of La Coruña, north-west Spain. The sea landing was successful in that the Catalina was not damaged and the crew immediately ditched all equipment and fired signal flares. The Catalina carried two H-type emergency dinghies with oars. The H-type dinghy was circular in shape with a seating capacity for five. It was fitted with a carbon dioxide cylinder for inflation and had small rope ladders at the side to improve access from climbing into it from the water. These were both prepared by the crew and made ready for any emergency or subsequent rescue. The documentation available and the personal papers of Sergeant Paul

Gees fails to mention if the crew used any of the sea anchors or other methods to steady the Catalina in the sea conditions.

About two hours after the landing, as daylight intensified, the crew spotted two small fishing boats approaching. Two more flares were fired to ensure they had been spotted and they launched the inflatable life rafts. The Catalina needed to be scuttled and the hull was smashed with an axe below the water line, which caused it to sink very quickly. One of the fishing boats took the crew from their rubber life rafts and transported them to Marin in the province of Pontevedra, Spain. Pontevedra is situated just north of the Portugal Spain boarder. Clearly a language barrier existed at that time and no doubt the crew were anxious about their destiny. They were landed by the fishermen at 2 p.m., just ten hours since their emergency landing. The Catalina crew were escorted to the Port Authority of the Merchant Marine where an officer questioned them on their fate, in particular the type of aircraft they flew, and he desired to know if they had been shot down. The crew refused to answer many questions and requested to see the British Consul in Vigo. Spain was tentatively a neutral country but Portugal, with its close relationship with the United Kingdom, was a far more certain alliance and no doubt seeking the assistance of the British Consul would resolve the matters of official internment for the British crew.

At 6.30 p.m. on 17 April, the British Consul, Mr Lindsay arrived at the Port Authority building and he organised the entire crew to be taken to Vigo. They were accommodated in a hotel with arrangements made for food and clothing by the British Consul. There was no official Spanish guard or any detectable containment placed upon the crew who remained in the hotel until the 19 April 1943. That afternoon, an officer of the Spanish Air Force took the men to Valladolid, a province more central within Spain. Once again, they were housed in a hotel and the Spanish officer gave them 500 Pesetas each and fresh civilian clothing. The crew were not under arrest or under surveillance.

On 21 April 1943, another official from the Spanish Air Force took the crew by car on the relatively short journey to Madrid. Further questions were put to them as to their aircraft and duties, and again, these went unanswered. In Madrid, they were taken to the British Embassy and were received by the British Air Attaché. Individually, all ten members of the crew were provided with a signed, embossed British Embassy of Madrid stamped letter of authority to travel to Gibraltar. These documents were all officially stamped and dated 21 April 1943.

The crew were taken to another hotel and remained there until the afternoon of 23 April 1943. Arrangements were made for the crew to take a train south to Gibraltar. They arrived in Gibraltar the following day where for the next five days they experienced the unique existence of living on the precious British rock colony. On 29 April 1943, the crew embarked on HMS *Bachaquero*, which sailed from Gibraltar and returned the crew to the United Kingdom on 14 May

1943. Much of this information originates from Sergeant Gees' personal papers and official National Archives escape evasion report, WO208/3313/120.

No. 210 Squadron had regarded the crew as missing in action after they failed to return. Adding to the mystery of their disappearance, search and rescue flights undertaken over their patrol area had failed to find any wreckage. Moreover, the homing pigeon that was carried within their Catalina was accidentally released without the necessary message affixed to the leg. The bird survived the long flight to the homing loft, adding to the unknown events that befell Catalina FP271.

The Directorate of Air Sea Rescue had been formed in early 1941. It became a most effective organisation, which additionally engaged in the education of aircrew personnel. Posters were displayed on crew room walls, emphasising the importance of sea survival. In 1942, the Directorate proposed the position of every airfield having an appointed 'Air Sea Rescue Officer' who was responsible for the education of survival after a ditching. The station's leading radio operator and the air sea rescue officer combined to educate the wireless operators in the drill required to achieve a successful SOS procedure. The most important aid to location was the dinghy-based wireless set. The carrying of caged homing pigeons that could be released with a position report messages were equally as important to ditched crews, particularly in the early years of the war.

Talks were requested from men who survived a ditching by the station rescue officers, a policy that continued and developed throughout the entire war. It became commonplace for survivors to be engaged in the touring of airfields, and included visits to the manufacturing factories of parachutes and dinghies. The workforce in those factories gained great satisfaction in knowing that they were indeed saving lives through their hard work. This practice led to the company, P. B. Cow Ltd, creating the Goldfish Club for survivors who used their life rafts or buoyancy life jackets to save their lives. Charles Robertson, the person responsible for the club, illustrated their 'K'-type dinghy upon the rear face of the boldly laminated Goldfish Club membership card. Enrolled members were issued with a fabric Goldfish Badge, which was frequently sewn onto their battledress flying jacket.

The heavy bombers' H- and J-type rubber dinghies were subject to modification and development works as the war progressed. Valuable information secured from rescued aircrews was analysed and fed back to the air ministry, and the directorate and the manufacturers of the survival equipment.

Additional dinghies were provided in an effort to afford the best opportunities of crew survival after a ditching. Heavy bombers were fitted with emersion switches which upon contact with the sea automatically operated the release of dinghies. This system was backed up by physical switches, which were failsafe measures designed to be operated by the crew if needed. The Stirling was constructed to hold the large J-type dinghy, capable of holding the entire crew and stowed in the port wing assembly. In addition to the J-type dinghy, at various locations were several K-type individual dinghy packs. The single man type K-type dinghy was tightly compressed and folded into an outer heavy canvas material pack. The cover had a stitched multilingual label to ensure instructions were clear to the various exiled pilots serving within the Royal Air Force. Internal pockets held survival equipment. This design was proven to be ideal for operational deployment across the entire Allied air forces.

Later developments enabled multi-crewed aircraft within other commands the opportunity to hold personal K-type dinghy packs. These were capable of being deployed with the observer-type parachute packs simply attached by secure clip fasteners. This facility proved to support the standard large crew dinghy support structure already in place. The K-type dinghy packs were responsible for saving additional lives across the Royal Air Force Commands.

Bomber Command circulated the following report within their routine orders admin appendices, No. A 212. BC/S.23054/B. This report serves well to illustrate the vital duties of a flight engineer's work in the most pressing of circumstances leading up to a ditching:

The Commander-in-Chief wishes to bring to the notice of all ranks in the Command the fortitude, courage and perseverance of the under mentioned NCOs of 214 Squadron:

    1485104 Flight Sergeant G. A. Atkinson, Pilot. (Missing)

    1388280 Sergeant H. J. Friend, Bomb Aimer.

    1807915 Sergeant D. C. Hughes, Flight Engineer.

    1513213 Sergeant W. B. Edwards, Navigator.

    1892607 Sergeant R. L. Bouttell, Mid-Upper Air Gunner.

    1368303 Sergeant J. C. Wilson, Wireless Operator.

    R.79844 Sergeant W. Sweeney, Rear Gunner. (Missing)

The above-named formed the crew of a Stirling aircraft (Stirling III, EF445, BU-J) detailed to bomb Berlin on the night of 22–23 November 1943. Just before they reached the target area the oil pressure on the port outer engine began to drop and the captain noticed that the propeller was revolving at excessive speed. He decided to complete the bombing run and the Bomb Aimer sighted and released the bombs correctly one minute after E.T.A. dangerously low and the propeller was feathered to prevent a seizure with the result that the aircraft was losing height. At 9,000 feet it was dropping into icing cloud and the pilot restarted the engine to gain more height for crossing a bad front. The engine started but had to be stopped almost immediately to prevent it catching fire and the propeller then failed to re-feather but continued to windmill. The aircraft lost height steadily until it was only 1,500 feet above ground at a position given by the Navigator as 20 miles east of Hanover. Near this place, the aircraft was engaged by anti-aircraft flak which wounded the Rear-Gunner in the right leg but he refused to leave the turret.

The Wireless-Operator sent out an S.O.S. at about 21.45 hours and repeated it until it was acknowledged. It was picked up at 22.30 as a very faint signal and he was given a fix. From then onwards, although reception was very bad, he maintained communication with the ground sending the height, speed, course and D.R. position, obtained from Navigator, at intervals.

Near the Zuider Zee, the aircraft was picked up by the searchlights which were attacked by the gunners and, crossing the island at about 50 feet the aircraft was again engaged by flak and searchlights; fifteen to twenty-five of the latter were shot at by the gunners and doused. A F.W. 190 intercepted the Stirling but was shot down in flames by the Rear-Gunner.

When the Flight Engineer reported there was only 10 minutes of fuel remaining, the captain ordered the crew to take up their ditching stations. Because of icing, a head wind and the wind-milling airscrew, the speed had been very low. Information of their plight was signalled to the ground station and the aircraft was fixed accurately as the Operator pressed his key down when the aircraft ditched halfway across the North Sea at 00.34 hours. Prior to ditching, the Captain called out the height of the aircraft as it approached the water and the Navigator gave him a surface report. The aircraft bounced off a swell and then made a very heavy impact with the water which caused the nose to sink in and the fuselage to break in half. The pilot was trapped in the nose and went under as the aircraft broke in two. The Navigator jumped into the dinghy and dragged in the Mid-Upper Gunner from the water. They heard the Wireless Operator calling, paddled up to him and helped him on board. The Rear-Gunner, who had been observed to jump into the sea, was also heard to call but they failed to find him and he was not picked up. After drifting for about an hour blowing their whistles, they heard an answering whistle, in the darkness, and eventually picked up the Flight Engineer from his 'K' type dinghy. When the Stirling hit the sea, the Bomb-Aimer got out of the astro hatch but was swept into the sea by the waves. The Flight Engineer passed him a 'K' dinghy which was swept away. The Bomb-Aimer re-entered the almost submerged fuselage, found another 'K' dinghy, held his breath and swam out again as the aircraft sank, three minutes after ditching. He inflated the dinghy and climbed in, but although he heard other members of the crew shouting and answered, he was too weak to paddle towards the sound and lost touch with them. After sunrise, he hoisted a red sail and fired a star cartridge when an Air-Sea Rescue Hudson approached.

The Hudson crew dropped smoke floats alongside and he was shortly after taken on board a high speed launch which continued the search and picked up the other four surviving members of the crew from the big dinghy about 40 minutes later. The Captain and Rear-Gunner could not be found.

This crew exercised very strong determination to inflict as much damage on the enemy as possible in spite of their difficulties and they showed an excellent team spirit. It was this good team work and initiative that made possible the long and difficult flight to the point when the aircraft finally ditched and the successful rescue of five members of the crew after attacking their target successfully.

Sergeant Paul Gees was a survivor of a ditching. It may not have been as traumatic as the events evidenced by the commander-in-chief of Bomber Command, nor was it as testing for the flight engineer within the events mentioned. It did, however, entitle Paul to apply to become a member of the Goldfish Club.

In respect of the missing Catalina crew, the procedure of next of kin being informed took place with great efficiency. Paul Gees's parents had received a sequence of telegrams and letters delivered to their home address in Woolston, Southampton. In August 1943, he resumed operational flying with 210 Squadron against the German submarine fleet operating within the Bay of Biscay. Squadron Leader Lobley gave way to Flight Lieutenant Chamberlain as the regular pilot for Paul and his crew. In just three operational searches that month, he accrued a total of fifty-four hours and twenty minutes flying. It needs little emphasis to appreciate the arduous nature of a flight engineer manning the cramped station of a Catalina for durations of twenty hours at a time. These were exceptional duties. By example, in November 1943, Paul recorded seven operations where he accumulated 106 hours and thirty minutes in the air. Such long endurance operations meant that Coastal Command aircrew were primarily regarded as tour expired by hours and not the numbers of sorties.

On 14 April 1944, another anti-submarine patrol took place for Paul and his crew in Catalina JX202. Operational from Oban, Flight Lieutenant Chamberlain lifted the flying boat safely off the surface of the sea at 2.40 p.m., intent on actively searching for enemy submarines. This particular anti-submarine patrol took place over a period of nine hours; at 11.25 p.m., they set course to return to Oban. However, the return sortie was to become significantly difficult. The flying log book entry written by Paul detailed some of the difficulties:

The weather had been particularly bad, icing was experienced from sea level up to 8,000 feet and the ice formations had broken the aircraft aerials. The Catalina was fitted with de-icing systems which when operated the Flight Engineer had three temperature indicators fitted to the left of his seat position. No doubt the engine speeds needed manipulating to assist in dislodging the ice forming on the propellers, the Pilot controlled the de-icing pump to the propellers from his control yoke. As they progressed south the freezing fog intensified and the aircrafts transmitters and radar stopped working effectively making them blind in the seriously detreating conditions.

Tentatively the Pilot found an opening in the fog and sighted a small fishing vessel. It was decided to land on the sea as soon as it was safe to do so. They jettisoned the six depth charges and dropped lower to affect a landing having assessed the sea by the wind and wave movements. At 06.50 hours, they safely landed onto the water and contacted the fishing vessel by semaphore signalling.

The trawler responded and offered assistance informing us that Stornoway lay west south west 40 miles away with mines protecting the entrance. Possible miss communication saw the fishing vessel depart. The Catalina was riding on the sea with engines off and bucket drogues out to assist with stability. Paul assessed the fuel supply as critical, 250 gallons remained but lengthy taxying was likely to use excessive fuel and induce engine overheating despite the gills being fully open. He devised an option of taxying and cooling the engines as they started heading for Stornoway. Additionally, the bilge pump needed to be monitored. Differing methods existed but normally driven by a small electrical motor, it was vital in these circumstances to ensure effective operation for obvious reasons.

The wireless operators combined their skills to get one transmitter working and having made contact, the response was to accept a tow if conditions allowed. The taxying and engine resting procedure which was closely monitored by the Flight Engineer led to the sighting of the fishing trawler *Boulona*. Responding to a request for assistance the trawler connected to the towing cable shackled upon the keel and commenced to tow the Catalina for nearly six hours into Stornoway. On reaching the outer harbour the local lifeboat took control at the entrance into the harbour.

Paul Gees recorded sixteen hours forty-five minutes duty for that eventful patrol. Many hours were spent waterborne. His skills as a flight engineer assisted greatly, and the endurance of such a long period of engine management ultimately led to a safe return.

On 16 June 1944, Paul flew the final anti-submarine hunt of his tour. It was an eighteen-hour uneventful patrol, but no doubt the crew were additionally elated at the news of the Allied landings holding and bridgeheads developing. His operational hours totalled 311 hours and forty-five minutes and he was classified as tour expired. Further service as an instructor at an operational training unit followed with Paul surviving the war.

It is appropriate to reflect back upon his fellow Halton apprentices from the 1937 entry. Unbeknown to Paul, many had likewise volunteered to join the ranks of flight engineers. These are the names of those apprentices who were not so fortunate and paid the ultimate sacrifice:

Flight Engineer Sergeant Frederick Armstrong crashed on outskirts of Paris. 30.5.42 aged twenty-one

Flight Engineer Sergeant Edward Leslie Belk shot down Holland 26.3.42 aged twenty

Flight Engineer Pilot Officer Rowland John Bowen failed to Return Berlin 2.1.44 aged twenty-three

Flight Engineer Sergeant Dennison Pierce Broomfield flying accident 8.9.42 aged twenty-two

Flight Engineer Sergeant John Alfred Carter flying accident 25.6.42 aged twenty-two

Flight Engineer Sergeant Lennox Ashton Crossley crashed off Dutch Coast 17.9.42 aged twenty-one

Flight Engineer Sergeant Leonard Clinton Fenton shot down France 16.6.42 aged twenty-one

Flight Engineer Sergeant George Green shot down France 4.10.42 aged twenty-two

Flight Engineer Sergeant Arthur Stanley Greenwood shot down France 30.12.41 aged twenty

Flight Engineer Sergeant Aubrey Hunter shot down Holland 13.6.43 aged twenty-two

Flight Engineer Sergeant Kenneth Roy Johnson crashed Germany 25.2.43 aged twenty-one

Flight Engineer Sergeant John Douglas Johnston flying accident 26.8.41 aged twenty

Flight Engineer Sergeant Richard Archibold Riddle crashed Holland 27.4.44 aged twenty-two

Flight Engineer Sergeant Derek Arthur Soggee flying accident 30.11.42 aged twenty-two

Flight Engineer Sergeant Henry Charles Walton failed to return 23.1.44 aged twenty-two

Every intake of Halton apprentices holds similarly sobering statistics appertaining to flight engineers.

28

Flight Engineer Davis: Far East, B-24 Liberator, Prisoner of War

The European air war tends to hold great audience, perhaps it could be suggested, to the exclusion of other theatres of operation. The flight engineers who flew in the American-built B-24 Liberator most certainly deserve recognition for their work in the Far East. Flying from India over very long endurance flights, these men performed extraordinary long duties frequently in challenging circumstances.

Winston Churchill wrote upon his meetings with the United States President, Franklin Roosevelt, at the Quebec Conference, 12–16 September 1944:

> For nearly three years we had persisted in the strategy of Germany First. The time has now come for the liberation of Asia, and I was determined that we should play our full and equal part in it. What I feared most at this stage of the war was that the United States would say. We came to your help in Europe and you left us alone to finish off Japan.

A few weeks after the above statement took place, a conference within the Far East 231 Group agreed that flight engineers were unquestionably required to fly in B-24 Liberators. No. 231 Group comprised of three wings, equipping six squadrons commanded by the Strategic Air Force. The Allied Lend-Lease Agreements supplying the B-24 aircraft to the Royal Air Force continued as the war in the Pacific progressed against stiff opposition. The January 1944 Arnold-Courtney agreement, with Air Chief Marshal Courtney and Major General Giles representing General Arnold as signatories, endorsed the supply of B-24 aircraft destined for the Southeast Asia theatre, all of which was supplied from the United States.

Wing Commander James Blackburn, Commanding Officer of 159 Squadron, had been instrumental in revolutionising the use of the Liberator in the Far East theatre where the targets were a considerable distance from India. Most importantly, by changing the manner in which the Liberators were flown to and from these long ranging targets, the flight engineer and his pilot would utilise the technique of climbing above the required altitude and then diving back with an increased speed before levelling out at the nominated cruising altitude. This process created more speed and less drag, inducing good fuel efficiency for the Pratt and Whitney Twin Wasp engines, which were effectively able to run at a reduced airspeed.

The Mk VI model Liberators, known as B-24J types, required the rear gunner to only occupy his turret once the aircraft was in the air and to extract himself from it before landing. This was to assist with the pitching of the airframe on its tricycle landing wheels. The B-24 was a most versatile aircraft. The tricycle undercarriage provided the crews with excellent vision for both landings and taking off, and the ground crews also enjoyed a very stable and level aircraft to work upon on the ground. The crew accessed the aircraft through the nose wheel opening or through the entrance hatchway, built into either the bottom of the rear fuselage section or through the bomb bay doors. In the air, the two main wheels retracted outwards and swung into large wheel wells within the wing—a very different configuration to the British heavy bombers. The forward nose wheel retracted into the fuselage, which was positioned just forward of the two twin doors, which opened inwardly. Those two doors acted as emergency exits for the forward crew members who were able to activate them by a quick release mechanism within the fuselage. The advanced design feature with the high lift wing created minimum drag to give the aircraft a heavy load capacity over a greater distance. The B-24 had rather unique corrugated sheeting bomb doors, with both sets operated on rollers opening outwards and upwards upon a central beam running along and up the lower fuselage. A small bulkhead structure divided the bomb compartment creating two bomb bays.

Emergency crank handles were situated to enable the flight engineer to open the doors in the event of any hydraulic failures in the air. The most common bomb load deployed was ten 500-lb bombs or five 1,000-pounders. The individual bomb shackle that carried the bomb had three securing points, the end two held the bomb by releasable hooks, and the third held the arming wire. The arming wire was a long wire that was inserted into the fuse and when the bomb was released, the arming wire pulled from the fuse as the bomb dropped. This allowed a small arming vane fitted on the nose fuse to rotate as it fell and, by doing so, arm the bomb.

Taking off fully laden in a Liberator required the pilot to hold the aircraft on the brakes while applying full power to the engines. The noise was immense and the airframe would shake and rattle as the physical forces were applied. The pilot and flight engineer would hold the straining aircraft with the flaps fully down and then set the fuel mixture at 'full rich' while ensuring the props were in fine pitch. The throttles were opened wide before the brakes were released and all four engines hauled the full weight of the B-24 down the runway until sufficient lift on the wing lifted the aircraft off the ground.

The hot climate naturally induced Far East aircrew personnel to consume more water than their counterparts in the European theatre of war. This fact, combined with exceptionally long sorties into Burma and further afield, required the crew to use a relief tube device situated at the front end of the bomb bay. The aircraft carried large thermos containers with hot water to make tea and pre-packed rations were carried for meals. These were essential for the crew during their exceptionally long and arduous sorties, some in excess of fourteen hours. In 1944, experimental caffeine tablets were issued to assist with maintaining the ability of enduring such extraordinary lengthy flights. These caffeine tablets were benzedrine, which was a trade name for an amphetamine-based product. These tablets originated from research carried out by the Flying Personnel Research Committee and at the Medical Research Council based at Cambridge University.

The men serving in the Far East Liberator squadrons were issued with a specially designed flying suit. The unique weather conditions and incessant mosquito bites had led to the design of what became known as the Beadon suit. Constructed of a green cotton material, it was both lightweight and showerproof, with only the head and hands exposed when worn. The suit had numerous pockets sewn into the material, all of which were to hold various escape and survival aids. This popular garment simply became known as a coverall.

Flight engineers were well aware that the Liberator was capable of sustaining severe battle damage, but, like many aircraft, it was dependent upon an effective hydraulic system that operated the landing gear, wheel braking, flaps, and bomb bay doors. The hydraulic system was driven by the number three engine and supplemented by an emergency auxiliary electrical pump as well as an emergency hand-operated pump. The number three engine was one that the flight engineer was likely to pay additional attention to.

In comparison to the European War, the Far East prisoners of war were treated appallingly. One flight engineer, Norman Davis in 159 Squadron, was to suffer great hardship when imprisoned in Rangoon Jail by his Japanese captors. Norman had been working as a butcher when he volunteered to serve in the Royal Air Force. He had taken the first opportunity to enlist on his eighteenth birthday in September 1941. Norman had distinctive auburn hair which during his military service ultimately led to him being addressed as 'Red' by way of a nickname. In September 1943, Norman completed his training and attached his flight engineer brevet onto his tunic at St Athan. In anticipation of serving on a Lancaster or Halifax-equipped squadron, he would have eagerly awaited his instructions. While among a large group of fellow flight engineers, an instructor called for all men with a service number ending with a zero to stand aside. Norman had a service number of 1545800 and was therefore included. All of those men who stood aside were duly gathered together and collectively assigned to serve as Liberator flight engineers.

Most men only knew it to be an American-built four-engine heavy bomber and very little else. The school at St Athan certainly had no Liberators. Norman

Davis received instructions to be vaccinated and was shipped to India by Allied convoy where he would eventually see the B-24 Liberator in which he would operate following his posting to 159 Squadron. India was effectively an extensive network of aerodromes for both heavy conversion and operational flying. The Strategic Air Force, 231 Heavy Bomber Group, consisted of six squadrons equipped with B-24 Liberators. The aerodromes at Digri, Salbani, and Dhubalia were where 159 Squadron operated from at one time or another between 1942 and 1945. These airfields were relatively close together—Dhubalia situated north of Calcutta, Digri and Salbani to the west of Calcutta.

Norman quickly adapted his skills to the Liberator at the heavy conversion unit and eventually flew with his newly formed crew. The captain of his aircraft was Flight Lieutenant Edward Stanley, who originated in Middlesex. His crew consisted of Dutch, Australian, Scottish, Welsh, and English men. The war had thrown this extraordinary diverse group of men together to take bomb loads huge distances from India into Burma and Thailand, primarily attacking Japanese infrastructures, including the famous Burma railway that had been constructed by the Japanese in their attempt to invade India.

All flight engineers on Liberators were responsible for the deployment of the small auxiliary power units, which needed to be started simultaneously with the engine start-up procedures by the pilots. It was a small capacity two-stroke petrol engine that powered an electrical generator. The small engine was situated under the flight deck and was started electrically to initially supply power to the essential electrical circuits. Once the aircraft's engines reached sufficient power to energise their own individual four generators, the auxiliary unit was shut down.

During the long flights deep into Thailand, flight engineers would transfer fuel from the outer wing tanks to the inner tanks. This procedure required using an electrically powered pump that was operated within a safety isolation process, transferring the fuel and then re-isolating parts of the electrical fuel circuit. Working with the pilot, the fluid movements caused an imbalance to the aircraft that would always need to be trimmed. There were twelve self-sealing fuel tanks built into the central wing section. Each engine was primarily fed by dedicated tanks and the power unit was capable of pumping its own individual fuel supply while in the air. Likewise, each engine had its own independent oil supply system, each unit holding some 56 gallons of circulating oil.

For Norman Davis, life as a flight engineer on 159 Squadron presented several challenges when he commenced operations in February 1945. On the flight deck, he was able to communicate directly with his pilot. The pilot had no access to the fuel transfer or electrical generator systems. On the rear bulkhead of the flight engineer's position were the electrical controls for the engine-driven generators attached to each of the four engines. Norman was responsible for monitoring the generators during flight and he was to some extent fortunate in that he had his own independent oxygen supply, provided by two bottles beneath his seat. That said, the oxygen system was in many cases stripped from Liberators to lessen weight as a heavy load restricted the height at which those aircraft were able to operate.

The fuselage of the Liberator was effectively divided into five compartments, comprising of the nose section, nose wheel, flight deck, bomb bay, and rear. Movement from the nose and flight deck was by means of a passageway through the nose wheel compartment, which required manoeuvring around the actual nose wheel. The dorsal upper turret was normally unoccupied unless required, in which case it was manned by the flight engineer. The turret was positioned immediately behind the pilot and readily accessible for the flight engineer. It was an electrically operated turret renowned for its reliability and ease of operation. Norman would sit with his feet resting on footrests as the turret turned in rotational movements. The control handles provided access to the two safety switches, which activated the turret. To move the turret, the handles were turned to the right to go right, and to the left to go left. Pressing down on the handles raised the guns. Pulling up on them lowered them. The slightest movement on the wrists regulated the turning, raising, or lowering motions. The index finger on both handles accessed the triggers. As a secondary duty, Norman was quite capable of effectively defending his aircraft from this turret. Air gunnery was normally instructed at Amarda Road Aerodrome, India.

Norman flew operations to several targets in February 1944, including Japanese aerodromes and railway marshalling yards. At the end of the month, Norman was to complete his first month of duty with a briefing to attack the Mahlwagon marshalling yards in Rangoon on 29 February. Flight Lieutenant Stanley would fly with eight additional bombers from the squadron. Liberator BZ926, with a winged Pegasus painted upon the forward fuselage, would carry the crew that night. It was an aircraft that Norman had grown to know well. BZ926 took off at 4.30 p.m. from Digri aerodrome and made for the target. It was normal to fly independently to any target, a practice far removed from the large European bomber streams. Rangoon was the lifeline for the Japanese, with its port and railway connections. It was the beating heart of Burma, a country that had elevated ranges separating it from India in the west, China in the north, and Thailand in the east. The Japanese had enforced their defences around Rangoon, making it one of the most heavily fortified areas in all of Southeast Asia. Heavy anti-aircraft guns and batteries of searchlights were concentrated at strategic positions. The larger part of the Japanese fighter pilot strength in Burma was based within easy striking distances of the city. It was a city of great value, possessing a river front with miles of jetties and wharves. Steamers berthed and unloaded cargo directly into huge storage sheds, which were in turn served by multiple railway sidings. The Burma railway then fed into the countries supply structure, enabling the Japanese to distribute supplies with ease.

At around 9 p.m., Liberator BZ926 approached Rangoon where it became illuminated by searchlights. Once held in the intense beam of light, two Japanese night fighters attacked with great ferocity, following which, in response to an order to parachute out of the stricken aircraft, six men tumbled from the Liberator. The pilot, Flight Lieutenant Stanley, his navigator, Flight Lieutenant O'Donohue, and his air gunner, Sergeant Chalcraft, never escaped and to this day, these men remain lost as does any trace of the stricken aircraft, Liberator BZ926.

The pair of Japanese night fighters worked in tandem, cooperating with the searchlight over Rangoon. It was an effective strategy, which was also responsible for shooting down Liberator BZ962, her entire 159 Squadron crew perishing. On that Liberator, the flight engineer was twenty-one-year-old Flight Sergeant John Leak, who had trained initially as an aircraft fitter and flight mechanic and in June 1943, he had volunteered to train as a flight engineer at St Athan. The destruction of BZ962 resulted in an inability to identify the individual men. John Leak died alongside his crew; however, the individually unidentified remains of only seven of the crew were buried in Rangoon War Cemetery.

The six men who survived from Norman's Liberator BZ926 fell towards inevitable capture. The reputation of harsh treatment to POWs would have been prevalent as they descended on each parachute, each man knowing that the Japanese mentality was that any prisoner of war was regarded as the lowest form of existence. Norman Davis was a young flight engineer who unfortunately fell into the custody of both Japanese and Korean guards who guarded Rangoon Jail. The Korean guards exceeded the reputation of the Japanese, conducting particularly brutal and intimidating daily routines upon the inmates held in the filthy, rat-infested jail, which contained around 100 British and Commonwealth airmen.

The flight engineer brevet itself brought Norman additional interrogations from the Japanese because the brevet was an unknown commodity to them. Norman, with his distinctive coloured hair and wearing a special brevet was assumed to be an important person in the crew. Little doubt exists that he would have also suffered at the hands of the *Kempeitai*, the Japanese secret police. Norman was selected for special interrogation where he was also requested to take part in broadcasting propaganda messages over the radio. Refusing to do so, he was subjected to additional beatings. These were terrible circumstances, which included mock executions in order to create terror and mental trauma on a regular basis. His survival was remarkable bearing in mind that four men, including Flight Engineer Robert Snelling, survivors from Liberator BZ938 had been executed by beheadings at Rangoon on 7 February 1944.

Gordon Clegg, commanding officer of 159 Squadron, wrote to eighteen next-of-kin to the airmen shot down on 29 February 1945. Six men had parachuted from Liberator BZ926 to become prisoners of war; four survived that experience to be liberated from Rangoon Central Jail on 3 May 1945. Among them was Norman Davis. Against great odds, this flight engineer survived and after medical treatment, he was eventually repatriated to his home in Northampton.

29

Awards and Decorations
by the King

During the Second World War, there was an allocation system that determined the number of awards available to each military service. In respect of the Royal Air Force, it was relevant to each respective command. The allocations were further disseminated between the individual decorations capable of being awarded to the respective ranks. The allocations were calculated by (among other matters) the number of hours flown. Flight engineers served in several ranks and were therefore likely to be in receipt of medals in differing configurations.

During times of war, the most prevalent gallantry awards to flight engineers were the Distinguished Flying Cross and the Distinguished Flying Medal. These could be recommended or awarded as immediate and non-immediate. Immediate awards were recommended for conspicuous deeds or individual acts and it was desirable for the recipient to be recognised as soon after the event as was possible. The latter, also known as a periodic, was more commonly made on completion of a first or second tour, or in recognition for a long period of competence.

Awards were effectively rationed and allocated on the basis of a mathematical formula. The number of operational hours flown by a squadron became relevant to how many awards were available. This system had been worked out at the beginning of the war. The number of awards granted would be modified by a 'divisor'. The divisor also varied with the degree of hazard associated with the Command. At the outbreak of war in September 1939, Bomber Command was considered the most dangerous of all formations, so the divisor was 300. For Fighter Command, it was 1,000, and for Coastal Command it was 2,000. This system in 1939 can be explained by the example of Bomber Command flying 6,000 operational hours, which would have resulted in an allocation of twenty gallantry awards. The same number of hours in Fighter Command would bring six awards, while in Coastal Command it would have brought three.

These figures were periodically modified during the war. The author has been unable to locate evidence of the formula for Fighter Command during the period we now regard as the Battle of Britain. However, the divisor would have been reduced significantly from the above. In the National Archives Air 2/6085 Non-Immediate Awards, 1940–1941, details can be found as to how Bomber Command awards were allocated for June 1940. With the Battle of France concluded, the divisor had by then been dropped to 150. Bomber Command flying for June totalled 16,090 hours, to which were added 506 hours that had been held over from May, creating a total of 16,596 hours. With the divisor of 150 applied, Bomber Command was deemed eligible for 110 awards, from which ten immediate awards were subtracted for a total of 100 eligible awards. The complexity of this subject is further explained by communication between the Dominions Office in London to the Government in Australia in April 1943, which stated:

> One award of the Distinguished Service Order, Distinguished Flying Cross, Conspicuous Gallantry Medal (Flying), or Distinguished Flying Medal can be made for every 360 aircraft flying hours of operational flying in an operational command. Not more than 50 per cent of those to be granted as Immediate Awards and the balance as periodical or operational awards …

The award process began with a recommendation made by the squadron commander, who in respect of immediate action would have received reports from operational sources. The recommendation then passed through several hands, increasing in seniority—station commander to base commander to group commander. In the case of Bomber Command, awards to flight engineers from 1942 onwards were presented before Air Marshal Arthur Harris. In practice, the original recommendation was supported by those going up the line but occasionally, changes were made. In some instances, awards were being downgraded, a practice that tended to be associated with immediate as opposed to periodic awards. Once the recommendation had been approved by the Air Officer Commander-in-Chief, the confirmation of the award was published in the *London Gazette*.

A document distributed by 6 Group, Royal Canadian Air Force, on 7 June 1943 advised on how recommendations were to be made, including comments on specific types of awards. The appendices to the document are particularly interesting and provide detailed information that offers a greater understanding of the awards system:

> The Victoria Cross, awardable to all ranks for most conspicuous bravery or some daring or pre-eminent act of valour or self-sacrifice or extreme devotion to duty in the presence of the enemy. The Air Council has advised that in their opinion this decoration should be awarded more often for getting into danger (i.e. in the furtherance of operations) than for getting out of the kind of desperate situation

which is latent in all operations. Exception to this general rule may, however, be made when there is clear evidence of actions of the highest gallantry. Commanding officers should consider whether any officers or airmen under their command might be regarded as suitable for recommendation for the VC for sustained gallantry over a long period, rather than for some specific act of gallantry alone. It will still be desirable that officers or airmen so recommended should have performed some outstanding act, but this should be the climax to a series of gallant exploits, e.g., a large number of sorties in the face of heavy opposition. The outstanding act need not of itself justify the highest award, but it would do so in a context of prolonged and heroic endeavour.

The Distinguished Service Order, awardable to officers (usually not below rank of Squadron Leader) who have been mentioned in despatches for distinguished services under fire, or under conditions equivalent to services in actual combat with the enemy.

The Distinguished Flying Cross, awardable to Officers and Warrant Officers for exceptional valour, courage, devotion to duty while flying on active operations against the enemy.

The Distinguished Flying Medal, awardable to all Non-Commissioned Officers and aircraftmen, for exceptional valour, courage or devotion to duty while flying in active operations against the enemy.

The Conspicuous Gallantry Medal (Flying) awardable to Warrant Officers, Non-Commissioned Officers and aircraftmen as an award superior to the Distinguished Flying Medal for conspicuous gallantry while flying on active operations against the enemy.

The appendix that set out the above criteria also laid down some administrative procedures for submitting recommendations. It stated that recommendations for posthumous awards could not be submitted except when a Victoria Cross or a Mention in Despatches was involved. However, the processing of recommendations for other awards would progress forward, even if the person involved had in the meantime been killed, but only on the condition that the initial recommendation had been submitted while the person was still alive. This was a rule that was evidently relaxed on many occasions to allow what would otherwise be ineligible 'posthumous' awards. It is occasionally evidenced in such awards with 'since deceased' against the official announcement procedures.

There were periodic awards of other honours, which fell within the duties undertaken by flight engineers, the most likely of which would be the following:

The Air Force Cross, awardable to all Officers and Warrant Officers for exceptional valour, courage or devotion to duty while flying, though not in active operations against the enemy.

The Air Force Medal, awardable to all Non-Commissioned Officers and Aircraftmen for exceptional valour, courage or devotion to duty while flying, though not in active operations against the enemy.

Mention in Despatches, an award which facilitated the posthumous honouring of personnel.

To assist commanding officers in drawing up recommendations, the document distributed by the Canadian 6 Group provided, in Annex IX, a compilation of phrases deemed useful for the task. No doubt, this was created as a means of inhibiting the drafting of extended exciting and heroic accounts. Similarities of many citations suggest that these were frequently written to adhere to the formula, particularly with periodical recommendations. Many of these phrases were pertinent to some wording found in non-Immediate awards to flight engineers:

1. By his fine fighting spirit.
2. His coolness under fire.
3. Complete disregard for personal safety.
4. By his coolness and presence of mind.
5. His fearless courage in combat.
6. This Officer's (NCO's) dogged determination, skill and devotion to duty.
7. Showed a magnificent example by.
8. Regardless of imminent danger.
9. By prompt action and with complete disregard of personal safety.
10. By skilful airmanship under most trying conditions.
11. Displayed exceptional skill and coolness in extricating his aircraft from a most perilous situation.
12. By his skill, courage and determination extricated his crew from a perilous situation.
13. To which action his crew undoubtedly owed their lives.
14. Thereby saving the lives of his crew and much valuable equipment.
15. His superb captaincy and airmanship.
... 19. Undeterred by intense flak.
20. In spite of physical suffering through intense cold, or hunger, or fatigue, or heat, or lack of oxygen, or thirst, or loss of blood, etc.
... 24. The successful completion of this operational flight was due to the initiative, resourcefulness and skilful airmanship of this officer or NCO.
... 35. Gallantry of the highest order.
36. Fine record of achievement.
... 42. Proved himself to be an outstanding member of a gallant crew.

A wartime investiture at Buckingham Palace was an awe-inspiring event for those individuals lucky enough to be invited. Most gallantry award recipients would have hoped for an invitation to the Palace, but to give every recipient their award personally would have been a physical impossibility for the Sovereign.

Medals were occasionally sent to operational bases during the war and the status between ranks was reflected in the quality of the cases in which the medals were sent. The Distinguished Flying Cross was encased in a fitted velvet-lined box, the box lid embossed with the initials of the enclosed award. The equivalent award to non-commissioned officers, the Distinguished Flying Medal, was sent in a cardboard box with no particular fittings other than tissue wrapping.

Occasionally, the King presented medals during official visits to operational units; these arrangements were particularly noteworthy as the entire squadron strength was inevitably present at such an important event.

At Buckingham Palace investitures, the recipients included men and women from across all of the fighting services, civil defence workers, Merchant Navy and others whose bravery had merited official Royal recognition. Each medal recipient was entitled to nominate one or two close relatives or friends who were allowed to witness the ceremony. Entry was only provided to individuals in possession of a numbered and stamped entry ticket. These small tickets were issued in differing coloured card to enable easy recognition for the staff managing the presentation ceremonies which were timed accordingly.

The King received each recipient separately in the Grand Hall. An official would read a summarised account of the deed for which the honour was being conferred before the King pinned the medal to the uniform tunic. Recipients were instructed to attend in their normal service dress with air raid wardens and other civil defence heroes attending in uniform, often with tin hats scarred as a result of their heroic work. On 4 March 1943, permission was granted for this previously most private function to be photographed for the very first time.

Campaign Medals and stars for service in the Second World War were accordingly governed by rules determined by the Monarch on the advice of the British Government. Winston Churchill spoke on the subject of medals on the 22 March 1944, his words are worthy of consideration:

> The object of giving medals, stars and ribbons is to give pride and pleasure to those who have deserved them. At the same time, a distinction is something which everybody does not possess. If all have it, it is of less value. There must, therefore, be heart-burnings and disappointments on the borderline. A medal glitters, but it also casts a shadow. The task of drawing up regulations for such awards is one which does not admit of a perfect solution. It is not possible to satisfy everybody without running the risk of satisfying nobody. All that is possible is to give the greatest satisfaction to the greatest number and to hurt the feelings of the fewest.

In June 1946, a United Kingdom committee known as the 'Committee on the Grant of Honours Decorations and Medals' produced a document setting out the conditions for the award of War Medals and Campaign Stars. This Command document was known as Command Paper 6833 (AIR 2/6723 TNA) and within the document, Sir Arthur Street suggested that the Battle of Britain clasp could be uniquely awarded to Battle of Britain participants and worn on the 1939–43 Star. The matters concerning the complicated award of the various campaign stars and their entitlements were also addressed in the same document. Sir Arthur Street had lost his son, who served as a pilot within Bomber Command. His son was among those men murdered after the 'Great Escape' from Stalag Luft III. Sir Arthur was well aware that Bomber Command had been hugely significant in the Allied victory over Germany, yet it was a bitter statement to those men that no campaign medal for Bomber Command was ever struck to commemorate their achievements. The immediate post-war Labour government appears to have given these men little recognition. Air Vice Marshal Harris was particularly concerned for the ground crews who served all hours in abominable conditions only to receive a Defence Medal.

The 'Bomber Command Memorial' that now proudly stands in Green Park, London, is a fitting testimony to all those men that bravely served, and goes some way towards addressing the perceived failings of those who held the ability to honour the men of Bomber Command in the immediate post-war years. The sculptor Philip Jackson CVO DL MA FRBS explains the significance of the flight engineer within this memorial:

> There are seven figures in the group and they represent the crew of a heavy bomber. Five of the figures are looking at the sky for the aircraft and their comrades that will not return. As it is a war memorial this is the important link between the living and the dead. Two of the figures are looking downwards to give the group a feeling of sadness and pathos. The Flight Engineer has his hand up shielding his eyes as he looks for the missing aircraft and this gives the groups gaze direction. The men stand closely together in a slightly flattened circle with a gap at the front so that the viewer can see the pilot. The pilots hand is raised to his face as he realises the scale of the night's loss. The figures are non-triumphal, reflective but quietly heroic but most of all they are a band of brothers welded together in the heat of war. They stand immortalised in bronze in memory of the 55,500 who did not return.

Bibliography

Article/Newspaper

National Archives, Recommendations for honours and awards, under the terms of the Open Government Licence.

National Archives, Squadron Records forms 541 (Operational Flights) and forms 540 (Operational Activity) supported by Appendices. All Squadron numbers are prefixed AIR27 and recorded daily

National Archives, Air 14/1880: Operational Research Section Sct122 Examination of Emergency Escape Arrangements for Operational Aircraft (28.1.44)

National Archives, Operational Research and Strategic Bombing. Section Head, Box2 622-page manuscript, Author Dr Basil Dickins (1945)

Air 14/0365 Aircraft losses and casualties reports, information and data.

Air 24/258 Bomber Command Intelligence Appreciation Peenemunde (1943)

Air 27: Squadron Operational Record Books

Air 28: Station Operations Record Books

Air 29: Miscellaneous Units Operation Record Books

Air Ministry., Air Publication 1660A, Stirling I, III and IV Pilot and Flight Engineer Notes, (Air Ministry 1944)

Air Ministry, Air Publication 1719C, Halifax III Pilot and Flight Engineer Notes, (Air Ministry 1944)

Air Ministry, Air Publication 2036A, Catalina Pilot and Flight Engineer Notes, (Air Ministry 1943)

Air Ministry, Air Publication 2062B, Lancaster II Pilot and Flight Engineer Notes, (Air Ministry 1943)

Hultons National Weekly, Vol. 19 Number. (*Picture Post*, 7 May 1943)

Book

Allison, L., and Hayward, H., *They Shall Grow Not Old*, (Commonwealth Air Training Plan Museum, 1992)

Bower, C., *For Valour the air VCs*, (Grubb Street, 1992)

Blanchett, C., *From Hull Hell and Halifax an Illustrated History of 4 Group 1937 – 1948*, (Midland Counties Publications, 1992)

Carter, N. and C., *The DFC and How It Was Won*. (Savannah, 1998)

Chorley, W. R., *In Brave Company 158 Squadron Operations.*, (P. A. Chorley
    Publication 2nd Edition, 1990); *Royal Air Force Bomber Command Losses of the
    Second World War, Vol. 9, Roll of Honour 1939–1947* (Midland Publishing, 2007)

Clutton-Brock, O., *Footprints on the Sands of Time – RAF Bomber Command
    Prisoners of War in Germany 1939–45*, (Grub Street London, 2003)

Dunn, R. L., *Exploding Fuel Tanks*, (Publisher Richard Dunn, 2011)

Firkins, P., *Strike and return: the unit history of No. 460 RAAF Heavy Bomber
    Squadron*, (Australian Military History Publication, 2001)

Gibson, E, and Kingsley Ward, *Courage Remembered*. (HMSO, 1989)

Harris, Sir A. T., *Despatches on war ops* (1995)

Hearns, D., *Distinguished Service Order Air Awards*, (Naval and Military Press, 2011)

Jefford, C. G. Wing Commander MBE, BA., *Observers and Navigators* (Airlife
    Publishing, 2001)

Lax, M & Kane-Maguire, L., *To See the Dawn Again; A History of 462 Squadron,
    RAAF.*, (Published by authors, 2008)

Maton, M., *Honour those mentioned MID despatches*. (Token Publishing, 2010);
    Honour the Air Forces. (Token Publishing, 2004)

Mason, F. K., *The Avro Lancaster* (Aston Publications, 1989)

Merrick, K. A., *The Handley Page Halifax* (Aston Publications 2nd Edition, 1990)

Middlebrook, M., and Everitt, C., *The Bomber Command War Diary* (Penguin, 1985)

Rapier, B. J., *Halifax at War* (1987) and Bowyer, C., *Wellington at War* (1982),
    Combined edition, (The Promotional Reprint Co. Ltd, 1994)

Robertson, B., *British Military Aircraft Serials, 1912-1969*, (Ian Allen, 1969)

Royal Air Force 1939–1945 Vol I, II, and III (HMSO, 1953)

Seymour, M., and Balderson, W., *To the ends of the Earth*, (Paterchurch Publications,
    1999)

Sweetman, J., *The Dambusters Raid* (Cassell, 2002)

Tavender, I., *The DFM A Record of Courage 1918–1982* (J. B. Haywood, 1990)

Tunbridge, P., *History of Royal Air Force Halton* (Buckland Publications Ltd, 1995)

Units of the Royal Australian Air Force: a concise history. Volume 3, bomber units,
    (Canberra: Australian Government Publishing Service, 1995)

Website

www.cwgc.org The Commonwealth War Graves Commission (CWGC)

www.awm.gov.au-catalogue-research. (National Archives of Australia)

www.flensted.eu.com (Airwar over Denmark)

www.stirlingproject.co.uk